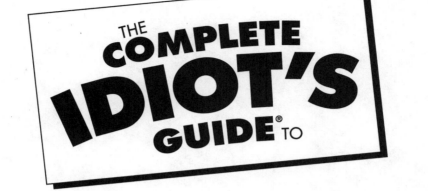

Landscaping

Illustrated

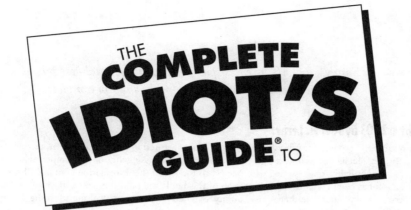

THE COMPLETE IDIOT'S GUIDE® TO

Landscaping

Illustrated

by Joel M. Lerner

ALPHA

Penguin Group (USA) Inc.

To Sandy, my wife, greatest passion, soul mate, and best friend.
It is your love and support that make my life complete.

Copyright © 2003 by Joel M. Lerner

THE COMPLETE IDIOT'S GUIDE TO and Design are registered trademarks of Penguin Group (USA) Inc.

International Standard Book Number: 0-02-864445-X
Library of Congress Catalog Card Number: 2002117448

05   04   03   8   7   6   5   4   3   2   1

Interpretation of the printing code: The rightmost number of the first series of numbers is the year of the book's printing; the rightmost number of the second series of numbers is the number of the book's printing. For example, a printing code of 03-1 shows that the first printing occurred in 2003.

Printed in the United States of America

Note: This publication contains the opinions and ideas of its author. It is intended to provide helpful and informative material on the subject matter covered. It is sold with the understanding that the author and publisher are not engaged in rendering professional services in the book. If the reader requires personal assistance or advice, a competent professional should be consulted.

The author and publisher specifically disclaim any responsibility for any liability, loss, or risk, personal or otherwise, which is incurred as a consequence, directly or indirectly, of the use and application of any of the contents of this book.

Most Alpha books are available at special quantity discounts for bulk purchases for sales promotions, premiums, fundraising, or educational use. Special books, or book excerpts, can also be created to fit specific needs.

For details, write: Special Markets; Alpha Books, 375 Hudson Street, New York, New York 10014.

Publisher: *Marie Butler-Knight*
Product Manager: *Phil Kitchel*
Senior Managing Editor: *Jennifer Chisholm*
Senior Acquisitions Editor: *Mike Sanders*
Development Editor: *Tom Stevens*
Senior Production Editor: *Christy Wagner*
Copy Editor: *Ross Patty*
Illustrator: *Chris Eliopoulos*
Cover/Book Designer: *Trina Wurst*
Indexer: *Brad Herriman*
Layout/Proofreading: *Angela Calvert, John Etchison, Trina Wurst*
Graphics: *Dennis Sheehan*

Except where otherwise credited, all photos and figures are by Jason Heath Lerner.

Contents at a Glance

Contents

Foreword

When I first met Joel Lerner some decade and a half past, it was during his service in the capacity of President for the Association of Professional Landscape Designers. We were, it seems, two peas in a pod in that we both enjoyed the field of landscape design and construction as well as publishing various pieces on many aspects of ornamental horticulture. Having read and reviewed previous works Joel penned and subsequently spent many an hour in discussion of leafy subjects at length, I discovered that he was and indeed is a very special personality with unique perspectives that most in our industry do not enjoy.

The Complete Idiot's Guide to Landscaping Illustrated is a work of both passion and spirit. It has the power to convert the most inept into an enthusiastic member of the gardening and landscape community. Although the intelligence required to perform in the art of creating natural beauty is not greater than that possessed by the average gardening citizen, with a bit more knowledge comes greater success—for when it comes to arranging and nurturing plants and their counterparts, we can always employ more knowledge. One might even reflect that when it comes to manipulating nature, humans really are a bunch of idiots!

When the first landscape designers and builders set to their tasks millennia ago, I'm sure any guidance would have been a welcome guest. I can almost picture the original designers of the hanging gardens of Babylon or the Roman promenades wondering why no one had thought to scribe a *Complete Idiot's Guide to Landscaping* in their day. Only through much toil and trouble, trial and error did our ancestors begin to gain the wisdom that has been passed along from generation to generation until it was refined into the art that I consider landscaping to be. Whether your tastes run toward the properly ordered, disciplined designs the Europeans and Early Americans composed or the Asian endeavors to emulate nature, the ability to envisage your landscape will be enhanced through these pages, thus weighting your probabilities of an end product worthy of pride and admiration.

Landscapes are more than simply a good investment in your property. They should inspire! A well-thought-out and well-executed landscape design is an example of living art in three dimensions. A canvas that one can stroll through, find time for reflection, and commune with nature. We have firm ties to the earth for it supplies us with nourishment, resources for shelter, heat from fuel wood burning on the hearth or cooking our food, medicine, and even the oxygen we breathe. It is not, however, essential that one carry an innate love of plants for success in the landscape. Simply heeding advice and learning the basics of the trade will ensure some degree of success.

So-called brown thumbers exist only in the minds of those unwilling to take the time to develop simple skills. There are no real complete idiots when it comes to landscaping, only practitioners with varying degrees of success. The fact that you have chosen to avail yourself of this guide in an attempt to reap greater rewards from your landscape only illustrates that you are not a complete idiot, but a thinking person who deserves every bit of the success I'm sure you will realize with Joel as your guide and mentor. Happy landscaping!

Peter C. Benjamin
group publisher, Cenflo, Inc., publishers of trade magazines for the ornamental horticultural industries

Introduction

I believe the greatest satisfaction derived by anyone who gardens is in seeing the finished product. It may be as simple as a perfectly groomed lawn, or as complex as a wildflower meadow, a shrub border, water garden, or some combination. It doesn't matter. The gratification of having a beautiful garden is worth every minute of effort.

A well-groomed lawn can be a pleasing sight, such as this one at Brookside Gardens in Wheaton, Maryland.

My earliest recollections of gardening are of helping my parents on their half-acre in Pensauken, New Jersey, when I was five or six years old. I remember planting vegetables and flowers, pulling weeds, trimming with grass shears, and, under highly supervised conditions, using a gas-powered mower on the lawn. None of this was meant to be fun. It was a way of earning an allowance. But, even at that age, I delighted in it. I loved seeing the whole garden "picture" emerge, the picture that my family and I had created using the raw materials of nature.

This beautiful garden was once just overgrown shrubbery and lawn on a hillside.

That's what landscape gardening is all about. It's about taking the land and putting in the features such as hills, flat spaces, paths, fences, ponds, or fountains that give it shape and character, and then using the color and texture of living plants to create the ideal garden picture that's in your mind.

This gravel path with a stone wall defines a natural area at the
U.S. Botanic Garden, Washington, D.C.

Getting There

This book explains how you get from that picture of your dream garden to a real landscape that you can look at, walk about in, and change, and improve as you wish. You don't need fancy skills. If you can dig a hole, pick up a rock, or turn on a hose, you can remake your landscape. You don't have to start out with a complete idea of your perfect garden. If you like to look at nature, and if you can draw lines and circles, you can come up with a garden design. If you already like to plant, weed, and water, that's great. This book will show you how to move to the next level, and create a garden that is your own special place: something you have designed and brought into being. It's a great feeling, to be working toward that goal, and it's wonderful to see your vision coming to life.

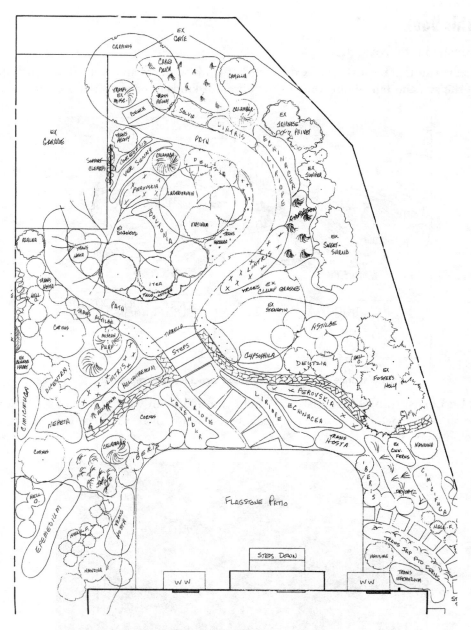

Simple shapes and lines indicate various elements in a garden design.

There will be some hard work involved, and some trials and some errors. Some things may not work. You will need flexibility and patience. But there will also be surprises and unexpected rewards. It's all part of the education you will be getting about the natural world, and your own little piece of it, and even about yourself.

What's in This Book

This book is divided into five sections:

Part 1, "Learning the Landscape," explains what landscaping is all about. It will include some of the history of the art, and talk about some of the different kinds of gardens that can be created.

(Elmer H. Lerner)

Renaissance gardens emphasized structure and repetition.

Part 2, "The Lernscaping Checklist," will help you figure out what you want to see when you look at your own landscape. This part of the book, based on my own system of Lernscaping, will help you develop your vision.

(Joel M. Lerner)

The yard of a new urban duplex offers a blank canvas on which to create a landscape design.

Part 3, "Looking at the Land," helps you determine what you have to work with—that is, the characteristics of the land you have to landscape and how to turn a collection of ideas into a workable garden plan.

(Joel M. Lerner)

The owner of this fountain placed every stone in the compass rose pattern.

Part 4, "The Hardscape How-To," explains how to plan and install the structural parts of your landscape, from walks and drives to decks, steps, and lighting.

Cacti and other arid-climate plants adorn a Southwestern-style garden in the conservatory of the U.S. Botanic Garden.

Part 5, "The Softscape How-To," de-scribes how to choose and install the trees, shrubs, and other plantings for your design and your location.

A gravel path winds through a natural-looking garden.

Photos and Illustrations

A big part of the book is visual examples of what's in the text, including photos of gardens—historic, finished, and in progress; illustrations of plans in all stages; and charts that help you define your environment and choose plants by their characteristics.

Extras

Throughout the book, there are several kinds of boxed tips and information.

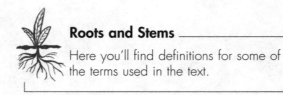

Roots and Stems

Here you'll find definitions for some of the terms used in the text.

Poison Ivy!

These are alerts letting you know to watch out, take care not to do something, or otherwise be cautious.

Planting Ideas

These provide tips for plants and planting.

Out of the Tool Shed

Here you find suggested tools for particular jobs.

Green Thumb Guides

In this special section, you'll get extra information, such as plant lists for the landscapes under discussion.

Acknowledgments

There are three partners at JML Environmental Design: Sandra Leavitt Lerner, Richard C. Levy, and yours truly. We undertake each and every project as a team, talking frequently into the wee hours of the morning, 24/7, and *The Complete Idiot's Guide to Landscaping Illustrated* is no exception. As always, Sandy, my wife of 33 years, did the heaviest lifting, lent her considerable artistic gifts to the design work, and kept our personal life asnormal as possible through this complex initiative. Richard, a marketing mastermind, put together this and every deal we have done. He is the company's driving force, chief strategist, and our mentor. There is no financial reward great enough to ever repay him for his belief in us, and his time and contributions to the company.

Karol V. Menzie, an exceptionally talented journalist, was the conductor and composer who turned my words and thoughts into a symphony. Her writing is the reason this book is so easy to understand and enjoyable to read. Our son, Jason Heath Lerner, utilized his photography training, tested his skills to the fullest, and put his life on hold to illustrate his book. He shot several thousand images in 12 weeks, and kept them in focus and well composed. My beloved, energetic, talented parents, Dr. Elmer and Matilda Lerner, once again, as they have done for my other books, developed ideas, created drawings, and pulled research that enrich this work.

The images were the vision of Mike Sanders, my acquisitions editor. We made it, Mike! Development editor Tom Stevens turned the manuscript into a book. Senior production editor Christy Wagner ensured that it all worked together. Thanks to the entire staff at Alpha Books who contributed their time and talent.

I thank my editor at *The Washington Post*, Maryann Haggerty, who understood the impact of this book on my schedule, and allowed me flexibility in the filing of my weekly "Green Scene" column.

I very much appreciate everyone who permitted their properties or plantings to be used in the illustrations. And of course, thanks to my readers, one and all, without whom there would be no impetus for me to put words on paper.

Trademarks

All terms mentioned in this book that are known to be or are suspected of being trademarks or service marks have been appropriately capitalized. Alpha Books and Penguin Group (USA) Inc. cannot attest to the accuracy of this information. Use of a term in this book should not be regarded as affecting the validity of any trademark or service mark.

In This Part

Part 1

Learning the Landscape

Humans have a long history of interacting with plants—even ancient peoples buried their dead with flowers. The first gardeners grew only what they needed—grains, fruits, vegetables, nuts—to feed themselves and their livestock. But as soon as people got down to the business of creating enclaves, city-states, and suburbs, they began to grow things just for fun.

Whether you're an absolute novice or an enthusiastic amateur at gardening, you'll find it helpful to learn how landscapes developed, and how garden styles evolved to fit their time and place. Knowing why Chinese designers placed rocks in the landscape (to represent mountains) or why Renaissance rulers insisted on symmetry and repetition (to establish order) will help you decide what techniques and ideas to use in your own landscape. You'll be happy to know that you can enlist Mother Nature for help with your gardens. And finally, you will learn a few simple principles that give your landscape comfort, serenity, fascination and, yes, even a little mystery.

In This Chapter

◆ Art of the outdoors

◆ Laws of the landscape

◆ Home comforts

◆ Making the garden glitter

◆ Landscape dollars and sense

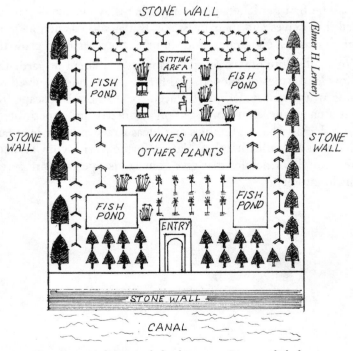

Egyptian gardens used shade trees, vines, and shelters.

Chapter 1

Landscape Matters

Humans have an innate desire to observe the natural landscape, and a companion urge to want to do something to change it. In the garden, it seems, everyone is an artist. Over the centuries, we have discovered certain rules about what makes landscapes and gardens beautiful and comfortable. Applying these rules to your own landscape can enhance your mental and physical health, and, bottom line, the value of your property.

It's Only Natural

The desire to interact with our surroundings likely began the moment man recognized he existed within an environment. It seems to be a natural instinct to want to create beauty and comfort outdoors as well as in. Records from Egypt 4,000 years ago describe gardens with shade trees, flowerbeds, and grape and ivy vines trained on rafters and trellises. The Egyptians and other ancients discovered benefits and principles of gardening and landscaping that endure today. Whether it's a tiny space stretching from the back of a townhouse to an alley or several acres surrounding a suburban mansion, spaces not covered by buildings or concrete call out to us for visual interest, with color, texture, fragrance, and maybe even a little mystery.

Planting Ideas

In an Egyptian garden of 4,000 years ago, you would find some familiar elements:

◆ Walls for enclosure

◆ Trees for shade

◆ Rows of grapes (a vineyard)

◆ Fruit trees

◆ Small pools for waterfowl

◆ Pavilions for sitting

What is landscape design? Everyone knows what a landscape is. Painters have been showing us for centuries. At its simplest, it's a vista, a slice of the natural world. It may include structures, such as a cowshed or a cathedral—or even people or animals, such as children playing, dogs, or shepherds watching sheep. Some landscapes are stylized and complex, like the backgrounds in Renaissance paintings. Some are realistic, like the great Hudson River painters of the late nineteenth century, or the spare egg-temperas of contemporary Andrew Wyeth. Some are full of wild colors and shapes, like the Impressionist works of Monet and Cezanne. Some are no more than shapes or colors, like the abstract works of Helen Frankenthaler or Richard Diebenkorn. What all these "pictures" have in common is a pleasing arrangement of shapes and colors—just like a garden.

A statue stands at the center of this vista on the grounds of the U.S. Capitol, Washington, D.C.

Sizing Things Up

A garden by itself isn't quite a landscape. What's the difference? It's a matter of scale. Gardens are "small picture" while landscapes are "big picture." The landscape is your canvas, and gardens are part of the picture you paint on it. In your own landscape, you get to be the artist. You can be a minimalist, a modernist, a traditionalist, an impressionist—or you can combine elements you like from a number of styles.

In the rose garden at Brookside Gardens, Wheaton, Maryland, paths in various materials lead to and through a pergola.

Green Thumb Guides

Further reading on landscape design history:

Carpenter, Philip L., Theodore D. Walker, and Frederick O. Lanphear. *Plants in the Landscape.* New York: W. H. Freeman and Company, 1975.

Huxley, Anthony. *An Illustrated History of Gardening.* London: Royal Horticultural Society/Paddington Press Ltd., 1978.

Marinelli, Janet. *Stalking the Wild Amaranth: Gardening in the Age of Extinction.* New York: Henry Holt and Company, Inc., 1998.

Rogers, Elizabeth Barlow. *Landscape Design: A Cultural and Architectural History.* New York: Harry N. Abrams, Inc., 2001.

Your canvas might be 25 acres or 25 square feet. However big or small it is, you can use the principles of Lernscaping, a technique I developed in my 30 years of garden design, plus a few basic artistic concepts, and the myriad tools available to today's home gardener, to turn your space into the landscape of your dreams.

Steppingstones lead to a sheltered bench in a small garden in suburban Maryland.

Look around your outdoor space. Is it the bare dirt of new construction, or is it a collection of weeds and overgrown brush? It may be the misguided or simply not-to-your-taste remnants of a former owner's efforts. As you examine the landscape, it may seem like a daunting task to create an Eden out of this nothing or this chaos.

Relax. It's not that hard. Whether you recognize it or not, you already know some of the principles of good design.

In the Beginning

Where do these principles come from? It's one of those chicken-and-egg questions. Was it good landscaping or good design that first attuned the human eye to pleasing outdoor settings? I believe humans simply recognized the good elements in their surroundings.

Perhaps they notice that a clump of trees in the middle of a field appears to be a cozy and welcoming spot. Click! The old light bulb goes on in the head and someone says, "I see—trees in groups look good."

(Sandra Leavitt Lerner)

Trees in groups can be an appealing landscape feature.

Or maybe someone notices that after working outside in a field, or in the monotonous reaches of a forest, it feels good to step into the familiar confines of one's own backyard.

A wooden gate opens into a cozy
backyard retreat.

Stairs from a deck and French doors from a living
room aid indoor-outdoor transitions.

However it happened, people have discovered what kinds of outdoor spaces make them comfortable. Gradually, by putting these recognizable elements together, people were able to create more pleasing designs from the raw nature of their immediate surroundings.

People with absolutely no design experience and no garden experience are often at a loss to explain what they want from their landscape. While it's important that each garden reflect the individuals who use and enjoy it, there are a couple of general principles that underlie all landscape design.

Getting Comfortable

What contributes to comfort in a landscape? Well, it should be easy to get in and out of. The transition between indoors and outdoors should be comfortable. If you have a back door that opens from the kitchen onto a small porch and then there are 10 straight steps to get down to the yard, you are not going to be comfortable constantly making that trip up and down. But if you had French doors that opened onto a deck, perhaps with a grill area, then four or five steps down to a second deck level, perhaps with a waterfall, small pool, or hot tub, then a few more steps down to a terrace, going outdoors will be much more pleasant.

Green Thumb Guides

Let the outdoors in:

- Don't cover windows where privacy and light are not issues.
- Hang sheer curtains instead of drapes and use shades for privacy.
- Substitute a door for a window.
- Frame outdoor views through French doors, or use patio doors with dividers, or "lites" (the frames add human scale and a little mystery).
- Put matching containers inside and outside by a door or window.
- "Borrow" a neighboring view by framing it with trees or a gap in a hedge or fence.

Or say there are no stairs, just a pair of sliding glass doors opening from the dining room onto a square paved area. You could have French doors opening from a formal French drawing room onto a French *parterre* with formal plantings leading to a *knot* garden leading to a lion's head fountain on the far wall.

Roots and Stems

A **parterre** is a garden in which beds and paths are designed to form a pattern. A **knot** is a complex, compact, interlacing pattern of plantings in a garden bed.

Okay, maybe you don't have unlimited funds to recreate your space. Small touches can make a difference, and vastly improve the transition from in to out. Changing a solid door for a French door or a full-length glass storm door will bring the outdoors closer. Maybe you just need wider steps, with container plantings along the edges, or maybe you need to reconfigure the stairs with a landing, with plantings along the railings.

Ivy, santolina (lavender cotton), lamb's-ear, and boxwood form a knot edged with ivy at the U.S. National Arboretum, Washington, D.C.

Perennial groundcover plants form precise shapes in a formal parterre.

A flagstone grilling area is home to a gas grill.

A truly comfortable garden must accommodate all your needs. If you do a lot of summer entertaining, you need to have space for guests to move around, and a convenient place for outdoor cooking facilities. If you have a swimming pool, you need lounging space and smaller-scale plantings that won't overhang the water. If you've got a child who's a basketball fanatic, you need a place for a net standard so the kid can practice shooting hoops.

Small-scale plantings soften the stones around a swimming pool.

If you use the space to get to and from your car, you'll need easy access to the drive or garage, and perhaps some shelter from the weather as you move from one to the other.

You'll need traffic control, ways to move people easily from house to garden, house to vehicles, garden to garage or storage area, or, for city dwellers, from house to alley.

Finally, you will need to bring everything down to human scale. It may be another of those concepts that is hard-wired into the human brain: the need for shelter. It may be shelter from danger, or shelter from uncomfortable weather. It may be shelter from noise, or pollution, or even shelter from something ugly nearby. Whatever it is, people feel more comfortable when their landscape encloses them. This enclosure has a double effect. One is shutting out danger or discomfort and shutting in beauty and comfort. The other is bringing the vastness of the outdoors down to a human level, so that people will feel connected to their environment without feeling dwarfed or daunted.

Getting Interesting

A landscape might be practical and workable and comfortable, yet still be dull. In fact, this is what drives most homeowners to seek landscaping advice. Their outdoor spaces are all right, but they lack sparkle, they lack surprise, they lack color. Color is what gets a landscape noticed, and I hear this from clients all the time: "Just color it up, Joel."

There are all sorts of ways to make a landscape more interesting. The most obvious is by putting in interesting and colorful plants. You can use *annuals* for a splash of one-season-only brightness, *biennials* to display foliage the first year and flower profusely the second, or *perennials* for reliable color year to year. But a landscape is more than a collection of flowers, shrubs, and trees. You have a dozen more elements to add interest to your landscape.

Roots and Stems

Annuals are plants that don't grow back after freezing, so must be planted every year, including flowers, herbs, and grasses. **Biennials** are plants that grow foliage the first year, then flower, then go to seed and decline or die, with new plants often springing up from the seeds. **Perennials** are plants that come up year after year, including trees, shrubs, bulbs, grasses, ferns, and flowers.

The curve of a bed of creeping juniper echoes a curving path.

Some are simple, such as taking out a straight path and putting in a curved one. Curved paths can make a small space look bigger, because your eye has to meander to follow it. They can also make big spaces look cozier, because they keep your eye from shooting straight out to the horizon.

A statue of a woman in repose adds to the tranquil look of a small pond.

Or you can turn to more complicated measures, such as re-grading the area to create hills and valleys (and improving drainage into the bargain) or adding small ponds at various levels and connecting them with waterfalls. You can build a gazebo in a leafy bower. Fences, hedges, pergolas, trellises, gates, and arbors all add interest in landscapes large or small.

A statue of a woman stands out against a small Stewartia tree.

Relatively simple elements include adding a sculptural feature, such as a statue or a sundial. You can add a water feature with a tiny pond.

(Joel M. Lerner)

Adding soil gentled the slope of a lawn, improving drainage and creating more level space.

Green Thumb Guides

The following are some garden structures:

◆ **Arbor.** A garden shelter, often made of rustic branches or latticework, on which roses or other vines are grown

A wooden gazebo offers a sheltered spot to look out over a northern Virginia garden.

An iron arbor forms an arch over a garden path.

◆ **Belvedere.** A structure or open-roofed gallery sited to command a view

◆ **Gazebo.** An open pavilion from which to observe a grand view

◆ **Loggia.** A roofed but open-sided gallery along the front or side of a building

◆ **Portico.** A porch or walkway with a roof supported by columns

◆ **Pergola.** An arbor or passageway with a trelliswork roof on which climbing plants are trained

◆ **Trellis.** A frame that supports latticework, used to train climbing flowers and vines

Climbing roses, sweetautumn clematis, and passionflower vines decorate a pergola.

Finally, and possibly most important, you can use some or all of these elements to make your space interesting every single day of the year, every month, and every season. You can design a landscape that is constantly changing, constantly appealing, and constantly surprising. And once again, you can do this whether you have 2,000 acres or a dozen square feet.

Dollars, Pounds, and Sense

Maybe you're not quite convinced that landscaping is for you. You like nice flowers, and you enjoy your few tomato or pepper plants. Why go to the trouble of designing a whole landscape? There are three very good reasons.

Out of the Tool Shed

For neat lawns you need the following:

◆ A mower (manual reel, electric, or gas powered).

◆ Grass clippers, shears, or string trimmer (gas or electric powered) to trim near trees and plant beds.

◆ A string trimmer (gas or electric powered) or edger (manual, gas, or electric) for edging next to hard surfaces.

◆ Bags for grass clippings (optional).

The first one is that it's good for you. There is extensive documentation of the therapeutic value—both physical and psychological—of gardening and the tasks involved in maintaining attractive grounds. These activities offer good calorie-burning exercise—as much as 150 to 240 calories per hour for working in the garden, and as many as 360 calories per hour for mowing the lawn with a push mower. They also offer a great escape from the pressures and pace of daily life. Horticulture therapy has been used to help people who are confined by age or illness to reconnect with the world and to improve strength and concentration. The Chinese have long believed that participating in the natural order of life around you will bring serenity and harmony.

These beliefs are based on the idea that our lives and fortunes are enhanced or impeded by the flow of vital energy, called "chi" (*chee*), around us. The ancient art of feng shui (*feng SCHWAY*) is designed to harness and direct the energy so people can live more in tune with nature. A partial Western parallel might be the old folkways that told when to plant and when to harvest by the phases of the moon. It

is part of the doctrine of feng shui that everything changes, so it is possible to apply these ancient principles even to the modern world. Feng shui involves everything from determining the most propitious siting of a structure to the natural ways to promote growth and inhibit disease in the garden.

A wooden bench painted periwinkle blue offers a destination at the end of a path, which is good feng shui.

While the entire system is deeply complex and full of complicated symbolism, some simple elements can be applied in every garden. For instance, it is believed that chi travels in meandering lines, and that straight lines or abrupt barriers will overhasten or block the flow of beneficial energy. Thus, paths can be laid out to wander, and the placement and type of a fence or hedge should be considered for its role in directing energy. Establishing harmony can mean establishing plants that are beneficial to one another. There are many books about feng shui, including *The Feng Shui Garden*, by Gill Hale (Storey Books, 1998), and most urban areas have feng shui consultants (ask at garden centers).

Planting Ideas

Feng shui in the garden:

◆ Clematis vines like cool roots. Use low-growing or mounding plants at the base of the structure on which the plants are growing.

◆ Plant marigolds around vegetables to inhibit aphids.

◆ Follow the natural contours of the land in laying out paths.

◆ Add a small Zen feature: an interesting rock or collection of a few rocks represent mountains, and gravel raked in patterns around them represents water.

The second reason for good landscaping is that creating a landscape that works within and contributes to the environment is good for your community. The environmental awareness movement that started in the 1960s has gradually alerted most people to the dangers of exploiting natural resources instead of conserving them. Trees and other plants breathe in carbon dioxide, a major culprit in global warming, as well as absorbing the fossil-fuel particulate matter that is a large part of urban pollution. A decade ago, the American Forestry Association figured that planting 100 million trees around homes and businesses to keep them cooler in the summer would save $4 billion in energy costs and reduce carbon dioxide emissions by 18 million tons per year.

Creating a garden landscape that conserves water, reduces or eliminates the use of chemicals, offers habitat for beneficial birds and insects, and makes everyone who glimpses it smile will have a positive effect. Gardens as a part of everyday life are considered so important that Congress in 1989 authorized the construction of a National Garden on a three-acre site at the foot of the U.S. Capitol. The National Garden site, overseen by the office of the Architect of the Capitol, will contain rare plants, a rose garden, a water garden, a wetlands environment, and an environmental learning center, among other elements. Even if you have a tiny space, you can make a contribution to the larger environment. And if you have a large space, you owe it to your environment to preserve and conserve the best of it.

A table with an umbrella offers an inviting place to pause on the terrace of the U.S. Botanic Garden at the base of the Capitol in Washington, D.C.

The third reason is that good landscaping makes good economic sense. Studies show lower absenteeism and higher morale in workplaces with plantings. Hotels can and do charge higher fees for rooms with garden views. Good landscaping around a private home can increase its value by at least 15 percent. In fact, for a homeowner, landscaping is the only home improvement you can make that increases in value with time: It can offer a 100 to 200 percent return on investment, as opposed to an 80 percent return for a new kitchen or a 75 percent return for a new bathroom. And both the kitchen and the bath start depreciating as soon as they are installed. Landscaping is the most important home improvement you can make.

The Least You Need to Know

- The desire to create a pleasing landscape is natural.
- The landscape is your canvas, and gardens are part of the picture.
- Good principles make good garden design.
- A garden should be comfortable and interesting.
- A delightful landscape makes good sense and cents.

In This Chapter

- ◆ A brief history of garden time
- ◆ Friends, Romans, and countrymen
- ◆ Royal prerogatives
- ◆ This side of the Pond
- ◆ A great time to garden

Humans have a long-standing appreciation for flowers.

Chapter 2

Landscapes of the Past

Archaeological evidence exists to prove humans appreciated flowers as long as 150,000 years ago, but it wasn't until the development of agriculture that plants began to be grown for pleasure. The Romans were probably the first great gardeners, and their ideas were rediscovered and expanded upon by Renaissance royalty. While settlers in the New World at first followed European styles, over the past hundred years a new, looser style has developed. Today's gardeners have centuries of history and a newly exploded variety of plant forms to choose from.

Long, Long Ago

Proof of the power that plants evoke in humans can be found in some of the oldest archaeological findings and in the most ancient of records. Wildflowers have been found in graves of the prehistoric people of Eurasia known as Neanderthals, who lived some 150,000 years ago. The Bible begins—in the beginning—with the Garden of Eden.

If you're just beginning to look at your outdoor space as part of a larger picture, it might help you to understand something of how the art and science of *gardening* arose. Take heart from this. No matter how green you are as a gardener, you always have plenty of history to draw on. What follows is an abbreviated look at some of the ways *landscaping* and gardening developed.

Roots and Stems

As a verb, **to garden** is to cultivate a private plot of land with flowers, vegetables, and fruits. **To landscape** is to improve or adorn a plot of land by contouring and planting shrubs or trees

Green Thumb Guides

The earliest gardeners cultivated:

- Grains, such as corn, wheat, and rice
- Roots and tubers, such as yams and taro
- Vegetables, such as potatoes and onions
- Fruits, such as bananas, figs, grapes, quince, pears, and pomegranates
- Herbs, such as mint, sorrel, dill, coriander, and watercress
- Nuts, such as hazelnut, walnut, and chestnut

At first, all manipulation of the landscape by man was for purely practical purposes—to grow food to eat. According to noted English garden writer Anthony Huxley, early cultivating of crops, mostly grains of some sort, seems to have begun in the area of Palestine sometime around 8000 B.C.E. There are also records of cultivation around 6500 B.C.E. in central Anatolia (now Turkey), and in Mesopotamia (Iraq) and Crete around 6000 B.C.E. In China, agriculture was being practiced at least as early as 5000 B.C.E., in India and South America by 2500 B.C.E.

Grape arbors were featured in Egyptian gardens.

People who lived in these settlements supplemented a diet of meat and grain with wild fruit—grapes, figs, pomegranates, and apricots. Gradually, stands of these formerly wild products began to grow up around settlements. People discovered the seeds, or pips, from which these plants could be grown, and began to develop orchards.

The earliest gardens featured water elements, like this pool at the U.S. Botanic Garden in Washington, D.C.

We're Getting There

None of this is exactly what we would today call a garden, nor was it any kind of landscape plan. That had to wait until the settlements, or villages, were secure from marauders and had risen above the subsistence level. By 1500 B.C.E., Huxley writes in *An Illustrated History of Gardening* (Paddington Press Limited, 1978), the Egyptians had developed the decorative garden, adding walls, regular beds, pools, and trees, and shortly after, flowers. Other cultures, the Assyrians and Babylonians, and later the Persians, created huge parklike gardens, used in part for hunting. Their writings show that the ancient Greeks loved flowers and scenes of natural beauty, and some wealthy people were able to plant acreage for their own enjoyment. The Greeks also actively cultivated herbs and other medicinal plants.

Early gardeners built walls for enclosure, like this square block stone wall at Brookside Gardens, Wheaton, Maryland.

Pleasure Gardens

But it wasn't until the second century B.C.E. that the Romans, with their great riches and advanced technology, developed farming, market gardening—exactly like the farmers' markets found in cities today—and laid the foundations for decorative gardening. The Romans borrowed some elements from the Greeks—with courtyards surrounding the main house. They used rectangular beds with paved walks and edgings of box and ivy, with some plants in large containers. They added statues, ornamental urns, and water elements, such as pools and fountains.

Roman gardens featured pools with small statues.

Huxley reports that where space was limited, the Romans extended their gardens with *trompe l'oeil* paintings on the walls. The latter characteristic can be seen in excavations of the city of Pompeii, buried under volcanic ash from erupting Mount Vesuvius in 79 C.E. and excavated beginning in the mid-seventeenth century. Huxley says some gardens as small as one foot by seven feet were expanded visually by a painted wall or fence. Roman gardeners also put plants in large containers, and used urns, statues, and water elements such as pools and fountains. Where ground space was limited, the Romans went up, and used rooftops and terraces for plantings. In their town gardens, the Romans used beds raised two to three feet above the ground. Raised beds were easier to work, protected plants from careless trampling, and could be filled with better soil than the rocky or sandy ground might have offered.

Where space is limited, plants thrive in containers, an idea adopted from the Romans.

With the fall of Rome, the glorious Roman gardens disappeared, and much of their lore was lost. However, the rise of monastic culture in Western Europe revived the art of gardening and preserved many plants from older times. Religious orders grew flowers to decorate churches, and herbs were raised for culinary and medicinal uses. Cloisters and enclosed courtyards often featured beds of flowers or herbs, sometimes divided into small enclosures, or *parterres*.

Matched rows of sky pencil hollies create a classic sense of enclosure at Bartholdi Park at the U.S. Botanic Garden in Washington, D.C.

Cloisters offered seclusion and quiet, a place to meditate or simply contemplate the natural world. Meanwhile, in medieval Spain, ruled by the Moors, luxury villas with elaborate gardens were being built. Perhaps the most famous examples remain today, the Alhambra palaces and their accompanying Generalife gardens in present-day Grenada. Because the climate is so dry, water, in pools and fountains, was an important feature in Moorish gardens.

It's Mine, All Mine!

Roman garden principles were rediscovered after the Dark Ages, and formed the basis for the grand Renaissance gardens of fourteenth- to sixteenth-century Europe. Because it required having a certain amount of wealth and leisure, the early grand gardens were those of nobles. Kings and emperors wanted a place to hunt, a place to take diplomatic strolls, maybe a place for a little romance.

Roman ruins and Roman garden ideas were rediscovered during the Renaissance. These columns are at the U.S. National Arboretum in Washington, D.C.

The idea arose that the outside of a stately home or castle should be as beautiful as the inside. In Renaissance France, royal gardens in the form of parterres or terraces, many with water elements, began at the walls of the palace and stretched as far as the eye could see. It was a king's way of saying, "Everything you see is mine to control."

Kings and nobles wanted parkland for hunting and strolling, like this lawn at Brookside Gardens, Wheaton, Maryland.

What we think of today as English gardening, with its expansive parks and walled and hedged garden "rooms" for flowers and vegetables, began to evolve in the 1600s, during the relatively peaceful reign of James I. By the late 1700s, gardening had come to the villages, and it was a rare cottage that didn't have its bit of land growing fruits, vegetables, and flowers.

Peaceful times in the 1600s led to the development of kitchen gardening, like these raised beds at an urban Washington, D.C., community garden.

The New World

When the first European settlers arrived on the shores of North America, they found the Native Americans growing fields of corn and tobacco, as well as vegetables and fruits. On the West Coast, Spanish Jesuit missionaries planted orchards, sugar cane, and herbs. Fences were important, both to help secure crops and to establish ownership.

In the New World, fences became important for enclosing livestock and indicating property boundaries.

By 1724, garden excellence was typified in Williamsburg, Virginia, where the English-inspired landscapes had—and still have, in present-day restoration—walkways, arbors, knot gardens, and ornamental plantings, often surrounded by box hedges.

An ornamental knot garden is bordered with ivy at the U.S. National Arboretum.

After two centuries of borrowing from European and British culture, two landscape architects, Wolfgang Oehme and James van Sweden, began to champion a new-old idea, which they called the New American Garden. Oehme and van Sweden advocated using native plants, such as grasses and wildflowers, in dense but free-form plantings that borrowed from natural surroundings. The New American Garden was seasonal and year-round.

The New American Garden features grasses, natural stone, and year-round interest.

Oehme and van Sweden, based in the Washington, D.C., area, rejected traditional "foundation" plantings that obscured architecture and instead used ground forms, gravel, stones, abstract natural and created forms, and plants to create three-dimensional art through which garden and public art patrons could stroll. They rejected the manicured look inherited from British and French formal landscapes and instead sought to create free-form, casual plantings that caress the land rather than constrict it.

Putting It All Together

What does all this mean for you, the modern-day homeowner? It means you can pick and choose from every bit of historical context. For instance, from the Greeks and Romans we learn the importance of statuary. All you have to do is place an urn or a terra cotta planter in a space and it says "garden." You don't even need to put a plant in the container. It works as simple sculpture. A simple statue, a "found" piece of rusted metal, or a small concrete frog, can make a garden of an ordinary bunch of plants. The idea is that the space has been enhanced. Space enhancements can be accidental, as well. A stump, an outcrop of rock, or a self-seeded vine twining around an old pump handle can turn a collection of plants into a "garden." Even in a narrow townhouse yard, perhaps hemmed in by tall fences or neighboring garages, a bench at the end or on one side, flanked by a pair of containers, will create an inviting haven.

A rock outcropping enhances a landscape space.

Even a tiny fountain offers a big enhancement in the garden.

Also from the Romans, you can borrow the idea of painting a view or scene that can turn a blank wall into a whimsical extension of the garden. It may be a part of the house, a plain basement door, or even the side of a garage. It's probably not a good idea to get your five-year-old to scrawl something in the space. If you have minimal artistic talent, you can copy designs from a book or magazine, or even from a block of wallpaper. (Trace a scrolly ivy from a border across the top or cross pieces of a gate and paint it with acrylics from a craft store.)

Or hire a local artist to design and paint a scene for you. It may be less expensive than you think. Or offer to trade fruits, vegetables, and herbs for artwork. If you're waiting for plantings to mature, consider painting them in the meantime!

Embrace the idea that a "garden" needn't cover acres, or even a lot of square feet. If your back door opens onto the brick wall of the garage, use a trellis and container plants to make it a little haven of green. Like their ancestors the Romans, Italians today find space for plants in every nook and cranny, from the top of a hollow pillar to the grating over a window. Posts that hold up awnings are enhanced by vines, and tiny spaces between paving stones are niches for fragrant herbs.

Adding a water element can also create the feel of a complete garden. It needn't be as elaborate as a fountain of prancing steeds and cherubs. A simple recirculating wall fountain can have a big impact by a patio. A small pond with a tiny bubbly fountain provides a home for historic bog plants such as iris and lotus.

From the Egyptians, take the idea of shade trees to create cooling oases in a hot yard. You can also use vines to soften the hard surfaces of fences and walls. Train vines on a trellis to screen a driveway or air-conditioning unit.

A groundcover juniper softens the outlines of exposed aggregate and brick steps.

All you have to do these days is to take a walk through any garden center, and you can find elements of all of these threads of history. You can find dozens of kinds of herbs, and each herb in many varieties. You can find fruit trees—often planted for their spring flowers—and dwarf fruit trees suitable for small-garden "orchards." There are ivies in many varieties, and boxwoods and other hedging plants. You can even find frames for training topiary, artfully shaped greenery often planted in containers.

Fencing materials range from iron, like this one, to wood and wire.

Rustic stones form a naturalistic path at Brookside Gardens, Wheaton, Maryland.

You can find a dozen varieties of gravel for walkways, or paving stones, quarried and manufactured, in all shapes, sizes, and colors. You can find flowerpots and containers that look like Roman urns or French parterre planters. There are fencing materials from rustic to ultra-ornamental, and wire, wood, and terra cotta edgings in all sorts of shapes.

You can find heirloom roses, lavender varieties that grow on Greek mountains or hillsides in Provence. You can find herbs for medicinal purposes (St. John's-wort, chamomile) and for culinary uses (rosemary, thyme, sage). You can find flowers that stand tall, flowers that act like bushes, flowers that creep or cascade. And you can find dozens of native grasses, and all kinds of plants that work in bog or water gardens—from the iris of oriental style to the lotus so prized by the Egyptians.

This may be the best time ever for you to develop your landscaping skills, for you have the choice of plants and materials developed over millennia by gardeners from all over the earth. You can also benefit from the cumulative wisdom of all those who've ever used a stick to dig a hole or lifted a designer hoe from a fancy catalog. You can, within reason, bring the world home to your own plot. Even if your garden encompasses only a few square feet, landscaping it to suit you can provide an almost regal feeling of well-being.

(Sandra Leavitt Lerner)

A modern garden center offers a dazzling array of plants and garden materials. This one is located in Kensington, Maryland.

The Least You Need to Know

◆ Humans have cared about plants for more than 1,500 centuries.

◆ Early forms of gardening, mostly by and for nobles, included stylized and formal beds as well as wilder areas for hunting.

◆ After the discovery of the New World, garden forms gradually became more parklike and less formal.

◆ Today there's growing interest in gardens that are natural, native, and low-maintenance.

◆ Contemporary landscapers can pick and choose from every style imaginable.

In This Chapter

- Fashions in horticulture

- Addressing your favorite style

- A glance at garden types

- Elements of style

- Plants for every occasion

A small garden becomes stylish with trellised vines
against the brick wall of a garage.

Chapter 3

Garden Styles

Gardens, like people, have their own particular styles. Travel is one of the best ways to appreciate these differences. Gardens of certain eras and places will exhibit common characteristics. Studying the various styles can help you decide what features you want to include in your own garden space.

It Takes All Kinds

Gardens, like houses and clothing, come in a variety of "styles." Each has a palette of features and plantings that are characteristic. Some are taken from historic models, some come from international tradition. Although each style is distinctly recognizable, all of them borrow some characteristics from the earliest forms of gardening.

People often absorb ideas of what is fashionable in clothing or home design by reading magazines, studying movies and television, or observing what people on the street are wearing. Even people who don't care about looking as if they just stepped off a designer's runway can discover new fabrics or colors that appeal to them. Traveling to Paris is almost bound to awaken some kind of fashion sense in everyone, because Paris is a place where dressing well is an everyday occupation. This works in garden design as well. People who have never been interested in landscaping or gardening are sometimes inspired by something they read about in a book or magazine or see in a movie. (Frances Hodgson's *The Secret Garden*, in print or in its many movie incarnations, has drawn generations of people to the idea of an English-style walled garden.) Or they are excited by a place they have encountered while traveling.

The U.S. Botanic Garden, at the foot of the Capitol, borrows elements from classic French, Italian, and English gardens.

Even in North America, influences of French garden design can be found, as in this public park in Quebec City where *alternanthera* forms the classic fleur-de-lis design.

Maybe it's happened to you. Every summer my phone starts ringing with calls from people who have seen something they love on a trip and want to know how to re-create it at home. Many people are surprised when they first visit countries like Greece, Italy, and Spain by the sheer profusion of plantings. In public spaces, every light pole is a standard to hold hanging baskets, and every traffic divider strip is profusely planted. Every windowsill and balcony sports containers of billowing flowers. In Japan, where space is always at a premium, tiny but carefully designed gardens are astonishing

oases of tranquility. In England and France, the shaping of landscapes large and small creates "rooms" that can be as sweet and cozy as a cottage, or as grand and spacious as a palace.

In public spaces in Victoria, British Columbia, light poles are standards to hold hanging baskets. Every nook and cranny is profusely planted.

The United States is large enough to have a diverse range of climate, and thus a vast array of landscape styles, from the low-slung rock gardens of New England to the wildflower prairies of the Midwest, from the colorful and rocky mesas of the Southwest to the Mediterranean profusion of Southern California.

Rocks and cactus characterize a garden in the Southwestern United States.

Traveling is always an excellent way to get garden ideas. Even a trip around your neighborhood can be helpful and inspiring. You can see how other folks have solved landscape problems, and what plantings they have had success with. Taking pictures or videos or drawing sketches of plants, structures, and plans you like as you travel is an excellent way to make sure you remember what you've seen and to begin a catalog of pleasures to consult for your own landscape space. Postcards and magazines are also good sources of ideas. While not every element of every garden can be duplicated in your particular location, *every* idea can be translated into something that will work for you. And remember that you don't have to stick to one style. You can mix and match elements from several types.

The Conservatory at the U.S. Botanic Garden in Washington, D.C., combines a Moorish-style pool and Italian- or French-style plant containers.

Characteristically Speaking

To give you an idea of some of the choices you have, here are some of the most popular garden styles. People are drawn to them because they meet the needs of their day-to-day lives for aesthetics, culinary use, low maintenance, color, and privacy, among others. You can pluck ideas from each and be the creator of your own eclectic garden.

English Country

English country, or cottage, gardens abound in foliage and floral color. They were extensively developed during the latter part of the nineteenth century, and remain popular today. These gardens have their origins in the late 1600s, when commoners moved from castle enclosures to small places of their own near farms or in villages. Because space was limited inside the walls of a castle, plants grown there were herbs for medicinal and culinary use, plus grapes and small fruit trees. That's why cottage gardens contain mostly flowers.

English country gardens mixed flowers and herbs, typically in a small area around a cottage or in individual garden "rooms."

Flowers flank a brick path in English-style border gardens at the U.S. National Arboretum, Washington, D.C.

Cottage gardens often bordered the path to the door of the dwelling, and this feature began the traditional mixed border, which still tends to follow a hedge or fence. The borders, with a foundation of smaller shrubs and perennials, are densely planted so that each flowering is succeeded by another. Typically, taller plants form the background, while sprawling or creeping plants encroach on lawns or walkways in front. You can design borders with a riot of color, or choose just a few colors, or even focus on a single hue (plus green, of course). You can use fences, arbors, and trellises to expand the area for plants vertically.

Use holly, like this 'Dragon Lady' cultivar, in an English-style garden.

Planting Ideas

Combine English style with greenery that likes the local climate. Escalonia, a wonderful flowering broadleaf evergreen shrub in England, can't survive the harsher winters in North America. Instead, try cherrylaurel or holly. Instead of the tall spiky delphiniums and lupines, try foxgloves, hollyhocks, and liatris.

Cottage gardens may also include more than one "room." Each room has a particular style or focus. The rooms may be set off with hedges or other structures, or they may be simply groups of related plantings. Sometimes the rooms are planted in a single color family—the White Garden at Sissinghurst Castle in Southeastern England is a famous example. The rooms are linked with one another by paths that wind through the landscape. The walkways are often edged with beds full of mixed flowering trees, shrubs, and perennials. This meandering style was probably derived from the Asian influence that was beginning to be felt in Europe in the eighteenth century.

A bench offers a place to sit in a garden "room" at Brookside Gardens, Wheaton, Maryland.

Typical plants of a cottage garden include tulips, daffodils, iris, roses, delphiniums, lilies, phlox, daisies, dahlias, poppies, asters, box, yew, heaths and heathers, European beech, linden, and horse-chestnuts.

Phlox (this is the cultivar 'David,' a fragrant variety)
a typical English garden plant.

Flowers and foliage in strict geometric shapes form
a French-style parterre.

French Country

French country gardens typically combine vegetables with decorative plants and flowers. They
may also include fruit, such as strawberries or
raspberry bushes, and small trees, such as pear
or apple. There may be some more formal elements, such as a central fountain or a sundial,
or even a stylized "knot" of herbs and small,
trimmed shrubs.

An armillary sphere gives a French touch to a center
bed at the U.S. National Arboretum.

Planting Ideas

Some edible flowers and their culinary
uses include the following:

◆ Nasturtiums: salads, pasta, pasta
salads

◆ Violets: candied, as decorations for
cakes and pastries

◆ Marigolds: petals in salads, pasta
salads

◆ Squash blossoms: salads, or stuffed
like peppers

French country gardens can be practical as
well as pretty. Some flowers, such as violets,
nasturtiums, and marigolds, are edible and
make beautiful additions to salads or stews.
Vegetables such as eggplant, artichoke, and
asparagus have great foliage and interesting
shapes. If you use leggy plants, like tomatoes
or peas, they will need to be staked or tied up
so they don't droop or wander, but a bit of
inspired chaos is what makes a French *potager*,
or kitchen garden, so charming.

(Sandra Leavitt Lerner)

The foliage of candytuft is evergreen; white flowers appear in spring.

Typical plants found in a French country garden include nasturtiums, strawberries, santolina, candytuft, germander, box, and hazelnut.

French or English Formal

Symmetry and order prevail in a formal garden. Typically, it consists of a number of terraces, or parterres, usually square or rectangular, surrounded by clipped hedges and filled with often-elaborate plantings in curvy, scrolly shapes. Box and yew are popular hedging plants, and roses are often used in the centers. Paving stones or raked gravel may form paths between the beds, or separate plants inside the beds. Often the landscape was designed to show best at a level slightly above the ground, perhaps from the terrace or belvedere of a palace.

The Wedding Gazebo is the focal point of symmetrical lawns at Brookside Gardens, Wheaton, Maryland.

Planting Ideas

Topiary—evergreen foliage that is trimmed or trained to grow in a particular nonplantlike shape—is a common element in a formal garden. It's probably the most extreme example of manipulated nature, and people tend to love it or hate it for that reason, but skillfully used, it can be striking. Shapes may be as simple as cones or balls, or as elaborate as the fox, hounds, and mounted huntsman carved from living greenery at Maryland's Ladew Gardens.

Rosemary and other herbs are typical of a French garden.

Typical plants found in a formal garden include rosemary and other herbs, roses, boxes, yews, violets, and wallflowers.

Italian

The grand Italian villas of the Renaissance were often located on top of hills, and the slopes leading up to them would be divided into as many as three or four terraces. The main entrance would be on the lowest level, which might also contain the most formal of the rising gardens. Higher levels would be increasingly wooded, with the top level providing a forest retreat around the main dwelling. These Italian gardens were generally oriented toward the *hardscape;* that is, the structural elements were more important than the plantings. These elements included fountains and waterways, statues, balustrades, the walled terraces themselves, and walls on which plants could be trained. Stairways between levels were often elaborate and magnificently decorated with stonework and statuary.

(Joel M. Lerner)

A fountain is the central element in a formal design at the U.S. National Arboretum, Washington, D.C.

The design may be elaborate, with several gardens surrounding a central statue or fountain, or it may be as simple as a pair of matching conifers surrounded by low hedges confining a single type of flower or a single color family. Even if you like more informal plantings, you might want to use a more formal approach in areas that border the street or entryway.

(Joel M. Lerner)

A stepped fountain at Meridian Hill Park in Washington, D.C., echoes classic Italian gardens.

Roots and Stems

Hardscape is the walks, patios, sheds, arbors, trellises, pools, and other structural elements of the landscape.

(Joel M. Lerner)

Terraces, fountains, and symmetrical hedges are hallmarks of European grand design at Longwood Gardens, Kennett Square, Pennsylvania.

Water elements were important features of these gardens. A gigantic urn-shaped fountain pouring water over its sides would have a path directly underneath, so visitors could stroll around the base of the urn and look out under a curtain of water. Another garden might have a torrent of water pouring down steps into a pool at a lower level. Although the structures were more prominent than the plants in these gardens, Renaissance Italians were fascinated by exotic plants brought back by sailing merchants, and often included a greenhouse on the property to shelter tender plants.

Typical plants found in Italian gardens are box, yew, cypress, ivy and other vines and climbers, oak, chestnut, and stone pine.

Chinese

Enclosure is the hallmark of a Chinese garden, often designed as a series of interlocking shapes, like a jigsaw puzzle or game board. These garden rooms were often separated by covered walkways. Inside the shapes, the designs tended to be stylized, with architectural elements prevailing. Sometimes a large weathered rock stood for a mountain range, or sometimes a pond was the focal point.

A teahouse sits over a pond at Brookside Gardens, Wheaton, Maryland.

Other features of Chinese style include grade changes to emphasize an architectural feature, such as a pagoda or teahouse. Plantings tend to be sparse, though trees are treated with special respect.

(Joel M. Lerner)

Azaleas (this is the 'Delaware Valley White' cultivar) are typical of a Chinese-style garden.

Typical plants in a Chinese garden include azaleas, pines, flowering cherries, maples, iris, peonies, lilies, and daylilies.

Japanese

Tranquility and harmony are the goals of Japanese style in gardens that tend to pack a lot of impact into a small area. Water features, small structures such as pagodas, and teahouses are combined with statuary, wood and stone structures such as benches and gates, and beautiful, but often spare, plantings. In some Japanese "gardens," plants may be absent altogether. Instead, carefully designed structures are placed amid gravel raked into patterns.

Both plants and structures are used for symbolic effect, and the whole is rigorously planned to conform to the gardener's chosen theme. Japanese gardens are often meant to be enriching places that will encourage those who visit to think of loftier pleasures.

A meandering path constructed of randomly sized rock leads to a wooden structure, called a *torii,* that is a Japanese-style feature at Brookside Gardens, Wheaton, Maryland.

Planting Ideas

A noted example of an American Japanese-style garden is Hillwood, installed in the 1950s by Japanese designer Shogo Myaida on the Washington, D.C., estate of Marjorie Merriweather Post. The garden includes typical lantern, Buddha, and pagoda structures, but uses plants hardy to the region. Constructed on a hillside, the garden has huge rock structures and a pedestrian circulation pattern that you would be more likely to find in a Chinese or alpine rock garden.

(Joel M. Lerner)

The flowering cherry trees in Washington, D.C., were a gift of the Japanese government.

Typical plants of a Japanese garden include daylilies, maples, flowering cherries, Japanese plum yews, grasses, chrysanthemums, and lycoris (spider lily).

Southwestern

Spare forms and intense pastel colors are the hallmarks of the Southwestern style found from Arizona and New Mexico to Nevada and parts of Southeastern California. Because the climate in this region tends to be harsh, with dry, rocky soil and rainfall as sparse as 10 inches per year, the natural hues and rocky outcroppings may form the bare bones of the garden, with plants added as accents. Distinguishing elements are flat "mesa-looking" rocks and stone mulches. The dry regions vary considerably in altitude, and plants that thrive at different levels vary as well. Where lower levels might feature cacti and succulents, higher levels would be more like an alpine meadow with conifers such as spruce and pine. A bonus of the Southwestern look is that you'll have a drought-resistant planting.

(Peter C. Benjamin)

Weathered wood, crushed stone, and a dry-stack wall, augmented by a few carefully chosen plants, distinguish this New Mexican garden.

(Peter C. Benjamin)

Piñon pines are typical evergreen conifers found in the Southwestern United States.

Typical plants of a Southwestern garden include tanyosho pines, yuccas, armerias, artemesias, santolinas, lavenders, sedums, and cacti.

Prairie or Meadow

Wildflowers and a loose, natural look define this look from the Midwestern United States. Plantings tend to be in large sweeps, and may be combined with swatches of lawn. Meadow gardens have become extremely popular in recent years, in part because they renew themselves, are low maintenance once they're established, and offer a coordination of bloom. If you have room for it, this kind of landscape can be stunning when a wildflower population comes into balance. They do require proper site preparation, careful planting for proper timing, and patience for a balanced mix of flowers.

(Joel M. Lerner)

Wildflowers characterize a meadow garden.

Green Thumb Guides

The following are some suggestions for creating a wildflower meadow. If you follow this recipe for wildflower seeding, be patient because it takes a year to prepare the site properly before it can be planted. The decades of low-maintenance enjoyment that follow are worth it.

◆ Site in full sun.

◆ Spray with a nonselective herbicide three times in spring (around March 1), in summer (around May 1 through 15), and in fall (September through October), when weeds are present and actively growing.

◆ Spray weeds again the following spring.

◆ Ten days after the spring spraying, break up the soil surface one-half inch in depth and seed with a mix tailored to your site from a local garden center or a wildflower mail order company. Purchase from a supplier who can explain why one specified mix is better for your situation than another.

◆ Stake a fabric mesh on embankments to hold seed in place.

Note: Spraying herbicide can be avoided. Instead, cover area to be seeded with black plastic or landscape fabric, staked in place, for one full year. Lift fabric in late spring and follow last two suggestions for creating a wildflower meadow.

Typical plants found in a wildflower garden include lanceleaf coreopsis, tickseed sunflower, purple coneflower, Joe-Pye weed, cardinal flower, lupine, bee balm, wild bergamot, black-eyed Susan, blue phlox, goldenrod, bird's-foot violet, switchgrass, little bluestem, and Indiangrass.

The New American Garden

Landscape architects Wolfgang Oehme and Jim van Sweden, founders of Oehme, van Sweden & Associates, Inc., Washington, D.C., mix trees, shrubs, perennials, wildflowers, bulbs, and ornamental grasses for year-round interest and low maintenance in their New American Garden style. Van Sweden, who grew up in Michigan, and Oehme, who grew up in Germany, met in 1964, designed their first garden together in 1971, and formed their partnership in 1975. Over the years, they have developed gardens that offer year-round interest and require little maintenance. It's a natural style using plants that are self-sustaining and aesthetically pleasing. The garden is designed to highlight all the interesting characteristics of a plant, including its flowers, berries, fall color, winter form, or colorful, peeling bark.

Naturalistic plantings, including grasses, variegated hosta, and yellowtwig dogwood, are featured in a New American–style garden room in Washington, D.C.

Green Thumb Guides

Here's a selection of New American Garden plants from Wolfgang Oehme.

◆ **Feather reed grass.** Ornamental grass with spring and winter interest; leafs out early spring; early flower; good companion for shrubs; plant in full sun.

◆ **Spike winterhazel.** Wide-spreading shrub; 6 feet in height; fragrant yellow flowers in April; leafs out purple; displays a zigzag branching habit in winter; tolerant of partial shade.

◆ **Elecampane or Inula.** Yellow daisy flower in late summer; massive plant; perennial; best naturalized as a mass planting; informal, open setting; plant in full sun.

◆ **Sweetbay magnolia.** Pyramidal tree; clean, open branching habit; fragrant white flowers in summer; evergreen to semi-evergreen; likes moist, well-drained acid soil; shade tolerant.

◆ **Thread-leaf moonbeam coreopsis.** Lacy foliage; pastel yellow flowers.

◆ **Russian sage.** Fragrant, gray showy foliage; narrow erect habit; winter interest; blue flowering sub-shrub that grows to about 3 feet.

◆ **Moor grass.** Arching foliage grows about $1^{1}/_{2}$ feet tall; purplish lacy panicles grow to 3 feet in fall and look good in cut flower arrangements; best planted in moist soil rich in organic material; full sun.

◆ **Boltonia.** Plant this tall, 4-to-6-foot, aster-like perennial to the back of the border; late summer to fall bloomer; flowers are available in white, pink and purple; shorter variety named 'Snowbank' doesn't need staking.

◆ **Winter or black clump bamboo.** Very hardy, noninvasive bamboo; evergreen in winter; black stem; drought tolerant; handsome clump-forming specimen.

◆ **'Arnold Promise' witchhazel.** Fragrant yellow blossoms in winter; flowers dependably for about a month from February to March; plant in sun or partial shade; excellent in woodland gardens with rhododendrons and azaleas.

The New American Garden frequently employs margin-to-margin plantings, with no trace of the traditional lawn. Hardscape elements tend to be simplistic, consisting of paths, patios, and simple seating areas. *Softscape* elements provide texture and color. A typical pairing might place the feathery pink spikes of astilbe against the round fuchsia balls of *Allium giganteum*, ornamental onion.

Roots and Stems _____

Softscape is the trees, shrubs, foliage, and flowers in a landscape.

Miscanthus sinensis 'Gracillimus' and black-eyed Susans grace a New American style garden in Northern Virginia.

Typical plants of the New American Garden include: grasses, liatris, *Echinacea* (purple cone flower), allium, sedum, black-eyed Susan, wisteria, clematis, Japanese black pine, juniper, *Buddleia davidii*, and bayberry.

The Least You Need to Know

- ◆ Gardens come not only in all shapes and sizes but also in all styles and fashions.
- ◆ Popular garden styles range from English and French country through Japanese and Chinese to modern wildflower prairies and meadows to the naturalistic plantings of the New American Garden.
- ◆ Today's gardens can include elements from many styles.
- ◆ Need more stimuli? Check out your neighborhood, parks, schools, public buildings, and gardens.

In This Chapter

- ◆ The bad with the good
- ◆ Mother Nature knows best
- ◆ More fun, less fuss
- ◆ Making plants feel at home

Gardening trends toward low-maintenance plantings, as in the New American Garden, match homeowners' wishes for less fuss.

Chapter 4

Enlisting Mother Nature

The bad news—and we might as well get this out of the way fairly early, folks—is there's no such thing as a no-maintenance landscape. Even if you pour concrete over your entire lot and paint it green (and this is a surprisingly common reaction, mostly among guys, to the whole idea of landscaping), there will still be some work involved. Paint fades and wears off. Concrete cracks and chips. Rain and ice can turn painted concrete into glass under the feet of the unwary—you get the idea. If you have some kind of land, you will have to manage it and maintain it.

The good news, however, is that once you have a landscape design that suits you, that is uniquely your own, that matches your particular needs, you are likely to find that working in your garden is rewarding, even fun. And there are plenty of things you can do to make your landscape easy to maintain.

The Latest Trends

The latest trends in landscape gardening—most of those associated with the New American Garden—coincide with the goals of most home gardeners: less pruning, treating, and mowing, as well as less fertilizer and less water. No matter what kind of garden you plant, taking care of it will be easier if you enlist the help of Mother Nature.

You don't have to be a plant expert. You don't have to study the latest U.S. Department of Agriculture bulletins, or watch the Weather Channel 24/7. You just have to use some common sense when you envision and plan your garden. It may be called native planting, *xeriscaping*, or sustainable agriculture. All these terms signify ways of getting water to plants more efficiently and keeping it there as long as possible. A good way to describe the practice is "water-efficient" landscape design.

Roots and Stems

Xeriscape (*ZEER-is-cape*) is landscape design for dry conditions.

Green Thumb Guides

Watering to save water:

- Watering early in the day, before dawn, will conserve. Watering during the afternoon leads to excessive evaporation, and watering at night can encourage leaf spot and other fungi, because the foliage often doesn't dry until the following day.

- Don't water in hot, dry, windy, or rainy weather.

- On slopes and areas where water tends to run off, frequent brief waterings are best.

- During a warm, dry winter, if the soil is not frozen, water to soak the root zones of major plants.

- Even drought-resistant plants need to be watered while they are becoming established.

A Leaf from Mother Nature

Whatever you call it, it means using the plants and techniques that conserve water and keep flora flourishing. It means using plants that already enjoy the conditions available in your landscape.

In their purist form, native plants are those that evolved with the animals that inhabited a region. In their absence, an area's ecology is severely altered. There are many examples, the most famous probably being the panda. As bamboo forests are cut in China, pandas, which need this single member of the grass family for habitat and food, are becoming extinct. This loss of habitat could be reversed by stopping the assault on bamboo.

Planting Ideas

Many plants from other areas of the world won't display invasive tendencies. But before any are introduced, they should have their performance tracked for several years, until we know that they won't negatively affect our ecology. To learn whether your trees, shrubs, and flowers could be invasive, call the Cooperative Extension Service or Native Plant Society in your county or state.

(Sandra Leavitt Lerner)

Porcelainberry (*Ampelopsis brevipedunculata*), an Asian native, is invasive in the United States.

Sometimes we unknowingly cause habitat destruction in ways that can't easily be stopped. For example, purple loosestrife, a Eurasian native plant, has naturalized into wet areas from Maine to Minnesota and south into the mid-Atlantic states. An invasive plant that's been moving somewhat notoriously into the South is the kudzu vine, imported from Asia. As they move in, these plants crowd out native flora. This in turn removes the food and cover that local waterfowl and fur-bearing creatures depend upon, and as a result, they may disappear.

Native Good Sense

Before the New American Garden became popular, native plants were being researched as a sensible way of creating practical, low-maintenance landscapes. Natives are plants that have always grown in the United States, not introduced from other countries or continents.

(Sandra Leavitt Lerner)

The native yellow or pink lady-slipper orchid grows in the Appalachian foothills.

Darrel G. Morrison, landscape architect and professor at the School of Environmental Design, University of Georgia, Athens, promulgated the theory of "sustainable landscapes" years ago. His approach involves installing native plants in a natural setting and using natural control measures, such as burning, to encourage vigorous growth of the most desirable species.

Leslie Sauer, a landscape architect and pioneer in the field of restoring and managing native landscapes, designs native plantings because they are sensible choices. But she strikes a compromise to avoid the stereotype of native plantings as unkempt or weedy. In her designs, native plants mind their manners and "homes still look like homes." That is, they fit into their surroundings, offer year-round interest and low maintenance, and the landscape renews itself year after year.

Planting Ideas

Some popular drought-tolerant perennials
- ◆ Blanket flower (*gaillardia*)
- ◆ California poppy
- ◆ Celosia
- ◆ Garden verbena (*verbena hybrida*)
- ◆ Globe amaranth
- ◆ Gloriosa daisy (*rudbeckia hirta*)
- ◆ Marigold
- ◆ Pinks
- ◆ Wax begonia

And Less Fuss

A carefully designed garden requires much less preening than the tightly clipped hedges and manicured lawns of most landscapes, an attribute compatible with home gardeners' desire to prune, treat, fertilize, water, and mow less often. It's important to site plants far enough apart so they will grow full and develop to their maximum potential. When you design plants for low maintenance, always ascertain the mature size of a tree, shrub, or perennial at the point of purchase, so you know exactly what you will have as the garden develops. Not finding out how big a plant or tree is going to get is among the most common mistakes homeowners make. Some trees and shrubs can be kept in check with shearing or pruning, but it's better to buy the right one to begin with—even if it looks a little puny when you plant it. A major component of low-maintenance planting is patience—from the people, not the plants. The garden will look a little sparse at first. Stephanie Cohen, who teaches landscape design at Temple University's Ambler, Pennsylvania, campus, tells clients when she puts in a new perennial garden, "You won't even *like* it for the first three years."

Plants in a new perennial bed, properly spaced, might look a little sparse at first.

Planting Ideas

If you use a sprinkler, use several shallow bowls in various parts of the spray to measure how much moisture is being distributed during each watering session. The time it takes for an average of 1 inch of water to accumulate in the bowls is how long you should water shrubs.

Another important component of low maintenance is *mulch*. Mulch is any material that can be laid over a plant bed to conserve moisture. It might be pine bark nuggets, shredded hardwood bark, straw, cocoa bean hulls, wood chips, newspaper, landscape fabric, stone, or *compost*. My personal preference is some kind of organic material laid 2 to 4 inches thick. Mulch works best in a small area.

Mulching around the base of plants helps hold in precious moisture.

Roots and Stems

Mulch is a covering of protective material, usually organic, around plants to prevent moisture evaporation and root freezing, and to control weeds.

Irrigate according to plant needs rather than by fixed schedule. Group plants with similar water requirements in beds together. This allows you to zone your watering practices so that plants are only watered as necessary, with minimum waste. For example, an established planting of black-eyed Susans, liatris, and purple coneflowers together in a common bed might not require watering all summer long,

yet moisture-loving ferns, astilbes, and impatiens that prefer cool, protected sites would wilt and dry within a week without irrigation, especially in a sunny spot.

When zoning your landscape, take into account the differences between warm and sunny and cool and shady areas of your property. Sun and shade orientation affect the plants' need for water. You must monitor each area. South-facing slopes dry fastest, so they might require closer attention.

Roots and Stems

Compost is a mixture of decaying organic material, such as leaves and manure, used as fertilizer for plants.

Green Thumb Guides

For better watering, do the following:

- Use places with low-lying drainage or near downspouts for plants with high water needs.
- A soaker, drip, or bubbler system will release water much more slowly and efficiently than a sprinkler that shoots water into the air. But a sprinkler is the only practical way to water lawns.
- Consider using full-sun groundcovers such as junipers and groundcover roses that might survive drought better than lawns.
- When you mow a lawn, leave the clippings in place. They'll help preserve moisture.

To conserve moisture, leave grass clippings in place after mowing.

- Incorporate compost into the soil.
- Check for soil moisture at varying depths to make sure you've gotten to the base of the roots of the plants without watering too deeply.
- Use a rain gauge to keep track of how much natural precipitation your landscape has received. Then you'll have a better idea of when you need and don't need to water, without checking the soil.
- Avoid using a sprinkler that throws a fine mist into the air: Mist loses too much water to evaporation.
- Stay ahead of weeds to keep down competition for moisture.
- Move container plants to sheltered areas, away from excess wind and sun.

Some water conserving considerations include mulching beds with aged shredded hardwood bark, enhancing soil with generous amounts of compost, and planting naturally tough ornamental plants. Composting the soil can also help preserve moisture, as well as adding nutrients for plants. It should be laid over beds 2 to 4 inches thick and tilled into the soil to a depth of 8 to 10 inches.

So while there is no such thing as no-maintenance, this style of garden will grow full with little work. Just cut back perennials once a year; prune woody shrubs only when they're growing where you don't want them; *amend* soil with compost; mulch, and enjoy.

Roots and Stems

To **amend** is to add nutrients, compost, or other materials to improve soil structure.

Wild and Free

One popular method of ornamentation with native plants is the installation of wildflower meadows. Their popularity lies in the fact that they renew themselves, are low maintenance once established, and offer a coordination of bloom. In many states, this type of planting is being adopted for areas along interstates and highways. Not only do the "meadows" require less mowing by government crews, they also provide habitat for native insects and animals, and they give passing motorists a fleeting glimpse of natural beauty. The effect when a wildflower meadow comes into balance is truly lovely.

Cosmos and black-eyed Susans form low-maintenance drifts in Rock Creek Park, Washington, D.C.

But gaining this perfect balance requires proper site preparation, proper timing of planting, and great patience. According to Neil Diboll, nationally known wildflower expert and president of Prairie Nursery in Westfield, Wisconsin, "The successful mix of wildflowers is dependent on their geographic location, soil type, soil analysis, hours of and orientation toward the sun, and many other cultural considerations. You must understand proper management, and gain as much control as possible of existing undesirable plant species before cultivating. Only then can you create a successful mixed wildflower meadow."

You Don't Have to Be a Purist

Native plants are definitely in vogue, and it makes a lot of sense to stock your garden with them. Increasingly over the last few years in my own work, clients have been requesting indigenous plants. But I note that I've long been specifying these same plants, not because they are indigenous, but because they have great ornamental value. You don't have to be a purist. In fact, while some native plants can be beneficial, some of them can also be a nuisance. Some types of grasses are extremely invasive, and will take over a yard if not managed severely. And some non-native plants have become so familiar

that their absence would be a surprise. For instance, if you live in the Northeast region, it would mean excluding Colorado spruces, Douglasfirs, and Southern magnolias.

Although they will grow north of Virginia, Southern magnolias are most at home in the Southern United States.

If you want to have a lawn, choose turfgrass varieties that are drought tolerant.

If you have to have a lawn (and where else would you put the croquet hoops?), you can still conserve water. Turfgrass can endure as long as three weeks to a month of dry conditions. If that kind of drought is normal in your area, you might want to consider installing an irrigation system that will deliver as much water as needed most efficiently. Water lawns separately from plants and shrubs, because turf has different moisture needs.

Green Thumb Guides

To ensure that you're planting in harmony with your environment, here are some regional plants and their descriptions. You might already have them in your landscape, or you'll want to try several now that you know they're local natives:

- **Clethra or summersweet.** Native from Maine to Florida, this deciduous shrub grows 4 to 6 feet tall and gets its name summersweet for good reason. The fragrant summer flowers are a treat at a time when few shrubs are in flower. It likes wet sites, has handsome deep green leaves, is shade tolerant, and displays russet-red foliage in fall.

- **White fringetree.** A white-flowering large shrub or small tree, this native from southern New Jersey to Florida flowers in May. The flowers look like an "old man's beard," a name by which it's also known. Plant it as a tree at the fringe of the woods, or as a 15-foot-tall and wide shrub, and mix it with lower-growing shrubs in a deciduous border.

- **Itea or Virginia sweetspire.** From the pine barrens of New Jersey west to Missouri and south to Florida and Louisiana, itea has a wide range of habitats. It prefers wet sites in sun or shade, but has some drought tolerance. Long-flowering, sweet-smelling blooms in summer and maroon fall foliage hold their ornamental value for many weeks. The 2- to 4-foot height keeps it a low-maintenance shrub.

- **Witchhazel.** The selling point for common witchhazel is the late fall yellow fragrant flowers that bloom for three weeks. Depending upon how you prune it, this plant can qualify as a shrub or tree. It's at home anywhere in the eastern half of the country in sun or shade, from Maine to Georgia and west to Nebraska, provided the soil is moist. Fall leaf color is an outstanding yellow. Vernal witchhazel is a native of the southcentral U.S. and displays all of the same characteristics as the common variety, except it flowers from late winter into early spring.

- **Mallow.** *Lavatera argentiflora* is a native of the California coast and Catalina Island. It is a deep pink summer-flowering shrub that will grow 6 feet tall but should be cut back to 2 to 3 feet in early spring if it gets too large. This heat-loving native is a good choice for Southern California. A hybrid that is hardy to the Northwest and flowers in a lighter pastel is a mallow called Barnsley Pink.

- **Black-eyed Susan.** This is the state flower of Maryland, but there are some species of this summer-flowering plant that grow in almost every part of the continental United States. Few native perennials make a splash of color that can compare with its bright yellow flowers that appear for a month or more.

Joe-Pye weed, with its pinkish-purple flowers, likes moist soil and lots of sun.

- **Eupatorium or Joe-Pye weed.** This native of the world likes moist sites in tropical, subtropical and temperate regions throughout Europe, Africa, Asia, and North and South America. It has a tall, 5 to 6 foot, coarse-textured habit. Its pinkish-purple flowers, from August to September, are easily seen since they stand above the foliage. Plant in sun or partial shade to the back of a perennial border or on the edge of a stream or woodland.

◆ **Goldenrod.** A North American native, goldenrod can be found as a wildflower growing along roadsides, in meadows and prairies, and along river banks throughout the nation. Because its showy golden flowers open the same time as ragweed, to which many people are allergic, this perennial gets blamed as an allergen. It's not. Its long-blooming yellow flowers in late summer and early fall attract butterflies. It's best used as a meadow plant mixed with wildflowers or on the edge of woods.

◆ **Butterfly weed.** It's native to and commonly found growing wild in western and central North America. This hairy perennial with reddish-orange flowers and thick, unbranched stems requires a natural, moist setting. These perennials are gaining in popularity because they are magnets for butterflies. They are especially important as a host plant for the long-lived Monarch butterfly.

◆ **Purple coneflower.** An easy-to-grow, long-blooming perennial with purple flowers, this native perennial occurs naturally from southern Canada to Texas and is cultivated and grown from the East to the West Coast. It fits well as a companion to black-eyed Susans. Plant it in natural or formal gardens. It has no serious insect or disease problems, and flowers dependably in full sun.

So use native plants by all means, but you can also use the so-called exotics, plants from other areas of the world, if they are willing to behave themselves. Even native plants must be sited where they'll thrive. There's a notion that indigenous plants need less care and watering, but you need to research plants you like in order to match their needs with your maintenance schedule.

The Least You Need to Know

◆ There's no such thing as a no-maintenance landscape.

◆ Maintenance can be reduced by careful soil preparation, composting, and mulching.

◆ Water-efficient, self-sustaining landscape design, achieved with plants that can survive on the rainfall in your region, is a sensible way to garden.

◆ Regardless of their level of drought tolerance, without rain, all newly installed plants must be watered during their first year in the garden.

◆ Make astute plant choices, such as native plants that already like your local conditions, to reduce maintenance.

In This Chapter

- ◆ Landscaping basic rules
- ◆ Seeing the rules in all sorts of everyday settings
- ◆ Same rules for all design practitioners
- ◆ Less can be more
- ◆ Moving through the garden

Simple principles such as balance, contrast, repetition, and proportion underlie good landscape design.

Matching stone walls, mirror-image benches, and a central water feature illustrate formal balance at Brookside Gardens, Wheaton, Maryland.

The difference between formal and informal balance is symmetry. The classical design is symmetrical. Each side is a mirror image of the other. The park design is asymmetrical. The sides don't match.

Large, irregular stones form an asymmetrical path through a wooded area.

Green Thumb Guides

(Joel M. Lerner)

How symmetrical is your house? The red brick house is symmetrically balanced in features and plantings. The light brick house is asymmetrical.

If you're not sure how symmetrical your house is, a simple rough drawing can help you figure it out. On a piece of paper, draw a simple box outline of your dwelling. If it's a ranch, it will be a wide rectangular box. If it's a colonial, it will be a square box. If the garage is off to one side, make it a separate box beside the house box. Then use Xs or Os to mark the location of doors and windows. Draw a line down the center of the box. If the Xs or Os are about evenly distributed, your property is symmetrical. If there are more marks on one side, it's asymmetrical.

Symmetry

If you go to the farthest point from which you can still see the front of your house, you can easily check the balance. Where is the front door? Is it in the center? Or is it set off to one side? Where are the windows? Are there the same number on each side of the door? Colonial style is often symmetrical, and if you have a Colonial-style house, you can either emphasize the symmetry or de-emphasize it with your plantings. You could put a matched set of urns on either side of the door and fill them with identical plants. Or you could plant a curvy garden bed on one side and balance it with a medium-size tree on the other.

Asymmetry

Most modern houses are asymmetrical. They may have a picture or bay window on one side of the door and a bedroom window on the other. It makes sense in terms of balance to arrange smaller plantings under the larger window. Near the smaller window, where the wall is blanker, larger plantings, such as a group of small trees, would balance the picture.

The idea of asymmetrical landscape design grew out of English "park" design of the eighteenth century. These parks were the lands surrounding the great manor houses. The idea was to develop a more "natural" style in the landscape, which meant finding out what gardens were like before the formal style took over. Landscapers looked to the Renaissance, which they found portrayed in paintings of the time.

Leonardo da Vinci's masterpiece *Mona Lisa* depicts a mysteriously smiling woman against what appears to be a balustrade or railing with a rugged landscape behind her, a landscape of jutting rocks and winding roads and aqueducts that would have been, in the fifteenth century, the remains of Roman architecture. Landscape designers took elements, or sometimes entire vistas, from paintings such as this and recreated the look, with rocks and pools and crumbling stone. In its most extreme form, this adulation of the ancient landscape introduced some serious forms of silliness into English landscapes, as when huge rotting tree stumps were introduced, or newly erected "ruins" provided to fill in a background. But the informal, asymmetrical style that grew out of the eighteenth-century quest for naturalism has become the strongest influence in American landscape gardening today. Natural gardens are easier to maintain than rigidly formal ones, so the informal style seems a good fit with American lifestyles.

Informality seems to fit American landscapes. This garden, with its rustic fence and casual bench, is at the U.S. National Arboretum.

Radial Symmetry

There's a third kind of symmetry that offers a different form of balance, and this is radial symmetry. In other words, plantings are balanced all around a space. The form of radial balance most people are likely to encounter is a ballpark, with its rounded seating bowl on three sides balanced by a giant scoreboard or screen. At Yankee Stadium, the seating bowl is balanced by the scalloped Victorian façade, decorated by flags. At Oriole Park at Camden Yards, the seating bowl is balanced partly by the Warehouse, the long red brick structure that was on the site and was integrated into the design, and partly by the large scoreboard and a parklike area (used for fan picnics) with a small grove of trees that's behind a high green wall covered with ivy.

In a home landscape, radial symmetry might be introduced in a garden "room," perhaps set off by hedges and entered through "keyhole" gaps. It might have a single path, or right-angle paths that cross in the middle. Or there might be a water feature, a pond or fountain, in the center. If you could look down on it from above—maybe from a helicopter or small plane—you would see that the plantings are grouped evenly all around the space.

Contrast

Contrast is what makes certain elements stand out in any visual settings. It's an element of surprise, and one that has to be used judiciously. Too little and it won't be visible, too much and it won't be contrast anymore.

Fortunately, there are all sorts of ways to introduce contrast in the landscape. It's often something extremely simple, such as a piece of stone or metal sculpture that represents a hard edge or an implacable surface amidst the pliant and fluid world of plants. It could be a rock outcropping in a sloping lawn. It could be a flowering vine set against a plain brick wall, the vividness of the plant contrasting with the hard symmetry of the masonry. It could be the introduction, among a great deal of foliage, of a flower, perhaps a rosebush or the tall stems of white or purple hostas. The contrast can be striking—say, a few orange and red nasturtiums creeping into a garden of white flowers. Or it can be subtle—say, a single weeping spruce in a group of upright evergreens.

The implacable edges of the upright columns form a sharp contrast to the looping grasses and soft foliage in this garden.

The trick with contrast is to use just enough. You wouldn't want an entire garden filled with weeping evergreens—it would be sad, not striking. One small statue tucked under a shrub is fine. But you wouldn't want small statues tucked everywhere—that would be boring. Artists often use color opposites to provide contrast, especially in shadows. That means using the colors across from each other in the color wheel. Red and green are opposites, purple and yellow are opposites, and blue and orange are opposites. A blue and green garden would look all the brighter for having a few hot oranges introduced. Texture is another element that can be used to great effect. Plants of the same color can be livelier if one or two are ferny or frilly, as opposed to upright. What you don't want is a lot of different elements that create competition for the eye. Too many competing elements equal confusion, and gardens are supposed to be places where the eye can rest.

Proportion

When you walk into a great house of worship, or a great seat of government, you feel awed, perhaps dwarfed, by the grandeur of the architecture. This is deliberate on the part of the builders. It is designed to remind mere mortals of the power and glory of beings who rule us. It can be a thrilling feeling, but it isn't comfortable enough that you would want to live in the structure. Nature itself is thrilling and awe-inspiring. The sky is the limit when it comes to nature. Think of the Grand Canyon, a red-wood forest, or a triple-canopy rain forest. Think of Niagara Falls, or the Alps, or any ocean. Wonderful as they are, they remain things we want to see, and not things we want to live with closely. These are all things that are very, very big, while humans proportionately are very, very small.

(Joel M. Lerner)

Looking at the sky though a canopy of trees brings the very large scale of the outdoors down to the smaller human scale.

It is the job of landscape design to bring down the proportions, to lower the sky, and to make human beings feel equal to their surroundings. There can be grandeur in a domestic landscape—all those stately English manors with their Renaissance-inspired "parks" are quite dramatic. But the proportions must be more equal if people are to stroll in comfort along the paths or across the lawns. The scale needs to be less monumental and more human.

The first step is to address the ceiling—that is, the overhead plane or *canopy*. The best way to do that is to use trees. When you see the sky through the branches and leaves of a tree, it is somehow much closer, even though the tree may be 80 feet tall. A hedge may be 12 feet tall, but have human-size gaps. You can also use structures, such as an arbor or a pergola (a trellis-roofed passageway), to bring the canopy down.

Roots and Stems _____

In the landscape, a **canopy** is the covering usually created by shade trees or overhead structures.

A gate offers an invitation into an enclosed garden room, where comfortable human scale prevails.

(Joel M. Lerner)

Masses of flowers help frame the view from a swimming pool across a sweeping lawn to woods and a horse farm.

Enclosure is another way to introduce people-size proportions to the landscape. Instead of having one huge garden, you can divide the space into a number of garden rooms. Even in a small space, such as a long, narrow townhouse garden, dividing the space into three separate enclosures will make the space seem more comfortable. Oddly, enclosures will also make the area seem larger, because our human brains tell us that if there are parts we can't see, or if we can walk from one place into another, the space is "bigger" than we are. Landscape design can help bring the proportions of a structure into human balance. A long, low ranch house can benefit from a taller tree that opens up the space, as well as low plantings that echo the structure. A tall, narrow townhouse can be made more people-friendly with a tree that visually brings the height down.

Landscape features can also be used to bring the *horizon* closer. A distant vista can be brought into more human scale by framing it, perhaps with a grove of trees, or with a fence or hedge, or even with a sweep of flowers.

Roots and Stems

The **horizon** is the apparent intersection of earth and sky, or of skyline and sky.

I once worked on a design for a family who had a large modern house on five acres of ground, most of it in the back, where there was a deck and then a pool and then a long, sloping vista. The family loved their long sight lines and their acres and acres of mowed lawn. They could visually "borrow" groups of trees on neighboring land, and even borrow the sight of their neighbors' horses cavorting in their fields. My instinct was to do something to create interest in this unbroken openness, but the family resisted every idea (didn't want to tear out the pool and create an enclosed garden; didn't want trees or hedges interrupting their view of the horses). Finally, I simply massed naturalistic banks of black-eyed Susans and purple coneflowers and other "native" plants around the pool to create wide swaths of color and contrast to the lawn that would frame the views. Nothing interferes with their vistas, but having the massed flowers nearby brings the scale of the landscape into more human proportion. And they did let me plant a grove of trees in the front yard.

It is not the role of landscape design to subdue nature, not in any way. But careful application of proportion will bring humans and their landscape into better harmony.

Repetition

Using the same or similar materials over and over in a design tends to promote harmony, reduce confusion, and make you feel more comfortable in a space. It works indoors as well as out, and it works in some way you probably haven't ever thought about. For instance, the fact that all the acoustic panels in a ceiling are the same size and texture makes you feel more comfortable about them being overhead. Imagine the confusion if all the tiles were different. It might be a "statement," but it wouldn't be a comforting one. Architects use repetition, for instance making all doors the same size and material, or making windows the same size and shape, to help people feel their surroundings are familiar, and therefore comfortable.

Some of the most awe-inspiring vistas in nature are repetitious. Think of the layered curves of the Grand Canyon, repeating endlessly into the distance, or the jagged peaks of the Alps, one after the other as far as you can see. The repetitive curl of ocean waves is what makes the sea so fascinating to watch.

Like other landscape garden elements, repetition can be formal or informal. The classic French formal garden, with parterres stretching out to the horizon, is an example of formal repetition. A meadow garden, with its intertwining sweeps of several different flowers, is an example of informal repetition. Repetition is closely linked to contrast, and both work best when they are judiciously used. Curiously, large spaces demand more repetition, which has the effect of calming them down and making them more comfortable. You can get away with more contrast and less repetition in a small space.

(Joel M. Lerner)

Repetition of a visual element—cascading plants in matched containers is underscored by the fact that the cascades and the flowers below are all the same bright orange.

Informal repetition softens the hard and unvarying edge of a pool.

The visual push and pull of contrast and repetition are why today's huge garden centers are both wildly appealing and completely confusing. It's thrilling to see row upon row of brilliant azaleas and rhododendrons in all shades of red and orange and purple, with some whites and yellows for contrast, but if you're trying to choose just a few plants for your garden, the proliferation of choices can be confusing. The temptation is to buy 12 plants in 12 different colors, because the variety looks so good at the garden center. While 12 azaleas, even if they're all different colors, can be considered a form of repetition, the variety is likely to lead to too much contrast to be appealing in your home garden. Generally speaking, repetition of a single color, such as white, or of a single color family, such as fuchsia, will make a more pleasing statement. The one-of-each approach creates a collection. Repetition is what creates a landscape.

Variety looks magnificent in a garden center. This center is the Marché Atwater in Montreal, Québec.

Sequence

Sequence in the garden landscape means movement. There are two kinds of movement: that of the people who move through it and of the eyes of those who view it. Proper sequencing means that people can easily get from one point to another when they need to—such as from the walk to the front door, or from the back door to the trash site—and that they can be encouraged to linger when there is a reason—such as stopping to smell the roses, or to watch fish in a pond. It means that even when you're sitting still, your eyes are traveling in sweeps, up and down, back and forth, always finding something delightful to look at.

(Sandra Leavitt Lerner)

An informal stone path that follows the contour of the land causes one to meander and enjoy the surrounding environment.

Human nature makes one follow a sweeping path, just as movement is created by the eye following the sequenced plants located to the left of the walk.

Sequencing can be as simple as placing tall plants at the back of a bed and shorter ones in the front to draw the eye in and up. Or it can be a complex system of walkways and plantings that allows gentle meandering through a series of garden rooms, guides children to a play lawn, offers a gardener space for storage and plant work, and screens off utilities. In general, straight lines imply or encourage rapid movement, and curved lines imply or invite meandering.

Although moving people around the landscape is a practical consideration, it doesn't have to be boring. Sweeping lines and curves are visually more interesting and entice the body to follow the eye. Even if your purpose is as mundane as getting people from the street to the front door, you can do that in a number of interesting ways. I've done walkways of feathered stone, which involves placing the stones in a staggered pattern that is visually soft and beautiful and is still a straight shot from Point A to Point B. I've also done entryways with a circular drive where people can be dropped off from a car leading to a short walkway to a half-circle at the front door.

Sequencing is just as important from the back door. You want to make it easy to get to the trashcans, but you don't particularly want to draw people's attention to them. You could create a path that leads to a screen, a fence, or a hedge, or some lattice with vines growing on it. The cans are behind the screen, but the path goes on, perhaps into another garden room. Or you could put an unobtrusive path along the edge of the yard that goes straight to the trash area, but put a sweeping, welcoming path leading from the porch or deck that will draw the eye and most people.

Moving the eye can be playful as well, and even a little mysterious. And what attracts the eye can spark physical movement to follow it. A keyhole arch in a hedge will draw the eye, and a glimpse of what is beyond the greenery can draw the person to walk through it. This is what's called progressive realization. In other words, the garden doesn't show all its charms at once. The great English park designers employed progressive realization in setting up vistas on the long drive up to the manor house. Visitors would catch a glimpse of a roofline, or a turret, or a series of windows, but not until they pulled right up to the house would they see the entire structure. But there are simpler ways to employ progressive realization, and they work in small spaces, too. You might, for instance, arrange it so that visitors hear a fountain before they can see where it is. The sound of water will draw them to it.

A keyhole sculpture invites the eye and then the person into a mysterious vista at the Smithsonian Institution in Washington, D.C.

Progressive realization reveals as it teases the eye and the footsteps of a child forward. At the Children's Garden in Brookside Gardens, Wheaton, Maryland, a rustic bridge leads to a steppingstone path, which leads to a tiny log hut.

Sometimes sequencing can take advantage of natural tendencies. For instance, it's human nature for people to hesitate when they come to intersecting lines. Behavior that's extremely irritating on the interstate can be encouraged in the garden: intersecting lines are a perfect place to put a bench.

The Least You Need to Know

◆ There are five basic principles in landscape design, which are shared with all forms of art.

◆ Three kinds of balance appear in landscapes: symmetry, where all sides are equal; asymmetry, where one side is weighted more than the other; and radial, where the balance is circular.

◆ Contrast employs the element of surprise. The trick to using it is to use just enough.

◆ People feel most comfortable when the proportion of a space is brought down to human terms—enclosure tames the horizontal plane, and a tree canopy brings down the sky.

◆ Repetition in the landscape promotes harmony.

◆ Sequence in the landscape is the art of motion—paths and plantings should be designed to move the eye through the garden and to move people along the most efficient or most pleasing path.

In This Part

Part 2

The Lernscaping Checklist

People who are seeking landscape advice often have strong feelings about what they want but have trouble coming up with specific items. With 30 years of landscape experience, I have come up with a way to help people organize and discover their thoughts. It's called the Lernscaping Checklist, and it presents a broad palette of ideas and garden elements that you can use to make your landscape a truly personal place.

As you work your way through the checklist, you'll establish how you *do* make use of your space (to decide what practical elements to include, such as a driveway and a walk to the back gate), how you *could* make use of it (to decide if you want to include a lawn for games, or devote all the space to flowers), and how you'd *like to* make use of it (dream of a swimming pool/hot tub combo? A walled English rose garden?). Then you'll learn how to select plants and other landscape features to do exactly what you want them to be doing.

In This Chapter

- Intro to Lernscaping
- Getting in touch with your property
- Making the tough decisions
- The working garden
- The fun garden

What's on your landscape wish list? One thing that comes up often is an English-style perennial border.

Chapter 6

The Garden in Your Mind

The big difference between landscape professionals and you, the ordinary homeowner, is that the pros have *ideas*. Lots of ideas. They've seen it all before, and they know what will work. They have a whole catalog in their heads of design solutions and plantings that will enhance or disguise as needed. This chapter is where you put your mind to work. You can let it roam over the possibilities and probabilities. Along the way, I'll be giving you *ideas*. This kind of thinking—pulling ideas together—is how you create your landscape design.

Learning Lernscaping

If you're thinking about landscaping your space, you probably have some idea about what you want to see when you drive up, look out the window, or stroll around the outdoors. Over 30 years in landscape design, I've developed a technique called Lernscaping to help clients figure out exactly what they want. It begins with a checklist that lets you organize your priorities—and wish for the stars and the moon and a tennis court and a swimming pool and an English border and a patch of baby lettuces.

(Sandra Leavitt Lerner)

Dreaming of a swimming pool? This Italianate pool in Florida has a mosaic fountain and exposed aggregate paving patterned with pavers.

Well, it will at least let you consider all those options. It's always been my belief that I can't *give* you a landscape. Your landscape has to grow out of your own needs and desires. It has to fit your practical considerations, and it has to encompass your dreams. I've found that having *you the client* sit down and fill out the checklist helps you focus on what you want and what you expect.

If your yard has rocks, you might want to turn them into a rock garden.

Putting That Landscape to Work

Let's start with some of your goals for the landscape. What do you want your garden design to do for you? Think in both Big Picture and Small Picture terms. Be honest about your likes and dislikes. Consider the needs of every person and creature that will be using the garden—people, pets, and wildlife. Think as well about the environmental conditions that prevail in your landscape. Is the climate harsh or mild? Do wind, noise, or pollution cause a problem?

What do you want your garden to do? Will you use it as a private refuge? A place to read a book in solitude, a place to work on your tan, or a place to watch wildlife? A place to play with your dogs? Do you need family space? Will your kids need a lawn to romp on? A place to store their bicycles, scooters, and sports equipment? Do you want to use the space for entertaining? Outdoor entertaining can be fairly formal—as are many wedding receptions—or it can be quite casual, with people in shorts gathered around a barbecue grill.

Make notes to yourself as you fill out the checklist. Think carefully about your choices, but don't hold back. This is your chance to explore and to dream a little, while the only thing at stake is some paper and pencil lead.

How will you use your landscape? Do you need a place to sit and relax or read a book? A bench tucked into an alcove is a perfect spot.

Here's the checklist:

❏ Relaxation

If benches are too formal, consider a
hammock for a relaxing spot.

❏ Enhance privacy

A simple screen of ivy trained on a metal frame creates a private "room" at Hillwood Museum and
Gardens, Washington, D.C.

A hedge of yews can screen out an unpleasant view
or protect privacy.

Green Thumb Guides

For screening purposes, you may not need the
monolithic look of a fence or hedge. There's
another alternative, and it's something I try to think
about first. It's what I call "guerrilla" screening.
Instead of presenting a linear plane, guerrilla elements look like they are part of the overall ornamental design. For instance, to block a view of a
neighbor's swimming pool, visible off one corner
of the property, how about using three large
conifer trees, such as Norway or blue spruces?
The *evergreens* would give more immediate
screening than a line of young shrubs. Maybe you
just want to lose that view of your next-door neighbor's tarpapered doghouse. A simple grouping of
small evergreen shrubs with year-round interest
might be all that's needed. Here are some plants
that are good for spot screening:

◆ Evergreen rhododendrons: large glossy
leaves, late-spring or early summer flowers in
every shade of red, plus white.

◆ Heavenly bamboo (*Nandina domestica*):
willowy bamboo texture with evergreen
foliage that turns brilliant red in winter.

◆ 'Alta' Southern magnolia: evergreen, narrow, columnar habit, fragrant white flowers.

A new introduction,
southern magnolia
'Alta,' is ideal for spot
screening.

◆ Hollies, such as 'Nellie R. Stevens,' 'American,' 'burford,' and 'fosters': evergreen,
glossy foliage, winter berries. (The types with
spikier foliage have the added benefit of
resisting browsing by deer.)

◆ Conifers, such as blue spruce, Norway
spruce, Douglasfir, and hemlock: evergreen,
dense foliage, tall and parklike.

A simple lattice at the side of a deck is softened with clematis vines. It makes a beautiful and simple screen.

❑ Provide or eliminate shade

Mature elm trees provide excellent shade.

❑ Dry laundry
❑ Aid energy efficiency
❑ Reduce pollution

Trees can reduce pollution and if densely planted, can help reduce noise.

❑ Aid noise reduction
❑ Wind reduction
❑ Erosion control
❑ Other
❑ Dining

(Sandra Leavitt Lerner)

Is al fresco dining important to you? This enclosed porch features a gas grill, a counter with a sink, and custom-designed table and chairs.

❑ How many?

(Sandra Leavitt Lerner)

A table and chairs of South American hardwood provide informal dining on a deck.

❑ How often?
❑ Entertaining

Green Thumb Guides

Some steps to take when getting ready for a party:

1. Make arrangements to rent a tent or pavilion well ahead of time.

2. Arrange to borrow or rent enough chairs or tables for seating and dining.

3. If the party area is dusty, sprinkle it with water to keep down dust.

4. If you're using propane for cooking, make sure to have extra gas canisters available.

5. Figure out how much food and drink you need, then add extra, to be prepared for surprises or accidents.

6. If the party is at night, use candles in containers (such as sand-filled paper bags) to light pathways and tables. String lights across the yard. Follow fences, fill trees with tiny lights. (You might be able rent lights from a regular rental company.)

7. Visit a party/paper store to find plates, cups, utensils, tablecloths, and napkins that fit your theme.

8. Decorate tables and tent uprights with flowers from the garden.

9. Use signs to make the purpose of the party clear (an anniversary), to honor the main guest (a list of accomplishments), or to celebrate a party event (a birthday or wedding anniversary). Use a continuous audio-visual loop to introduce the honored guest (birthday boy or girl or bar or bat mitzvah).

10. Consider games to keep party-goers entertained. For adults, entertainments might include lawn games such as croquet or badminton or darts, or social games such as charades. For children, games might include blind man's bluff, musical chairs, piñatas, or hide and seek. Scavenger hunts work for both adults and children.

❏ How many?
❏ How often?
❏ Children
❏ How many?
❏ Ages?
❏ Playground/climbing for children

A slide and other playground equipment offer children a place to play.

❏ Growing vegetables

It's wonderful to grow vegetables to use, store, or share with friends and family.

❏ Growing herbs
❏ Shelter or hideaway

A simple, rustic seating platform in Northern Virginia offers a great spot for relaxing, reading, or simply watching the water.

Covered seating is welcome in all garden styles. This stone and wooden gazebo is at Brookside Gardens, Wheaton, Maryland.

❑ Athletic activities

If you provide a place for them to play, kids will come.

❑ Reading
❑ Listening to music
❑ Sunning
❑ Dancing
❑ Provide wildlife habitat
❑ Attract birds, butterflies
❑ Other

Poison Ivy!

There are some types of wildlife that you don't want to attract—even when it's cute. Most people know that deer treat gardens like a salad bar, and should be discouraged. But other cute little mammals can be a nuisance as well. For instance, squirrels and chipmunks eat more than seeds. They eat bulbs and plants. Squirrels can get into hanging baskets and containers. Adorable little chipmunks have been known to undermine stoops and steps. Rabbits will eat garden plants. Raccoons get into garbage and will come into your kitchen if they think there's food there. They'll use your fish pond as a bath tub and can really tax your imagination when it comes to keeping them out. You might need a steel trash can anchored to an iron frame to keep your lawn from being trashed daily. There are sprays and powders to discourage pests. Garden centers and local cooperative extension service offices can help you learn how to discourage these critters.

Green Pathways

If you've been a gardener, you may already have some ideas about what you want. You know what times of the day you want to sit quietly, and what times you want to get out with the gloves and a weeding tool. If you've lived in a spot for some time, or if you've made a study of sun and sky patterns, you'll know the best spot to watch the sun rise or set, or the best spot to watch the moon reflected in a pool.

An informal table and chairs offer a place to sit and read the newspaper with a cup of coffee. The seating visible at the left overlooks a small pond.

You may even know the best place to watch unobtrusively as birds come to feed and bathe, or to sit while butterflies flitter around you to their favorite plants. If you've lived in a place for some time and don't know these things, you need to spend some time outside, both sitting and tramping around, until you are familiar with every foot of your space. If you're landscaping a new place, you need to spend the time to get to know it. Make your survey with an open mind. Do you really need so much shade? Can you borrow a neighbor's view? Would you spend more time in the garden if you had a screened gazebo to sit in?

Times of day the garden will be used:

- ◆ Early morning
- ◆ Midmorning
- ◆ Noon
- ◆ Midafternoon
- ◆ Early evening
- ◆ After dark

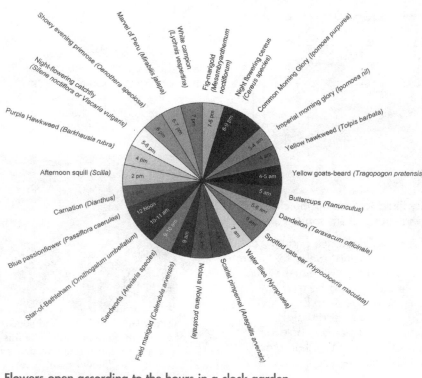

Flowers open according to the hours in a clock garden.
(Elmer H. Lerner and Robert Vaura)

Green Thumb Guides

A formal hedge at Ladew Topiary Gardens, Monkton, Maryland, clearly shows the influence of European travel on creator Harvey Ladew.

One of America's most noted amateur gardeners was Harvey Ladew (1887–1976), whose house and extensive gardens in rural Harford County, Maryland, displays its owner's well-traveled eye as well as his powerful fondness for topiary. Ladew, born into a wealthy family in New York, never lost his Gilded Age sensibilities, though he was no dilettante in the garden, being perfectly willing to pick up the clippers and nip a few boxwood swans into shape.

Harvey Ladew liked to take up the clippers and maintain the shape of his topiary swans.

He spent time in England, France and Italy and visited gardens everywhere. His love of fox-hunting was developed early, and the theme runs through both gardens and house. Among his extensive friends and acquaintances were the Duke and Duchess of Windsor, T. E. Lawrence, and Baltimore-born society decorator Billy Baldwin. Ladew's house is comfortable rather than grand, and the grounds, although they encompass 22

acres, are surprisingly intimate. Ladew was influenced by the English idea of garden "rooms," and his landscape reflects this. While most people visit to see the justifiably famous topiary, a couple of the intimate spaces are among the most memorable.

One of the favorite spots at Ladew Topiary Gardens is the Tivoli Teahouse.

One is the Tivoli Teahouse, a tiny oval structure with urn-shaped finials around the flat roof, set among lilacs and peonies. It's a lovely spot for afternoon tea or for morning coffee. Another unusual space is the Card Room, connected to the House's Oval Library by an open arcade. You might not think of having a room in the garden dedicated to playing cards … unless you take a cue from Mr. Ladew and consider the outdoors as space that is as versatile, personal, and useful as the indoors.

Ladew Gardens has grand spaces, but some of them are quite intimate, like this little garden room featuring a table around wisteria and 'New Dawn' roses.

White flowers along a walkway at Ladew Topiary Gardens, Monkton, Maryland, really pop out when the sunlight starts to fade.

Roots and Stems

Deciduous plants are those whose leaves fall off when temperatures drop in the fall. Often evergreens in marginal zones are considered deciduous because if it gets cold enough, they will drop their leaves.

Favorite seasons:

- Spring
- Summer
- Fall
- Winter

Favorite colors (list colors for every member of the family)?

Petunias, like the ones in this simple basket hanging on a fence, come in an enormous range of colors. Everyone in the family can choose their favorite shade.

Green Thumb Guides

Creating a white garden?

- **Yellowwood (*Cladrastis lutea*).** Large (40 feet) *deciduous* shade tree, blooms late spring to early summer.
- **Dogwood (*Cornus florida*).** Small (20 feet) deciduous tree, blooms in early spring, before leaves appear.
- **Japanese andromeda (*Pieris japonica*).** Broadleaf evergreen shrub (8 feet), blooms in late February, early March.
- **Common Jasmine (*Jasminum officinale*).** Semi-deciduous, twining woody vine, fragrant flowers summer to fall.
- **Moonflower (*Ipomoea alba*).** Annual self-seeding vine (related to morning glory), huge flowers throughout growing season.
- **Deutzia (*D. crenata* var. *nakaiana* 'Nikko').** Low-growing (18 inches) broad-spreading (4 feet) groundcover shrub, covered with flowers in spring.
- **Phlox 'David' (*P. paniculata* 'David').** Sturdy, tall, narrow perennial (2 to 3 feet), fragrant flowers throughout summer.

Phlox 'David' offers fragrant white flowers on tall stems throughout the summer.

Favorite style:

- Informal (natural)
- Formal (manicured)
- Curved rows or edges
- Linear rows or edges

Plantings around a cabin reflect its simple, rustic appearance.

Orientation?

- Inward orientation
- Outward orientation

What mood would you like to convey?

- Relaxed
- Cheerful
- Private
- Social
- Open

Green Thumb Guides

Things to lift your mood in the garden:

- A hammock
- A wooden swing
- A lounge chair
- Fragrant plants
- A fountain

(Joel M. Lerner)

A tiny fountain with a scalloped shape is a happy touch in a garden.

- A gazing ball
- Wind chimes
- Found art (driftwood, rusted farm implement)
- Garden stones
- Fish in a pond

Designing Themes

If you've seen a garden somewhere you'd like to duplicate, or if you just have an idea of a style you like, you can choose that as a theme for your landscape. Or you can choose a variety of styles. Here's a review of some of the styles I've discussed:

- English (colorful, naturalistic, mixed perennials, topiary, whimsical, eclectic)
- French or Italian (practical, symmetrical, hedged in, mixed herbs and vegetables)

Symmetrical design and curvy, scrolly shapes define parterres at Hillwood Museum and Gardens, the Washington, D.C., home of Marjorie Merriweather Post.

◆ Japanese (strong symbolism, simplistic, use of sand and gravel aggregates, stone sculptural elements)

The Japanese garden at Hillwood Museum and Gardens demonstrates Japanese style with American plantings.

◆ Southwestern (colorful, low maintenance, use of mesalike stones, desert- or alpine-elevation plants)

◆ New American (asymmetrical, colorful, 12-month interest, mixed woody perennial)

◆ Contemporary (single specimen plant or several trees, simple, uncluttered)

A mixture of textures and standout plants gives a garden a contemporary look at the U.S. National Arboretum, Washington, D.C.

The Least You Need to Know

◆ The more ideas you have, the more exciting your landscape will be.

◆ Figure out how you want your garden to work for you, from providing shade, to screening noise, to fighting pollution.

◆ You can design your landscape for relaxation, play, or usefulness (such as growing vegetables).

◆ The most interesting gardens are the ones that are the most personal.

In This Chapter

- Green themes
- Plant picks
- Selecting structures
- All on the surface
- Taking time

Flower memories can be quite specific, and
sometimes favorites are chosen for life.

Chapter 7

The Green Stuff

Almost everyone has favorite plants, and a reason. Maybe you remember your mother's roses, or your grandmother's carefully clipped box hedges.

If you've been doing your homework, you've collected pictures and drawings, maybe even clippings, of some plants you like. This is all good. But ... before you start naming names, or becoming a plant collector, you must understand that landscape design deals more with plant concepts than with nomenclature. What you need to ask yourself is what do you want a plant to do for you? Each plant has several characteristics that determine its usefulness. Specific plants serve specific purposes. You need to learn to think about plants by their characteristics:

- ◆ Height
- ◆ Width

It's important to know the size of a mature plant. This blue spruce is considered a "dwarf," but when it grows up, it covers a lot of ground!

◆ Shape

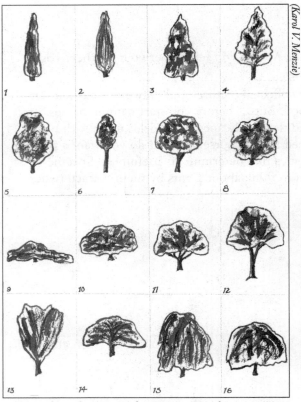

(Karol V. Menzie)

Some plant shapes: (1) fastigiate; (2) columnar; (3) and (4) pyramidal; (5) and (6) ovate (oval); (7) and (8) globose (round); (9), (10), (11), and (12) spreading; (13) vase; (14) fan; (15) and (16) weeping or cascading.

◆ Habit
◆ Texture
◆ Foliage
  ◆ Size
  ◆ Texture

Lenten rose, *helleborus orientalis*, has leaves with a coarse texture.

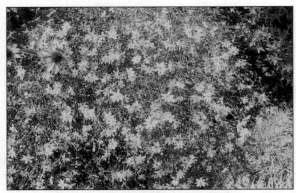

Coreopsis 'Moonbeam' has finely textured leaves and a ferny habit.

◆ Color

The foliage of the Japanese maple 'Bloodgood' has a fine texture and deep purple-red color.

◆ Duration

◆ Flower

◆ Form

(Sandra Leavitt Lerner)

Pennisetum setaceum 'Rubrum' has a "vase" shape and a reddish color that makes it desirable as an accent plant. It's an annual north of Zone 9.

◆ Size

◆ Texture

◆ Color

◆ Duration

◆ Cultural requirements

◆ Moisture

◆ Light

◆ Soil preference

◆ Hardiness

◆ Disease tolerance

◆ Geographical origin

Use the checklist to list your preferences. Check everything that you would like to include.

❑ Shade trees (40 feet to 100 feet)

❑ Small flowering trees (under 40 feet)

❑ Specimen trees (under 40 feet)

A weeping cherry, Prunus subhirtella pendula, makes a fine small deciduous specimen tree.

❑ Evergreen trees (15 feet and over)

❑ Deciduous hedges (5 feet to 15 feet)

❑ Evergreen hedges (5 feet to 15 feet)

❑ Deciduous flowering shrubs (3 feet to 10 feet)

Evergreen boxwood forms a hedge
around an herb garden.

❑ Evergreen flowering shrubs (3 feet to 10
feet)
❑ Deciduous groundcover
❑ Evergreen groundcover
❑ Vines

Nierembergia, an annual in frost areas, cascades
over the edges of a window box in the Georgetown
neighborhood of Washington, D.C.

❑ Vegetables
❑ Herbs
❑ Bulbs

Vines climb classical columns to a pergola at
Hillwood Museum and Gardens, Washington, D.C.

❑ Perennials
❑ Annuals

Cannas are a summer-flowering
bulb often used as an annual.

❑ Fruit trees and shrubs
❑ Flowers for cutting
❑ Winter interest

Witchhazel 'Arnold Promise' is covered in bright yellow flowers in late winter.

❏ Other

Spend some time dreaming. Imagine your ideal planted space. What would it contain?

❏ Plants
❏ Style
❏ Use

Ivy clipped into a low hedge shape surrounds a statue in a small formal garden at Hillwood, home of Marjorie Merriweather Post, Washington, D.C. In this stylized space, boxwoods are trimmed into V shapes inside the ivy.

Hardscape Happenin's

The part of your landscape that isn't plants is the hardscape. Hardscape includes the structures and installations that give your gardens shape and purpose. You might think of the hardscape as the bones of your design. Start by thinking about that landscape in your head. What are its shapes and textures? Check all the following elements that appeal to you:

❏ Curves

A curvy walkway winds to a circular patio.

❏ Rectangles
❏ Circles
❏ Squares

A circular fountain has a square surround at the U.S. National Arboretum, Washington, D.C.

❑ Crescents

Small boxwoods are trimmed into crescents on either side of a memorial to Andrew Jackson Downing, designer of the Smithsonian Institution's grounds, Washington, D.C.

❑ Tiered/stepped

Two sets of stone steps lead up into the woods at Brookside Gardens, Wheaton, Maryland.

❑ Sunken
❑ Raised

A dry stone wall elevates a raised garden bed.

❑ Hidden

Boning Up on Garden Basics

Some of the bones of your landscape will show. These are the structures and infrastructures on which your gardens will be built. Think about how you'll be using the space, and check the elements you find necessary or appealing.

❑ Deck(s)
❑ Pond

A small pond features a waterfall and overhanging plantings at Brookside Gardens, Wheaton, Maryland.

❑ Patios
❑ Walks/paths

A block-laid path is softened by plantings that arch over it.

❑ Seating
❑ Trellis
❑ Table(s)
❑ Fence(s)
❑ Gates(s)

A wrought-iron gate dividing a front garden from a rear garden was custom-designed to match an old gate at the front of this property in Washington, D.C.

❑ Swimming pool
❑ Hot tub

Total relaxation: A swimming pool, a hot tub, a hammock, and a lounge area.

❑ Statuary

Adam and Eve rest in a leafy bower at Ladew Topiary Gardens, Monkton, Maryland.

- ❏ Sauna
- ❏ Driveway
- ❏ Arbor
- ❏ Ramp(s)

A simple metal rail makes it easier to negotiate a ramp at Hillwood Museum and Gardens, Washington, D.C.

- ❏ Portico
- ❏ Gazebo
- ❏ Retaining wall(s)
- ❏ Planter(s)

Two different styles of containers flank a small pond.

- ❏ Irrigation
- ❏ Greenhouse
- ❏ Barbecue grill
- ❏ Lighting

Utility Structures

Utilitarian features are those that you must have and usually are not aesthetically pleasing. The way many designers and homeowners address them is to hide, disguise, or place them in an area not used for recreation and entertaining.

- ◆ Clothesline
- ◆ Storage

A clothesline stretches from a storage shed in a Washington, D.C., garden.

- ◆ Parking space(s)
- ◆ Garage
- ◆ Pets
- ◆ Firewood
- ◆ Potting shed
- ◆ Compost
- ◆ Maintenance shed
- ◆ Trash/recycling bins
- ◆ Rainwater collection
- ◆ Service/utilities area

A covered plastic barrel captures
rainwater for use in the garden.

Bricks and Mortar

The building materials you select have a pro-
found effect on the look of your landscape.
The materials will help make the difference
between formality and informality, between
simply casual and positively rustic. Certain
materials are associated with certain looks, or
styles. For instance, gravel paths can be formal
if they are carefully bordered, and will convey
a European feeling. Mulched paths are more
informal and rustic. Textured, colored, shaped
paving stones seem to give a more Southern or
Western feeling to a space such as a driveway
or patio. Think about the "placeness" you want
to convey when you select building materials.

- Brick
- Flagstone

Gravel paths surround formal parterres at Hillwood
Museum and Gardens, Washington, D.C.

- Rock
- Pavers
- Lumber
- Textured, colored, patterned concrete
- Asphalt
- Gravel
- Mulched paths

A mulched path offers a rustic entry into woods at
the U.S. National Arboretum, Washington, D.C.

- Interlocking block

- Epoxied gravel
- Fiberglass
- Steel
- Rubber
- Reed or landscape fabric
- Exposed aggregate

Steps of exposed aggregate material
are edged in brick for interest.

Time and Effort

When you think about how you will use the garden, you must also think about how much of your effort is going to go into maintaining the space so it's always fit to use. How much maintenance you do will be determined by your plant and structural choices. For instance, if you have a lawn, you'll need to spend some time mowing it. If you build a wooden shed to store garden tools, you'll have to apply paint or wood preservative every so often. Of course, you don't have to do everything yourself. You may be able to hire lawn-care professionals, or employ your own or a neighbor's children to mow or weed. Still, you need to give some thought to how many hours you can devote to maintenance.

Estimated hours per week, per task, for the following:

- Mow lawn
- Rake leaves
- Fertilize and treat lawn and shrubs
- Prune shrubs
- Prune trees
- Watering

The best way to deliver water to a plant is slowly,
where it can reach the roots.

- Weed and edge beds
- Mulch beds
- Paint/preserve/repair structures
- Plant trees and shrubs
- Plant perennials and annuals
- Install landscape structures

Also figure the following:

- Total hours required for working in the garden.
- Hours you intend to spend working in the garden.
- Hours you will require assistance from professionals or other helpers.

Dollar $igns

A rule of thumb is to budget 10 percent of your property's appraised value for landscaping, including both the hardscape and the plants.

Green Thumb Guides

Here are some tips for budgeting and planning to ensure that you get started:

◆ Doing something yourself will cost a fraction of what a landscape design and installation company has to charge for the same work.

◆ Erase a more expensive idea, and re-design the space to have a more realistic use. For example, your swimming pool might become an herb, vegetable, and cutting garden.

◆ Leave an ambitious element in the land-scape design, such as the water garden or a formal fountain and parterre, and be patient. Take it a step at a time. If all you can do is locate and install trees and some shrubs in the first year or two, do that. Per-haps the water garden could be installed in 10 years, or for your retirement.

◆ Give trees priority over other plantings. They are the slowest-growing element and add the most value to your property.

◆ Mail order is an inexpensive way to get plant material, but keep in mind that they send very young woody plants. You will usually get seedlings and bare root stock.

The Least You Need to Know

◆ Choose plants for your landscape based on their form, texture, habit, duration, and purpose.

◆ A wide variety of plants will make the most interesting gardens.

◆ Garden structures can be a decorative element in a garden.

◆ The materials you choose will determine the look and style of your garden.

◆ Choices you make in the garden will influence how much maintenance is required.

In This Part

Part 3

Looking at the Land

It's called a landscape design for a good reason: It's a piece of paper with your proposed landscape drawn on it, so you can see what is there (like the house and the driveway) and what will be there (the trees you want, the shed, the new gardens). These drawings take into account the site characteristics, including the soil, the climate and the prevailing winds), and your own personal wishes (a circular patio, a fountain with a quilt design in pebbles, a two-level deck, whatever your heart desires).

If you can use measuring tools, and draw circles and lines, you'll be able to create your own landscape plan. This plan is a blueprint for your project. It can help you estimate costs, stay on track while you're working on the space, and provides a simple and cost-efficient way to make changes. (That big tree's too expensive? Erase it.) Start by drawing in the functional things you need (driveway, walk, storage), and then add the fun things (a fish pond, a garden that attracts butterflies).

In This Chapter

◆ From dreams to drawing board

◆ Plats, plans, and plots

◆ Keep it legal

◆ Throw in a few curves

◆ Water, water everywhere

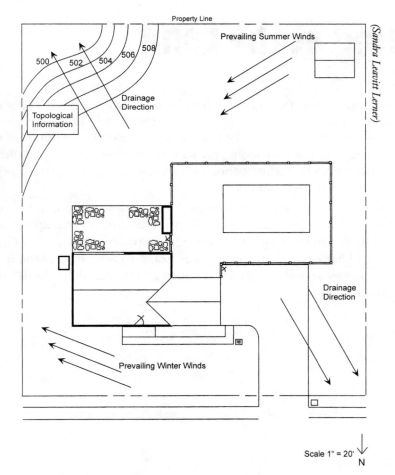

On your landscape plan, chart some basic information, such as structures and installations, land contours, and drainage patterns.

Chapter 8

The Plat Thickens

It's time to move some of your landscape ideas from your head—no, not onto the land yet—onto a piece of paper. This paper is your landscape design, and it will guide your path when you do begin to build and plant. To make the plan most useful, you need to chart some basic information, such as structures and installations, land contours, and drainage patterns.

Developing the Landscape Plot

In order to turn your dreams and schemes into a landscape, you have to have a plan. This is not merely a collection of ideas kept in your head, it's an actual drawn-up plan, on a real piece of paper. Your plan will be the most important tool you have in creating your landscape. It will take every element into consideration, from existing features such as roads and property boundaries; to such variables as prevailing winds, the location of power lines and other utilities; to the walkways, walls, and exact plants you want to add. The plan will define your landscape, and will chart your path as you work on bringing your vision into reality.

Although you can—and will—make changes as you go along, it's important at the outset to get down everything that characterizes and influences your style. At the end of this section of the book, you will have a blueprint for your landscape design. Then, and only then, can you begin digging and planting. Think about it. It's a lot easier to move a plant on paper than it is to move it in the ground.

In creating your landscape, take into consideration power lines and utilities.

The plan starts with a site analysis. This is a systematic, thorough review of all the physical characteristics of your patch of ground. You can measure your property yourself, but most real-estate transactions include an official-looking piece of paper called a plat plan. It may be labeled something like "House Location Survey."

The purpose of the plat is to define your property for tax purposes. It shows only the property that you own, with survey boundaries and rough dimensions. It will include the outline of any buildings on the property, again with rough dimensions, and may show such things as utilities, roads, driveways, and sidewalks. It may not show setbacks (land that is actually owned by the state, county, city, state, or township), and these may have some restrictions on what you can build or plant. Measure the exact distance from your house to your street. Compare that with the distance on the plat plan. The difference will be the setback. You need to check with the department that

maintains your thoroughfares for possible restrictions. If you don't have a plat plan, also called a tax plat, you can get one from the planning and zoning division of your municipality or other local jurisdiction.

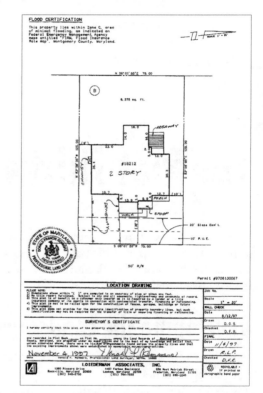

Use your House Survey Location, or tax plat plan, as a basis for your landscape plan.

A Plan with a View

The plat is especially useful for landscape purposes because it is an overhead view, a bird's-eye look at your property from the sky. This view is essential in deciding where to locate plants, and it's extremely helpful in plotting paths. With this view, you will be able to tell how far plants are from each other (so you won't have two trees competing for the same air space, for instance) and how far plantings are from paths and walkways.

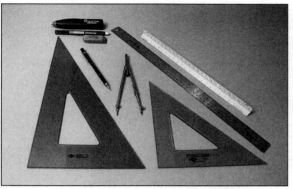

Drawing your landscape plan will be easier with the right tools.

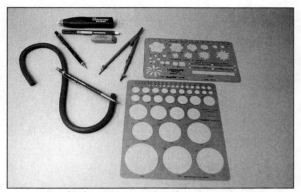

You can find some specialized tools, such as templates, flexible curves, and mechanical pencils and erasers, to help you draw landscape designs.

A sketchbook is good for drawing ideas. Use Vellum and parchment (tracing paper) to develop your landscape design.

There's something pleasing about starting a new project with all the right tools. Get some good medium soft-lead pencils (HB) and several different kinds of erasers (the push-up pencil types are easy to use) and a large pad of paper, the kind found in art supply stores; 18 by 24 inches is a good size. You can use newsprint, but it tends to shred if you have to erase. A tougher paper, such as a 60 pound Bond sketchpad, is better. You can make notes and sketches on small pieces of paper, but it's a good idea to keep all your landscape information in one place, and the bigger pages will be helpful when you start drawing. (Don't worry about your drawing skills. If you can use a ruler to draw a line and trace around a glass to get a circle, you can draw a perfectly usable landscape plan.)

Green Thumb Guides

The following are tools you need to create a landscape plan:

- Plat plan or property survey
- 18-inch ruler, compass (optional), protractor or set of triangles (optional)
- Medium soft lead (HB) pencils
- Eraser(s)
- Pad of artist's drawing paper, 18 by 24 inches, 60 pound Bond
- Tracing paper

The first step in drawing your plan is to transfer the plat plan to one of your large sheets of paper. It's probably easiest to use a 1-inch grid to 4-foot grid, in which 1 inch equals 4 feet, and every $1/4$ inch equals 1 foot. If your property is too large to fit on the paper at that scale, you will have to use a smaller one, such as 1 inch to 8 feet ($1/8$ inch equals 1 foot). Locate north; it's usually at or near the top of the plat plan. Direction is going to be very important when you start locating cold and warm areas and the path of the sun across your property.

It doesn't matter how you orient your drawing. Typically, the view is front to back, so the front yard is at the bottom of the paper and the back is at the top. If the front of your house faces north, you may be more comfortable putting north at the bottom. As long as you keep the proper compass orientation around the paper, you can put north anywhere you like. You may find as you draw that the plat plan doesn't include all the dimensions you need. It may give you the width of the house at the front, and the width of the property at the street, but it may give you only one side measurement from the front of the house to the property line. You'll have to subtract, or measure yourself if you know where the lines are, to get the width of the other side.

On your drawing, locate utilities, including poles, boxes, wires, and underground lines. Your local utility has a free service to tell you where underground placements are, so give them a call. If you have a septic system, you should also locate that. It's not uncommon with older properties for the exact location of the septic system to have become lost over time. If you're not planning major excavation, or major paving, you may not need this information. But if you do need it, you may have to hire a septic specialist to locate the tank and the drainage area.

Green Thumb Guides

To track the path of the sun across your property, buy a bag of craft sticks (like those found in frozen treats) from a craft store. Pick a single direction at a time, and label sticks by hour (7 A.M., 8 A.M., etc.), or by half-hour. (The smaller your property, the smaller the time intervals need to be.) At the appropriate time, lay the Popsicle stick down (or stick it into the ground, if possible) at the boundary of sun and shade. This will give you a sun map. If you want a plant that calls for full sun, you will need to know which areas are not shaded during the day so you can place it properly.

Cracking the Codes

While you are checking with various utilities, you will also need to check with your local jurisdiction about building codes and zoning restrictions. Building codes may determine how tall a fence you can install (and it may be different for different parts of your property), whether and where you can build a storage shed, and how much of your space can be taken up by a deck. The restrictions often require a certain distance from structures to the property line. Even if what you're doing doesn't seem significant, there may be some code restriction or requirement. It's much easier to check the codes first than it is to tear something out later because the inspector objects.

If you live in a designated historic district, such as this one just north of Washington, D.C., there might be some restrictions on what you can build.

If you live in a designated historic district, or in an area that is covered by its own covenants or restrictions, you need to find out what those rules are as well. For instance, many new subdivisions have strict rules governing the height and placement of fences and the location of decks and porches.

Check Out Those Contours

Next on your drawing, you need to mark the topography. This is usually a series of concentric lines, separated by intervals of 1, 2, 5, or 10 feet, that indicate the slope of the land. It may be called a relief or elevation map. Slopes are important in determining drainage, siting driveways (if not existing), and calculating possible locations of retaining walls or terraces. You needn't do an extensive geological survey of your property, but you do need to mark general slopes and any major variations such as rock outcroppings or steep drops. (Use arrows to mark the direction of the slope, long ones for a gentle slope and short ones for a steep incline or decline. Use a line to indicate a drop-off.)

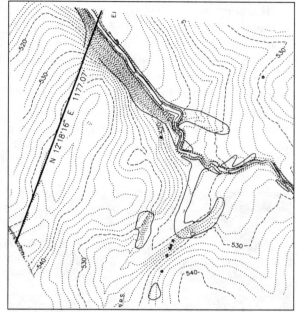

Land contours are indicated by lines on a topographical map. The numbers indicate elevation above sea level.

Planting Ideas

Label everything! This is important, because there are going to be a lot of marks on your drawing, and you will not be able to remember what they all mean if you don't label them as you draw them.

Topology matters because certain slopes mandate what you can do with them. If you don't have an existing driveway and your property is hilly or has one or more sharp variations in elevation, there may be restrictions on where you can build one. Slopes are measured in terms of rise and run—that is, how much the elevation rises over a run of a certain number of feet. A slope that rises 1 foot over 5 feet equals a 20 percent grade.

(Joel M. Lerner)

If a driveway is too steep, grading
can correct the slope.

Driveways should not be installed on slopes over 11 percent. Slopes that steep or steeper are candidates for a retaining wall or a groundcover. Mowing is dangerous on a slope of 15 to 20 percent. *Grading* can change the contours of your land, and is certainly something to consider if you have contour problems. It can be expensive—all *excavating*, even digging a hole for a mature tree, is pricey—so you may want to site drives differently, if that's possible, rather than grade.

Roots and Stems ____

Grading is altering the surface of the land, especially its contours. **Excavating** is removing soil by digging or scooping out.

Waterworks

The slope of the land is also important in drainage. If soil is poor or rocky, contour will determine how well it drains. (Oddly, perfectly flat land is not desirable from a drainage point of view either, especially if the soil is not especially spongelike. Water may pool or stand or simply race away into gutters.) Most homeowners don't think about drainage until water with no place else to go finds its way into the basement. It's important to maintain the natural drainage system of a piece of property where possible. You wouldn't want to build a patio at the base of a property's drainage field. You don't even want to put in a path that interferes with normal runoff. Ignoring natural drainage patterns can mean you end up with a pond or a mud-wrestling site!

(Sandra Leavitt Lerner)

It's important not to interfere with the
natural drainage system on a piece of land.

(Sandra Leavitt Lerner)

If paved areas are not properly installed, water will puddle after a storm.

A patio properly installed has a slight grade, so water will drain away.

One of my clients designed and installed a patio without giving any thought to drainage. As a result, the patio blocked the natural flow of rainwater. The dam created by the patio's raised edge turned the backyard into a rice paddy. He lived with this annoying mistake until the standing water worked its way into his basement. The solution was to tear out the patio and replace it so it followed the natural slope of the land. When water no longer pooled, it no longer found its way into the basement. When you install any kind of paving, always maintain the existing drainage pattern of your property. It's a common error to lay walks or patios perfectly level. If they are level, they will hold water and promote growth of fungus and algae. They must be installed with a slope so they will drain. Paved surfaces should drop 1 inch over 10 feet. Because this is less than a 1 percent grade, it will still seem level to the eye and foot.

Even if water in the basement is not a problem, before you do any landscaping you need to check the drainage patterns around your house while it's raining to make sure that all water rolls away from the downspouts and walls.

Planting Ideas

If you see that rainwater is not flowing away from building walls, you need to add soil to create a downhill slope along the walls. The soil used for fill should have a high percentage of clay in it and be low in rock, sand, or compost. The soil within approximately 2 feet of a wall should contain as little organic material (for example, composted leaves, wood chips, straw, etc.) as possible. You want the soil to direct water away from the house, not percolate it down.

When you've walked your property thoroughly, during rain and just after, you should have a good idea of what the natural drainage patterns are and what barriers exist to good drainage. Should your water problem be caused by circumstances beyond your control, such as underground springs, high water tables, or creeks that have been piped underground, they may need to be corrected with subsurface pipes or sump pumps. (Fortunately, these problems make up less than 1 percent of residential drainage problems.) If your survey for your site analysis reveals serious drainage problems, before you get into expensive solutions, call your county Cooperative Extension Service (usually a function of the state university) for unbiased information and help in mapping out a plan. They have soil conservation experts trained in *hydrology*, or water science.

Roots and Stems

Hydrology is the science that deals with the occurrence, circulation, distribution, and properties of the waters of the earth.

It's useful to know the general level of the water table in your area. If you've had to dig a well, you will already know this information, and if you live in an area where the water table is uniformly close to the surface, as in most of Florida, you will most likely be aware of that as well. If you don't have the information, it may be available from the extension service, or possibly from the planning and zone board.

Surface contours matter in one other respect: weather. Remember that elementary physics lesson that cold air falls? Unless you live in a climate that is tropical, you will have to worry at least some part of the year about frost. In the United States, virtually every single area can experience a freeze, even if it's not of long duration and doesn't happen every year. In landscape terms, this means that cold air rolls downhill. You need to know where the low spots are, because those will be the coldest areas, and are places where you don't want to locate tender plants.

At this point you should have a drawing of your property with the house and other buildings located on it. You should have the location of streets, sidewalks, and setbacks. You should have a general idea of the topology, the land contours, and the direction of drainage. These are important, but they're just a start on analyzing your site.

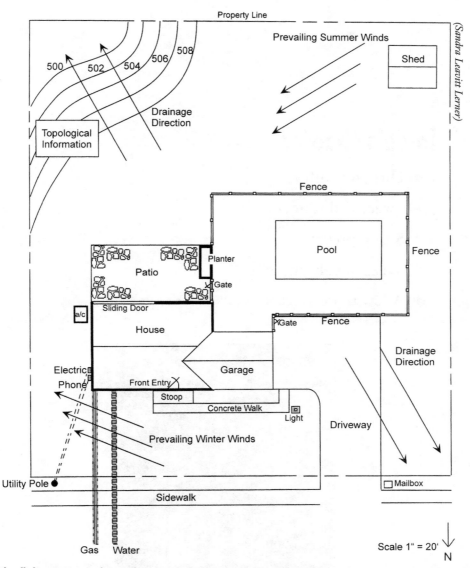

(Sandra Leavitt Lerner)

With all the structures located on your plan, you are ready to start working on your landscape.

The Least You Need to Know

◆ It's essential to have a good landscape plan before you begin any work.

◆ Make sure your tax plat matches the measurements of your property, especially in front where county setbacks frequently occur.

◆ Site analysis will give you the basic information you need to draw a landscape plan.

◆ Your site map should include existing buildings, driveways and walkways, if any, streets and sidewalks, utilities, and information on land contours and drainage.

◆ Always make sure water drains away from structures on your property.

In This Chapter

◆ Dirt and stuff

◆ Sweet and sour soil

◆ Siting pretty

◆ Trees, lovely and not

◆ A few trade secrets

(Joel M. Lerner)

A mature birch, with characteristic white bark,
is a desirable tree on any property.

Chapter 9

The Real Dirt

Soil is an important component of design, as the type of soil may dictate what types of plantings you can use. Your landscape plan will need to contain information about soil types. Soil is also a major factor in drainage. Your plan also will need to show existing plantings, such as trees and native species. Mature trees are prized, but weed trees should go. Your plan may be easier to read if you use some professional landscape architect's symbols.

Down and Dirty

Any landscape plans you have will be seriously affected by the type of soil on your property. Soil may be mostly clay, loam (the type that farmers desire), rocky, or sandy, or any combination. It's rare to find a site that has only one type of soil. Finding out what kind of soil(s) you have is important because soil provides not only nutrients that plants feed on to grow, but also determines how air and water will be held available for plants. Soil is the most important factor in determining the success of a plant.

You can have samples of existing soil tested at some garden centers, as well as at a county Cooperative Extension Service. The proper test measures nitrogen, phosphorus, potassium, and pH (acidity/alkalinity). Make up a composite sample, using a cup or so of soil from several spots in the landscape. Take the soil from about 1 inch below the surface. The test usually requires about a cup of this mixture. After the results come back, you can add nutrients as recommended, preferably in the spring. (If you have already discovered drainage problems due to the nature of the site, you need to fix those immediately.)

Planting Ideas _____

To correct soil that is overacidic, add ground limestone. At a rate of 50 pounds per thousand square feet, limestone will increase the alkalinity by one tenth. To correct soil that is overalkaline, add sulfur or iron sulfate.

Roots and Stems _____

pH stands for (p)otential of (H)ydrogen, and measures the acidity or alkalinity of a solution, with neutral being 7 and higher numbers indicating greater alkalinity and lower numbers greater acidity.

Sweet and Sour Soil

Woodland plants such as rhododendrons like more acidic soil.

Different plants prefer different levels of acidity/alkalinity. Most plants do best at a level of 6 to 7, though sun-loving flowering shrubs such as weigela, lilac, and forsythia prefer "sweeter" soil above _pH_6.6, and woodland shrubs such as rhododendron and blueberry like more acidic soil below pH6.0. Because the most desirable pH of your soil depends on what you are going to plant, you may wait to amend the soil until after you have decided on plantings. However, before you plant is the best shot you have at "fixing" the soil on your property. Once the plants are in the ground, you can't really get back to the root zone.

To find out how much organic matter your soil contains, dig a hole and remove 1 to 2 cups soil. Put the soil in a quart jar and fill the jar with water. Shake up the contents of the jar and let stand overnight. The next day, the soil will have settled itself into layers of clay, loam, and sand.

Generally, however, almost all soil can be improved by adding organic matter. To determine how much organic matter your existing soil contains, dig a hole 3 to 4 inches deep and remove 1 to 2 cups of soil. Put the soil in a quart jar and fill the jar with water. Shake up the contents of the jar and let stand overnight. The next day, the soil will have settled itself into layers of clay, loam, and sand. Organic matter will be floating on top. This simple test often reveals that your soil has almost no organic content—perhaps a mere ¼ inch floating above the clay. That's not a surprise, because organic matter is the hardest thing to keep in the soil. It leaches out over time, gets used up by plants, and washes away with rainfall. Test the soil in a number of locations around the property, especially where there are relatively large grade changes. By doing this simple test, you will also get a very general indication of your soil's texture. Measure the thickness of each layer in the jar. If the sand is the thickest but there is some clay, it's sandy clay. If the top layer is widest, it's clay, and if the middle level of silt equals the other layers, it's loam. Sand won't hold moisture well. Clay holds it too well and the plant can't access it. Adding compost makes moisture available to the plants.

Planting Ideas

A variety of comparative soil tests would make a good science project for a schoolchild—besides helping you chart soil types for your landscape plan.

Mark the results on your landscape plan. You might want to do this with soft colored pencils, so you can color-code the types—brown for clay, orange for loam, yellow for sand—and erase them as you improve the soil in various areas.

You can look at existing plants to determine if drainage is inadequate. Poor drainage around plants can mean a lack of soil *percolation*. This is a situation where water doesn't drain from the root zone fast enough. It's often referred to as "wet feet."

Roots and Stems

To **percolate** is to drain or seep through a porous substance or filter.

To check soil drainage, dig a hole and fill it with water. The faster the water drains away, the better your drainage.

To determine if you have a problem with standing water, dig a hole, fill it with water, and see how long it takes to drain. The exact length of time depends upon the size of the hole, but you'll know if you have poor drainage. I've dug holes, filled them, and had water standing 24 hours later. It does no good to plant in hard, undrained soil. Even if you add nutrients and compost, it's a watertight basin, and after the first good rain your plants could be floating. A container plant on your patio is in a kinder environment—at least it has drainage holes! The only solution is to improve the drainage at this site.

Green Thumb Guides

The way to encourage air and water circulation in previously undrained soil is to cultivate as widely and deeply as possible (8 to 14 inches or more) using my soil recipe:

◆ Spread 2 to 3 inches compost over the soil surface.

◆ Spread 50 pounds of agricultural limestone per 1,000 square feet over the compost.

◆ Spread 80 pounds of gypsum per 1,000 square feet over the lime.

◆ Dig deeply and thoroughly—as the British say, double dig (two spade depths).

◆ If the area is too large or the soil too hard to dig with a shovel, use a rototiller to break up the soil. If you don't own a rototiller, this device for cultivating soil can be rented from an equipment rental company.

Getting the Sights on Siting

While you are checking with various governing bodies about zoning, water tables, soil types, and other land characteristics, you will also want to determine if you are in a flood plain. Various restrictions govern land use in an area that has been determined to be subject to flooding. If the flooding is severe, you may be able to do nothing at all with the land. A couple I know who were looking for a small property in Pennsylvania thought they had found the perfect site, with 10 acres and a farmhouse. However, further research proved that of the entire 10 acres, only the land on which the house sat was not in an unbuildable flood plain. Some states also restrict activities on property that includes protected wetlands. Obviously, these are things you need to determine before you purchase the land.

Most people seeking landscape design help have bought an established property, or have lived with established landscaping for some time. These people are looking for a change. However, sometimes clients are buying property and want to make landscaping a priority.

The bare lots often left after new construction offer a blank slate for landscaping.

If you are buying unimproved land, you may have the opportunity to choose a site for your house. I say "may" because obviously there are certain jurisdictional and geological conditions that may limit your choices. If, however, you do have options, remember that the most comfortable place for people is a southeastern orientation with protection from southwestern sun. A slightly elevated setting, one third to two thirds the way up a pleasant slope (under 10 percent) will provide the best vistas. It will also keep the house and its inhabitants warmer, since cold air will continue down the hill. And, unlike plants, which need relatively loose soil to grow in, people need firm soil that bears compacting and will easily hold their weight. So while plants prefer loam, people are better off walking or building on clay and shale. Determining what types of soil exist in what locations on the property can help you decide where to build as well as where to plant. Even if you have an existing property, landscaping considerations may help you orient it more toward the pleasant parts of the land.

To Tree or Not to Tree

Once you have drawn your soil types onto your property map, you need to draw in the existing trees and plants. This is where the protractor and compass come into play. Or you may want to simply use a series of round objects, such as coins and the rims of small glasses or jars or their lids, to make circles. Measure the exact locations of the plants you want to keep. This, in conjunction with the structures, is your bird's-eye or *overhead* view of your existing landscape.

Roots and Stems

An **overhead** view is the view down on an object or set of objects as from a height.

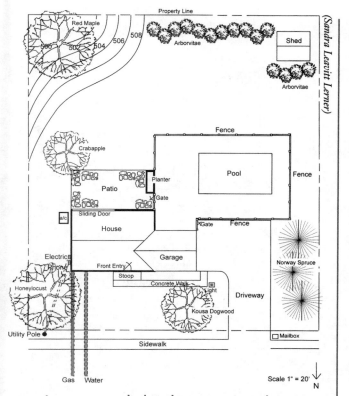

(Sandra Leavitt Lerner)

Locate trees and other plants you want to keep on your base drawing.

Remember that mature trees are usually considered a tremendous asset, and they are certainly expensive to replace. You may not want to keep them, however, if they are some species of "trash tree," such as locust, catalpa, sumac, or mimosa. Trash trees are giant weeds, and they can often be identified by the amount of debris they drop on your land over the course of a growing season. (Catalpas, for instance, though they have nice bark and pleasant rounded leaves, in spring drop large whitish flowers that will look like bits of dirty tissue on your walks and gardens. They then grow long seedpods, which split open and drop seeds, and then the pods themselves, which may be almost a foot long and immediately gum up the tines of any rake, drop. In the fall, the leaves drop. Frilly, fragrant mimosas are beloved in some southern climes, but they too spend the growing season dropping plant debris on your yard. Sumac, which grows like some evil alien life form in urban areas, has an odor some people consider unpleasant.)

You may also want to remove trees if your area is deeply shaded and you would like to grow sun-loving plants. Some people consider it blasphemy to remove existing trees, but you will have to decide what's best for your site and what best fits into your plans. In some cases, removal may be the best thing for the trees. If trees are growing too close together, they may become spindly or misshapen in the contest for available light and nutrients. If you are simply dealing with a previous owner's notions of what a landscape should be, and those notions are far removed from what you need and want, take courage, and get rid of things that displease you—as long as you can do so without damaging the overall environment.

Of the trees you want to keep, draw first the trunk to locate it, and then draw the mature canopy—that is, the circle that its mature burden of branches and leaves will encompass. Center the circle on the trunk or stem of the plant. It's important to draw the *mature* size, so you don't end up putting things too close together, or putting sun-loving plants where they will eventually be overtaken by the shade of a growing tree. Garden centers or nurseries can help you determine how big a tree or shrub will be at maturity. (Most plants come with tags that list such characteristics as light preference and mature size.)

Planting Instructions

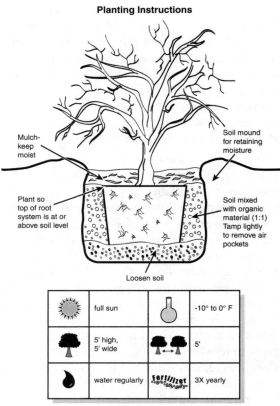

Mulch—keep moist

Soil mound for retaining moisture

Plant so top of root system is at or above soil level

Soil mixed with organic material (1:1) Tamp lightly to remove air pockets

Loosen soil

☀	full sun	🧪	-10° to 0° F
🌳	5' high, 5' wide	🌳↔🌳	5'
💧	water regularly	fertilizer	3X yearly

Look for a tag on new plants that tells you its characteristics and needs.

Nurture for the Natives

If you are landscaping property that already includes native vegetation—if it's a cottage in the woods, or a waterfront area with dunes—you will need to survey what is already growing on the site to decide if you want to keep it. In some cases, such as that of grasses growing on the dunes, you may be required by law to protect certain plants. Changing the conditions surrounding such plants, including disturbing the soil or altering drainage patterns, may doom them. If you are considering a suburban property where developers have left occasional large trees, you may want to have them evaluated by a tree expert to see if they will continue to thrive in the altered conditions.

Green Thumb Guides

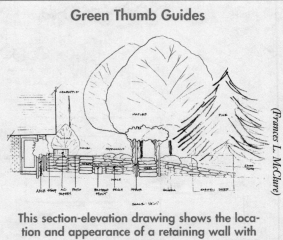

(Frances L. McClure)

This section-elevation drawing shows the location and appearance of a retaining wall with steps.

If your landscape plan includes building new structures, such as decks or sheds, you may need to get a permit from the local authority to install it. In that case, you will probably have to submit drawings of the proposed structure. One will need to be an *elevation* drawing, that is, drawn from the viewpoint of an observer on the ground, not the bird's-eye view of the landscape plan. An elevation drawing will show the cross section of a structure so it is clear how all the parts fit together. In the case of a deck, for instance, the elevation drawing would include the parts of the railing, the frame, the joists, the posts, the concrete piers supporting the posts, and the rise and run of steps. Few jurisdictions will accept a rough homeowner-type drawing, so you will need a contractor's or architect's drawing. If you need a *perspective* drawing, that is, an artist's rendering of your house, hang a piece of paper on the wall and project a slide of your home onto the paper. Then trace around the plants, house, and property details on it. This will make sure you get the proper scale and proportion in the drawing.

Roots and Stems

An **elevation** is a scale drawing of the side, front, or rear of a given structure. **Perspective** is a rendering of objects in depth, as viewed with normal binocular vision.

The Shape of Things

When you are creating your design drawing, you may want to use some of the shorthand professional landscape architects employ to indicate different types of plantings and structures. For instance, they use a heavy zigzag line with occasional outward spikes to indicate evergreens (if you've ever had an electrocardiogram, think of one line of the photograph curved into a circle). They use a solid line with occasional tiny inward spikes to indicate a deciduous shrub or tree. Drifts of flowers are represented by free-form amoebalike shapes. Formal or clipped hedges are squared off, while informal hedges are a collection of circles stuck together (a sort of caterpillar shape). Fences are lines interspersed with tiny squares to indicate posts. Walls are parallel lines with diagonal shading. Underground features are indicated by dotted lines and rocks by shaded zigzags. It isn't essential to adopt a style more complicated than you are comfortable with. Evergreens could be Xs and deciduous trees Os. Or all plants could be simple circles. But if you enjoy using professional trade tricks, they will enliven your drawing.

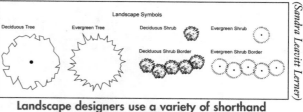

Landscape designers use a variety of shorthand symbols to make drawings readable.

Professional landscapers and designers use their drawings in part to show developers and homeowners what their landscape will look like, but they also use them to develop "specifications," or "specs." Specs list every new item covered under the plan, and are essential in preparing a budget. (One such item might read "15 rosebushes @ $24.95 each, total $374.25.") While you are preparing your drawing, you might want to keep a similar list of things you are including so you have them in one place when it comes time to match your plans to your budget.

The Least You Need to Know

- Simple tests will reveal how much organic matter your soil contains and how well it drains.

- Identify what plants and trees existing on your site will be kept and which will be removed.

- Draw your design from an overhead perspective.

- Show your plants at mature size or the size they will be within 10 to 20 years.

- You don't have to be an artist to draw a landscape plan, but it will help to use some shorthand symbols.

In This Chapter

◆ Blowing hot and cold

◆ Micro-climates

◆ Hardiness zone basics

◆ Calling for help

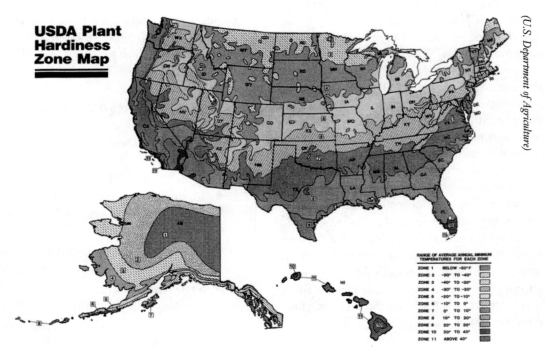

USDA Plant Hardiness Zone Map

(U.S. Department of Agriculture)

Horticulturists have divided the entire North American continent into a series of 20 plant hardiness zones.

Chapter 10

Climatic Decisions

Before you proceed with your landscape plan—and you're getting closer to the fun part, the wish list—you need to establish what kind of climate, or climates, dominate your property. You need to study climate on both a macro and micro scale, the Big Picture and the Little Picture. You already know if you live in a generally cool, wet climate, or a hot, dry climate, a climate with seasonal extremes, or a climate with less seasonal difference. But you may not know that horticulturists have divided the entire North American continent into a series of 20 plant hardiness zones.

Head in the Air, Feet on the Ground

The plant hardiness zones are based on the coldest average temperatures in a given area and range from –50 degrees Fahrenheit at Fairbanks, Alaska, and Canada's Northwest Territories, to more than 40 degrees Fahrenheit in Honolulu, Hawaii, and Mazatlan, Mexico. (Lebanon, Pennsylvania, and Branson, Missouri are in the middle, with temperatures as low as –17.8 degrees F to –23.3 degrees F.) The USDA Plant Hardiness Zone Map, issued in 1990, was developed by Dr. Henry M. Cathey, then director of the U.S. National Arboretum in Washington, D.C.

Every plant has its limits—that is, it will tolerate cold only down to a certain point. Virtually all plants that grow in the United States are subject to freezing, even if it's temperatures of only 30 or 31 degrees Fahrenheit. So virtually all the plants that grow in the United States have some degree of cold-tolerance. There are plants that will survive temperatures of –50. Some examples are arborvitae, spruce and other conifers, falsecypress, lupins, snowdrops, daffodils, and winter aconites. The cold-hardiness characteristics of various plants generally confine them to certain areas. Alders, for instance, are extremely cold-tolerant, but in the milder climate of the mid-Atlantic region, they easily succumb to pests.

(Sandra Leavitt Lerner)

Ferns and mature Douglasfirs characterize
a rainforest in the Pacific Northwest.

(Sandra Leavitt Lerner)

Groves of Colorado spruces and wildflowers
characterize a high mountain meadow.

(Peter C. Benjamin)

Piñon, juniper, and native stone are
typical of the Southwest landscape.

(Joel M. Lerner)

A pineapple palm, Norfolk Island pine, and Chinese
podocarpus are typical of south Florida.

Dr. Cathey, who has retired from the arboretum, is still active in horticulture, and has developed a companion heat-hardiness zone map that reflects the highest temperatures plants can tolerate. For instance, heaths and heathers, like the alders, do not grow well south of a certain area. The zone maps are geographical opposites: Cold hardiness is measured from south to north, while heat hardiness is measured from north to south. It is Dr. Cathey's goal to combine the two maps and produce a single map that reflects both highest heat and lowest cold for individual zones. Plants are almost always labeled or listed with their cold-hardiness zones. Most plants thrive in a band of zones. For instance, the sugar maple, *Acer saccharum*, likes full sun in Zones 3 through 8—roughly from International Falls, Minnesota, to Austin, Texas. (But they don't do well in cities anywhere.) Lavender, *Lavandula angustifolia*, likes full sun in Zones 5 through 9, or roughly from Des Moines, Iowa, to Fort Pierce, Florida. Verbena, a popular flower for attracting birds and butterflies, likes full sun in Zones 7 through 10, roughly from Oklahoma City to Miami. The cold-hardiness map is widely available in botanical books and on the Internet.

Locating your property within the cold-hardiness zones is only part of the battle, however. Within every macro-climate are areas of micro-climate. These are spots where specific conditions influence the local climate. The area can be as large as part of a city or as small as a section of your backyard. For instance, the Mall in Washington, D.C., normally in Zone 7, is one of the warmest spots in its entire region, and plants from as temperate an area as Zone 8, such as Darlington oaks, can be grown there.

The Mall in Washington, D.C., is a micro-climate that is warmer than the area around it. This live oak thrives here even though it's a Zone 8 plant growing in Zone 7.

There are various explanations for the phenomenon, ranging from the influence of the nearby Potomac River to the protective atmosphere created by the buildings of the Smithsonian Institution, which line both sides of the Mall. The U.S. Capitol dominates a rise at the eastern end and the Washington Monument dominates a hill on the west, creating a sort of long shallow bowl. Cities in general tend to be warmer than their zones, partly because of the press of people and vehicles in a small area and partly because of the predominance of hard surfaces that reflect sunlight and hold heat. Gardenias, definitely a tropical plant, have been wintered over in Atlanta, Georgia.

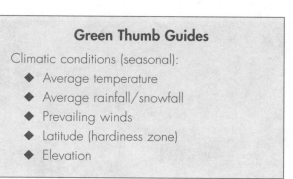

Green Thumb Guides

Climatic conditions (seasonal):

- ◆ Average temperature
- ◆ Average rainfall/snowfall
- ◆ Prevailing winds
- ◆ Latitude (hardiness zone)
- ◆ Elevation

You might experience a similar phenomenon on your own property. If your backyard is fenced in, hemmed on the north and southwest by trees, and faces south or southeast, it may generally be some degrees warmer than the unprotected north-facing front yard. Aspect, or the direction your land faces, influences the climate upon it. A south-facing aspect will be warmer than a north-facing one because the southern aspect will get more sun. (However, you will still need to track the sun's path across your land, as buildings, trees, and hills can block sunlight.)

Another climatic influence in which your property may vary from the norm is in rainfall. The information about your area's average rainfall is available from the National Weather Service or your local library. Keep in mind that in colder areas, part of the average annual moisture comes in the form of snow. Snow can be beneficial, because it delivers a lot of moisture to the ground slowly as it melts. But it can also be heavy, and can break limbs and damage shrubs and hedges. Some shrubs, especially boxwoods, need to be tied to keep snow from knocking them down. It's a good idea to brush snow off bushes and lower tree limbs so the weight won't harm them.

(Sandra Leavitt Lerner)

Snow can be beneficial because it forms an insulating blanket around plants and provides moisture.

(Sandra Leavitt Lerner)

Rosemary is listed as hardy to Zone 7 or 8. However, a series of mild winters in the mid-Atlantic area have allowed the plant to flourish.

How do you know if you have a warm micro-climate, or several of them, on your property? It takes experimentation. You can place outdoor thermometers at various locations to track variations. (The National Weather Service can supply average summer and winter temperatures.) You can set out a number of saucers or small bowls to check rainfall. You can check the prevailing winds, which might differ from what the television news lists every night. (Use a compass and simple stakes with streamers tied to them.) You might try to talk to a local meteorologist. But mostly you need to spend enough time on your land to develop an anecdotal sense of its climatic idiosyncrasies. In the end, you have to make plant choices based on your observations and best guesses. And you can simply experiment. If there's a plant you particularly like, you can try it and see if it survives. If it's a tender plant, it may require some extra trouble, such as covering before any suspected freeze. If it's a cold-zone plant you're hoping to nurture in Zone 7 or 8, you may have to be especially vigilant for insect damage or problems with excessive water.

You can influence the climate in various areas of your land by plantings. For instance, on the Eastern seaboard, winds generally blow from the southwest in summer and from the

northwest in winter. So you would want to channel the milder southwest winds and block the storm-bearing northwest winds. An evergreen screen provides an excellent wind block.

Planting Ideas

One way to keep less cold-tolerant plants happy is to plant them in containers and move them around with the seasons. In winter, you can move them in a dormant state to a cool, dark basement or root cellar, or take them inside to a sunny spot not too close to cold windows. You can be imaginative with movable containers. How about planting tender shrubs or perennials in a wheelbarrow? Then you can move them easily from cooler to warmer parts of the garden, or you might grow annuals in the sun and wheel them onto your shady patio for a party.

When you have determined the major climatic influences on your property, you can indicate them on your plan. Prevailing winds are usually indicated with an arrow (be sure to label the arrows). You can lightly pencil in dotted lines to indicate warmer or cooler micro-zones.

Tracing It Out

It's time to start creating your paper landscape. You'll do this by placing a piece of tracing paper over your basic plan. Everything that is within the boundaries and not otherwise occupied by house or other existing features is the playground of your mind. You can put anything you want on the tracing paper. If an idea doesn't work, you can tear up the tracing and throw it away. You can trace dozens, even scores of different plans—tracing paper is cheap. In fact, you might want to waste a few sheets just practicing. Professional designers start by drawing circles, or bubbles, to indicate general areas of activity:

◆ Public area

◆ Entry court

◆ Play

◆ Service/storage

◆ Lawn

◆ Games

◆ Planting areas

◆ Screening

◆ Sports/swimming

This will allow you to evaluate areas in relation to each other. Do you want the play area close to the house so you can supervise activity? Or do you want it out of the way so dirt and noise won't disturb adult activities? Do you have a choice of where you locate service areas? Do you have a garage where a service area makes sense? If you have, or want, a pool, where is the logical place? There's no rush to make these decisions. You can experiment with every possible variation until you find something that makes sense for your situation.

When You Need Professional Help

The following sections help you understand the skills of the most visible among the green industry professions. Contact these organizations. Or as you peruse the Yellow Pages looking for a landscape expert, check for membership in these associations. It shows that the professional participates in a program to make him or her more knowledgeable in the field, which is an excellent indicator that you are hiring a conscientious person. But it is not the ultimate qualifier; nothing beats references from a satisfied customer.

Landscape Architect (LA)

An LA oversees the landscape design of large-scale projects, such as the regional planning of parks, subdivisions, apartments, and other commercial sites. LAs also perform residential landscape design.

By training, they are the "structural engineers" of the landscaping industry. They do landscape construction design and develop planting and drainage plans. Their education gives them an understanding of plants and a sensitivity for the environment that most architects and engineers do not possess. LAs must pass the strictest licensing requirements of all landscape professionals, and their practice is regulated in about 40 states.

To obtain information about where to locate a Registered Landscape Architect and how to learn more about this profession, contact: American Society of Landscape Architects (ASLA), 636 Eye Street, N.W., Washington, DC 20001-3736; 202-898-2444; www.asla.org.

Landscape Designer (LD)

Through education, training, and experience, LDs engage in the consultation, planning, design, and/or construction of exterior spaces. Their designs locate plants and the incidental paving and building materials necessary to enhance a property, such as trellises, water gardens, paths, patios, walls, arbors, sculpture, furniture, and the like.

LDs might have a certificate, a Bachelor's degree, or a Master's degree in a landscape design curriculum. Training is usually in horticulture. But individuals using the title "landscape designer" are not required to have training in the profession. One way to know an LD's expertise and experience is through a nationally recognized certification program offered by the Association of Professional Landscape Designers (APLD). Ask if the designer is a Certified Professional Landscape Designer and a member of APLD. And of course, ask to see examples of work and references.

Information about finding a Certified Professional Landscape Designer is available by writing APLD, International Headquarters, 1924 North Second Street, Harrisburg, PA 17102; 717-238-9780; www.apld.com.

Growers and Retailers

In terms of information about growing and site preparation, much comes from plant growers and retailers. They represent the source of your plant material and are often employed at nurseries, garden centers, or large general landscape companies. There is overlap among landscape professions, and many of these nurseries, garden centers, and general landscape companies are set up to provide general contractors who can oversee entire landscaping projects from beginning to end. Some larger operations have complete staffs of LAs, LDs, masons, and maintenance personnel.

These folks may or may not be primary growers, but they generally keep abreast of state-of-the-art plant information. Most garden centers offer a full line of products and services for do-it-yourselfers.

For names of nurseries, garden centers, and landscape companies that offer "soup to nuts" design, installation, and care, contact the American Nursery and Landscape Association (ANLA), 1000 Vermont Avenue, N.W., Suite 300, Washington, DC 20005; 202-789-2900; www.anla.org.

Grounds Manager

The importance of home lawns and golf courses has catapulted these pros to the forefront of the greens industry. Lawn treatment companies get the most press because they were an overnight multi-million dollar success. However, overall grounds management includes pruning, fertilizing, mowing, pesticide application, seeding, weeding, mulching, snow removal, and much more. Grounds managers know general cultural practices for plants as well as how to operate and repair landscape equipment.

Professional grounds managers are employed to care for trees, shrubs, flowers, and lawns. Ways to certify expertise in this field are through the Professional Grounds Management Society (PGMS), the Professional Lawn Care Association of America (PLCAA), and/or investigating a firm's qualifications yourself.

PGMS can give you names of Certified Grounds Managers and Certified Grounds Keepers. PLCAA, in a program with the University of Georgia, offers a Certified Turfgrass Professional rating.

To locate certified grounds professionals, contact PGMS, 720 Light Street, Baltimore, MD 21230-3816; 1-800-609-7467; www.pgms.org. To find a certified lawn-care specialist, contact PLCAA, 1000 Johnson Ferry Road, NE, Suite C-135, Marietta, GA 30068-2112; 1-800-458-3466; www.plcaa.org.

Landscape Contractor

Contractors are the professionals who install the design. But as with general contractors associated with nurseries or garden centers, they oversee a wide range of projects from landscape architecture and design to grounds management. They have a variety of experiences and expertise. Check their work and references, especially if you're hiring one to oversee a project from beginning to end.

Licensing is required in many states, but it can range from basic registration, such as a home improvement contractor, to many different sorts of testing procedures. For more information, contact the Associated Landscape Contractors of America (ALCA), 150 Elden Street, Suite 270, Herndon, VA 20170; 1-800-395-2522 or 703-736-9666; www.alca.org.

Poison Ivy!

Everyone coming to your property to perform any work must be insured. If there is any doubt, ask for a certificate. Any landscape professional can have his or her insurance company mail or fax it directly to you.

Cooperative Extension Service Horticultural Experts

A Cooperative Extension Service horticultural information specialist can be found in nearly every county. They range from trained master gardeners to Ph.D.s, dedicated to providing thorough, unbiased information about every aspect of landscaping. They are the advisors to the industry. Whatever you need to know, they'll get you the answer. It's an invaluable service for do-it-yourselfers.

An idea can turn to dust or magic, depending upon the talent that rubs against it. An idea can be expensive to develop and execute, or economical. The more you understand about who does what, the fewer surprises you'll experience, and the more satisfied you'll be with the professional you hire.

The Least You Need to Know

- The USDA's Plant Hardiness Zone Map can help you figure out what plants will thrive in your area.

- Sun, shade, rainfall, and existing plants and structures may create a micro-climate in your yard.

- Locate general areas of use, such as an entry court, a play area, service storage areas, lawn, games area, and gardens, on your landscape plan.

- If you need help with your landscape design, professionals in a variety of fields are available.

In This Chapter

- ◆ Car parks and people paths
- ◆ Everybody on deck and take a seat
- ◆ Fencing in, fencing out
- ◆ No-snore storage
- ◆ Fantastic lights
- ◆ Sound gardening

(Sandra Leavitt Lerner)

Latticework gives a deck a comfortable sense of
enclosure. It's a place to sit and read, enjoy a cup
of coffee, or have a conversation.

Function First

Once you've established the general utility, storage, play, and planting areas of your landscape, you can begin drawing in the infrastructure—the practical parts of the plan. This means establishing traffic patterns for drives and walks. It means considering all seasons and how they will affect your landscape and your energy use. You need to establish boundaries and enclosures with walls and fences. You need to have a place to store tools and other garden items. Finally it means planning the space so outdoor living is as comfortable as indoor existence for all members of your family.

By now you should be getting the idea that your landscape is not a passive and pretty patch of flowers, but an active part of your life. If you design for utility, your landscape can help you get chores done quickly, fence children in and strange dogs out, and give you places to sit down and store your lawn equipment. It can provide security and light, and shelter you from winds, noise, and pollution.

Car Parks and People Paths

The first step in making your landscape function well is to map out the traffic patterns for the driveway, paths, and walks. Where do you go when you walk out of the house? To the driveway? To the car? How do you get the car to the garage? How do the children get to their play area? As with drainage, it's best to follow the most natural patterns.

Driveways can offer a formidable design challenge. Not only do they offer the problem of how to integrate a huge chunk of paving into the landscape, they also are beset with rules dictated by law, by safety, and in the name of common sense. Before you design a new drive, especially if you are planning to replace an old drive, the governmental jurisdiction that maintains your road owns part of your property and should be contacted to find out what the law requires.

In general, a driveway that runs perpendicular to the road is the easiest to enter. If there's room, the drive should be designed so you can drive out front-first. (Backing accidents are the most common.) When you are leaving your property, you should be able to see 300 feet in both directions. Plantings and fences should never get in the way of your visibility. In addition, you need to be careful with the grading of your driveway, lest you wake up one icy morning to find that your car has slipped down your driveway into the street. The ideal maximum slope to drive on is 12 percent, but for parking or unloading passengers, the slope should be no greater than 2 percent. Straight sections of driveway need be only 9 feet wide. However, paving a width of 10 feet will save the plants and help keep people on the paving. Where driveways curve, they should be 12 feet wide. Paving material can be stone, brick, gravel, asphalt, or interlocking block (a type of concrete brick laid without mortar).

While the shortest distance between two points is a straight line, one way to soften the hard surface of the drive is to curve it to make it follow the contour of the land. (Remember, curved lines are more interesting than straight lines.) Another way to make a driveway disappear from view is to install a raised bed in front of it to screen the mass of paving. You might also be able to install the driveway at a slightly lower level than the lawn, as long as drainage patterns are preserved.

The asphalt curb was installed on this driveway to keep cars from siding into the yard when the weather is icy.

Walk This Way

As for walks, when you are designing a circulation line solely to accomplish chores, such as taking out trash, tending the garden, walking the dog, or getting firewood, the walkway is better designed as a straight line. This invites rapid movement and gets you from point A to B very efficiently. Front walks are considered by most designers and architects as utilitarian and are generally installed as straight lines. But if a garden has been integrated with an entrance walk, curved paths work nicely.

Most designers and architects consider front walks to be utilitarian, so they are generally installed as straight lines.

In all areas of the yard, paved pathways should be designed to keep people out of planting beds and off roots. A path begins to form if only one person walks over the land. You may have seen this happen where the mailman crosses your property, or where schoolchildren take a shortcut over your lawn. Foot traffic destroys the friable, aerated, well-drained soil that plants require to thrive. It causes soil compaction, which helps pedestrians maintain their balance, but which destroys plants. Before you determine the shape of a paved walkway, you must know how you want to use it. If you're interested in admiring the garden as you walk through it, install a pattern of circulation that encourages meandering. A curved line, or even offset sections of paving, have the effect of slowing movement, causing you to notice your surroundings.

A brick and stone path encourages people to admire the garden, but discourages them from stepping on the plants.

The minimum width of a walkway is determined by basic needs. Average human shoulder width is 18 inches. Allowing an extra 6 inches, the walk should be a minimum of 24 inches wide for one person. It must be twice that wide, 48 inches, if it must accommodate people walking in two directions at the same time. Walks that lead to main entrances and exits should be wide. Large homes can support walkways 6 to 10 feet wide to fit the proportion of the building.

Green Thumb Guides

A wooden plank ramp accommodates wheelchair users and people for whom steps are a problem. This one is at Brookside Gardens, Wheaton, Maryland.

Do you need to consider paths that accommodate people with disabilities? The minimum path size for people in wheelchairs is at least 6 inches wider than the vehicle, which equals 36 inches in width. However, 60 inches is sufficient for two-way traffic. At entries and gates, wheelchair paths should be a minimum of 32 inches wide. Another important issue for wheelchair accessibility is the grade or slope of a walk. According to the Americans With Disabilities Act, maximum grade for wheelchair accessibility on walks and ramps is 5 percent. That means a wheelchair-accessible walkway should rise or drop no more than 6 inches per each 10 feet in length. At entrances, steps, and tops of curbs the grade should be reduced to a maximum of 2 percent. For complete guidelines on accessibility for disabled individuals, call 202-514-0301 or 1-800-514-0301.

Decked Out

Decks and patios are among the most practical ways for people to interact with the landscape. They provide vantage points for views, space for entertaining, and protection for plants from the tramp of heavy feet. Plus, almost everyone wants a place to sit, and perhaps a place for al fresco dining. They're a natural extension of living space. Think about it: Decks work well whether they're off the living room, den, kitchen, dining room, or even a bedroom.

If you're thinking about a deck, think outside the box. Why should a deck or patio be square or rectangular? Why shouldn't it be curved, or pentagonal, or a couple of irregular shapes joined together? Why should it be a single level? Why not put seating, cooking, and spa bathing on different levels? Why not have a two-story deck, with the top level opening off a bedroom and serving as a roof for part of the deck below? Or perhaps as the ceiling of a screened porch? There's no need for the planking to be a simple back and forth. Why not lay the floor planks diagonally, in a herringbone pattern, or even in a sunburst? Railings can complement the planking, the house, or even the garden style. Think of rustic, or Chippendale, or neat, white-painted balusters with a white or gray top rail.

Planters on top of a brick wall and plants around a stone patio soften and screen the outdoor space.

Patios can be any shape and any size, and can be paved with a wide variety of materials. One of the more interesting aspects of choosing a paving material is that you can choose it by color—terra cotta or soft pink brick, blue or green slate, tan, white, brown, or multi-colored pavers. Patios can be coordinated with decks. Low walls can contribute a feeling of enclosure to a patio and double as seating.

A patio made of carefully placed facing stone from a Baltimore quarry is set in stone dust in a circle of cemented granite.

You can use plantings to soften or screen the deck. You can combine railings with planters, though keep in mind that plants in containers may need more care than plants in the ground. One look that is appealing for its ecological value as well as its elements of whimsy, or mystery, is to build the deck around a large existing tree.

Flagstone steps edged in brick lead the way up a gentle slope to a swimming pool.

Steps and stairs can be integrated into the design of a deck, or even as part of a pathway. Wide deck stairs, perhaps incorporating planters, can make the deck look more inviting. If there is a slope, the steps need not be made of wood. They might be paving stone to match the patio, or to form a more natural entrance to the yard or garden. Steps needed as part of a path can also be made of natural-looking stone.

Good Fences

Fences and walls mark property boundaries, keep young children and pets safely inside, protect wildlife, and provide comfort and privacy. Barriers can be inviting or ominous, depending on style. Psychologically, a low barrier (3 to 4 feet) implies privacy, but is still inviting. A tall fence or wall (6 to 10 feet) is forbidding and says "Private." The style and construction material used for a barrier can make it look like it belongs. You would expect to see a white, wooden picket fence around a colonial style home or a bamboo fence defining the boundaries of a Japanese garden. Ornamental iron would be an expected touch to a Spanish or New Orleans–style home, and brick for a country estate. A stone wall wouldn't seem incongruous if it surrounded a mountain cabin or complemented rock outcroppings. Fences should flow with the landscape.

A board-on-board fence with a lattice top establishes privacy and enclosure.

A good fence should flow with the property. This 4-board fence is typical of horse farms.

Don't let them dominate the property. Plantings can make barriers appear less obtrusive. If you don't want total spatial enclosure, short sections of fencing may be enough. A section or two around a patio or other private space may be enough to add contrast and create an element of interest. If you want something besides a level fence line, an arched or dipping pattern is eye-catching. (The arched pattern says private; a dipping pattern, lower in the center than at the posts, is more inviting.)

An 8-foot-tall chain-link fence means business. This one is designed to keep deer out of Brookside Gardens, Wheaton, Maryland.

Green Thumb Guides

No, deer:

- Install fences first, to establish boundaries. Then install plants inside.
- Fences should be at least 8 feet tall. Woven wire, with openings no more than 6 inches square, is best.
- Don't leave gaps in fencing. Deer will find a way through.

Before you design a fence or wall, call your local government or neighborhood association to find out maximum heights allowed for fences, and any other rules and regulations that might apply. Most jurisdictions require a building permit before fencing can be put up. Generally, fences between the house and the front of the property must be 40 to 48 inches. This height is required for safety, because clear lines of sight are crucial in order to see pedestrians and vehicular traffic. If rear fence heights are regulated, maximum allowable height typically ranges from 6 to 7 feet.

Masonry walls add an extra touch of beauty to gardens, and low walls can double as seating. Retaining walls can turn slopes into multilevel terraces. Slopes are an interesting element, and there are nonstructural ways to stabilize them, such as groundcover, rock gardens, and tree-shrub combinations. But retaining walls add horizontal stability to a house or property. They can also help reclaim level yard areas for sitting, croquet, or other activities requiring a flat surface. Retaining walls are more complicated to build than a freestanding wall. A retaining wall must be able to withstand hundreds of pounds of pressure from elements pounding down on the soil.

Stonework adds an elegant touch to a mortared masonry wall.

Flat stones placed without mortar form a "dry-stack" retaining wall.

Take a Seat

You can also separate plants and people by designing seating along with walkways, and greatly enhance comfort in your garden as well. Any object that you can comfortably sit on is appropriate to consider. Garden seats exist in every configuration and material. Remember that picturesque objects such as rocks, tree stumps, walls, and planters can also double as seating. The comfortable sitting height for most people is 17 to 20 inches, and the seat depth is 12 to 24 inches, depending on the use, if any, of cushions and back supports.

A rustic wooden bench fits in well next to a simple stone-lined pond.

Seating should blend with the style of the garden. In addition to the old standards—brick, flagstone, and concrete—many new forms of paving materials are available, such as brick-size blocks that interlock, concrete in various colors and textures, and gravel mixed with epoxy and laid like concrete (a modern form of the terrazzo so popular in classic Italian and French landscape plans).

What's in Store

While you're considering structures for your landscape, you need to think about storage. It's better to do this early in the process, rather than as an afterthought. You will probably discover that you need to store landscape maintenance and recreational equipment, tools, lawn and garden supplies, and almost anything else that requires protection from the elements or just doesn't need to be in view. One solution is to build a shed. Besides holding things, a shed can be used as a screen for trash cans, a heat pump, gas meter, or other utility. Storage can also be built into the landscape in the form of a cottage, a playhouse, or a rustic log cabin, whatever fits with your design. If your storage shed looks like a springhouse, for example, it could be planted with shrubs and perennials and serve as a focal point that you can see from other parts of your landscape. You can build the structure or buy one prefabricated.

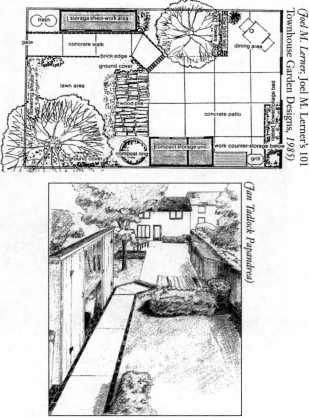

Joel M. Lerner, Joel M. Lerner's 101 Townhouse Garden Designs, 1985

(Jan Tadlock Papandrea)

A small yard is designed for maximum storage. There's a place for trash cans, tools, and potting materials, as well as a counter for cooking and a dining area.

An approach I recommend to clients whose homes have decks is to use the area underneath for storage. If the deck is not too high, say 5 to 6 feet, you can put up plywood, cover the area underneath with roofing felt, drain the water away from it and install siding to make it look like an extension of the house. This makes a house look bigger, as well as offering the benefit of storage. Even if a deck is too low to walk underneath, it may provide an excellent spot to store lawn furniture, hoses, and gardening tools. Put something around the outer edge to block the space from view, such as exterior wooden siding or a heavy duty, frame-mounted latticework. Fashion an access door to match. You might also include some camouflaged storage in your plantings. Build a compartment under a bench or padded outdoor hassock. Mass large shrubs or small trees around it, and orient the seating toward a pleasant view. A storage container could be tucked away and out of sight, surrounded by plants or under seating, but very functional to store gardening tools or other outdoor utensils.

The sharp spines on the end of 'Dragon Lady' holly leaves can discourage unwanted visitors.

Fences will provide security, but plants can also help discourage unwanted visitors, two-legged and four-legged. You can use a thorny thicket to create an impenetrable barrier. It can provide security at the edge of a property or in a dark corner. If I don't need a tall screen, I'll keep shrubs pruned to 3 feet or lower.

A low hedge of thorny barberry can provide a barrier without interfering with sight lines.

However, while shrubs provide privacy, they have the potential to be a screen for criminal activity and might have to be removed or cut back regularly in order to secure an area. Shrubs shouldn't cover your windows. This creates the opportunity for an intruder to get in without being seen. It's a common misconception to think that covering your windows from the outside keeps others from seeing in. The fact is you create a security risk. You can't see out, and an intruder could stand between shrub and window looking in. Remember that a thorny plant is a trash and leaf catcher so it will need to be cleaned periodically. To minimize the possibility that a wall or fence will conceal an intruder, consider a picket-type lattice with large openings, walls with an open pattern, or other see-through fencing such as chain link.

A Little Light on the Subjects

Another aspect of security is lighting. This is one of those features that you never feel you need until you have it and see the difference it can make. Lighting extends the time the garden can be used and, besides offering an element of security, it also adds safety, especially when used to top-light stairs, walks, and entries. Good lighting adds enormously to property value.

Uplighting provides drama in the landscape, because we are used to seeing light come from above.

(Bruce LaPierre, SiteLight, LD, Richmond, Virginia)

Green Thumb Guides

Here are some tips to help you conquer what I call "landscapeluminiphobia" (fear of installing landscape lighting):

◆ Buy good-quality, low-voltage lighting (12v). There is no reason to install a special 120v line, unless it's needed for other uses.

◆ See what is out there in terms of design and fixtures; try different combinations. Consider walkway, pole, and low-accent lights for trees and shrubs. Design security lighting, if necessary, and consider areas you may wish to darken. One of my clients requested that his rear garden be as dark as possible, for his telescope.

◆ Use front light to show the color of a plant's flowers, leaves, and/or bark.

◆ Use back light to silhouette a plant and accentuate it. The effect of back lighting in winter is tremendous, especially behind specimen trees such as a Contorted Filbert or Weeping Norway Spruce.

◆ Use side lighting to cast shadows. Light placement can bring romance and mystery to a garden and/or completely change a garden's identity.

◆ Hide fixtures. Make lights as unobtrusive as possible, and keep light beams from aiming toward people's eyes.

◆ Buy quality lights. Many garden centers stock lighting supplies. Fixtures and more information are available from outdoor lighting specialists. See Lighting Consultants in the Yellow Pages.

◆ Remember that you need the brightest lights only at entry points. While all landscape illumination can enhance safety, it's not to be confused with parking lot security lighting that sprays the property with brightness. Accent lights should be low (10- to 40-watt bulbs), unless you're lighting a tall tree. A little wattage goes a long way at night. If you use lights for security, put them on a separate switch so they don't wash out any you're using for aesthetics.

Finding the Energy

While you're worrying about finding the energy to work in your garden, remember that your garden can be working to save you energy—energy costs, that is. Most heat that is lost from a home is lost through the windows. Shading the windows in summer can save on air-conditioning costs. In the winter, when the leaves fall off the trees, the lower winter sun will pour warmth in through the windows.

Besides arranging so conveniently for the leaves to fall off in the appropriate season, nature has cleverly arranged that humans inhale oxygen and exhale carbon dioxide, while plants, including trees, take in carbon dioxide and give off oxygen. Trees thus help prevent the buildup of greenhouse gases, which contribute to global warming. They also remove particulate pollutants from the air.

Trees are in fact among the hardest workers in your garden. Besides helping save energy and removing pollutants, trees can also protect you from the chilly winds of winter. When you have established the prevailing wind patterns, you can use a windbreak of evergreen trees full to the ground, or possibly a hedge, to deflect winter winds. To protect your property completely, you need to stop not only the blowing winds, but also the turbulence that occurs when wind meets a barrier. There is a formula to block prevailing winds. For example, to screen the wind for a distance of 80 feet across your yard you would need an unbroken barrier 8 feet tall and 11 times the height in length, or 88 feet. The windbreak can be evergreen or deciduous, depending on the direction and nature of the wind. In hot and humid climates, you want to block wind in the winter and channel cooling breezes in the summer.

Turn Down the Sound

Finally, there's one more service plants can perform for you. They can deflect noise. This is important for urban gardeners who may live among busy city streets, or in the country with an interstate highway in the backyard. A buffer of mixed plants can absorb and deflect sound waves. The mix of plants is important since different types of leaves—coarse to fine—reduce noises of different frequencies. How well they control noise depends on the intensity, frequency, and direction of the sound and the location, height, width, and density of the planting.

These tall columnar evergreens provide a strong windbreak at Ladew Topiary Gardens in Monkton, Maryland.

There are two kinds of noise screening: psychological and actual. Sometimes it's enough that you simply can't see the traffic streaming past. In the first case, the philosophy is, if you can't see it, it won't bother you. You screen the sight and the noise with a variety of plantings. However, if you have a major metropolitan traffic artery in your backyard, you'll need an actual barrier. An actual barrier needs to have some heft. You can cut back on the decibels with plants, but to keep serious traffic sounds from invading your property, you'll need solid barriers—fences, or mounded earth berms topped with plants.

Concrete panels with an exposed aggregate finish are the standard way to screen noise from a major highway.

Like a windbreak, a noise break needs to wrap around the area you want to protect, to keep noise from coming in at the ends. Earth berms can be as tall as 8 feet, with plantings on top to help absorb and deflect noise. A serious noise barrier should be 15 to 25 feet wide and include tall and short plants and all heights in between. A well-planted solid berm can cut auto and truck noise by 70 to 80 percent and substantially reduce it from other sources, such as playgrounds, sporting activities, manufacturing companies, or other industries. A wide variety of plants works best.

For year-round noise reduction, plant a mix of evergreens such as arborvitaes, spruces, pines, and hollies. To be effective sound barriers, all of these trees must have foliage that reaches to the ground. Deciduous plants are also effective for noise abatement, but only when the foliage is on. Like evergreens, these must also have foliage from the ground up to really do the job. Thickets of sassafras and pawpaw have been found to be relatively effective for this purpose.

Include lawn or some other groundcover in shady areas. Turfgrass or other low vegetation has a muffling effect on sound, compared to hard-surface areas of bare soil or various paving materials, which are more likely to bounce sound off their surfaces. You can also effectively dampen noise for a small townhouse or postage-stamp-size property, if you install a fence or wall with no openings that's tall and dense enough to shield outside clamor. It will work like the barriers you see along the highway.

The Least You Need to Know

◆ Driveways and walkways can be attractive as well as efficient in moving people and vehicles around the landscape.

◆ Fences and walls can be off-putting or inviting, private, or merely pretty—the materials you choose should be in keeping with your overall design.

◆ Low walls can double as seating.

◆ A well-designed landscape is more than a pretty picture. It can provide security, light, and storage, as well as sheltering you from wind, noise, and pollution.

In This Chapter

- ◆ Remember the basics
- ◆ Bubbles and sprays
- ◆ Striking sculpture
- ◆ Sound ideas
- ◆ A few furry or winged friends

(Cary Levenson)

All five basic principles of landscape design appear in this space at Longwood Gardens, Kennett Square, Pennsylvania: There is symmetrical balance in the arrangement of the pools. The circular central fountain contrasts with the squarish forms of the other pools. The hedge provides enclosure, for a sense of human proportion. The plantings and the finials exhibit repetition, and the pathways move the eye and the person through the garden.

Aesthetically Pleasing

It's great that a landscape can be a protector and a partner in your daily endeavors, but you'll truly want to spend time in it only if it is pleasing to your eye and to all of your senses.

When you begin to deal with issues of pleasure and beauty in your landscapes, there are two types of aesthetic principles that apply:

◆ Artistic
◆ Personal

The artistic principles appear in Chapter 5:

◆ Balance
◆ Contrast
◆ Proportion
◆ Repetition
◆ Sequence

These are the underlying elements that ensure harmony and appropriateness in your design. They guarantee cohesiveness and comfort; however, there's no need to follow these rules off the end of the pier, and there's nothing about them that limits individual taste and inventiveness. It's always *your* garden, but keeping these guidelines in mind will help you get the best from your design.

These principles represent broad landscape strokes. Following them will give you "good bones" to build on as you make the myriad choices, the thousands of tiny decisions that will create your landscape.

It's time to pull out your wish list—those parts of the Lernscaping checklist where you let your heart rule. What will be the loveliest thing in your garden? Here are some specific aesthetic elements to think about.

Water, Water

The number-one item that clients ask me for is "water." Indeed, the appeal of water in the garden is so strong that almost every area can benefit. Fountains are extremely popular. In addition to being beautiful in themselves, fountains add the appealing sound of flowing water. Fountains are available in fiberglass, metal, ceramic, stone, and concrete. Styles can be simple or elaborate, rustic or formal, bubble or spray. Prices vary with elaborateness and difficulty of installation. You can install a self-contained unit yourself or hire a specialist to design and put one in.

It might help to visit a garden where there are fountains. Ask a staff irrigation specialist for ways to ensure maximum efficiency and water pressure. Network with experts and you will be more qualified to choose a fountain or water feature. When installing the fountain, experiment with water delivery to achieve a certain stream or flow. Alter the shape of the outlet pipe to change the effect. Move the pipe around to try different angles of flow over the surface of the fountain. But whatever you do, keep it simple. Your garden isn't Versailles. If you dominate it with water features or sprays shooting in too many directions, you risk losing the beauty of the feature.

A fountain doesn't have to be huge. This little urn is at the U.S. Botanic Garden, Washington, D.C.

A two-tiered pool in Maryland features aquatic plants and a small waterfall between levels.

If you want aquatic plants, you will need to separate them from the fountains. Plants prefer undisturbed water. They grow better in pools. Pools should be located in a sunny area so plants and fish thrive. The pool should not collect a lot of leaves and debris. It should collect exotic flowering plants (for some shade), snails (to clean the water), and fish, especially Koi. These fish can be trained to eat out of your hand. The pool will provide many hours of enjoyment.

Building a pool can be a simple task. Today you can buy pre-formed fiberglass or install a plastic liner.

Green Thumb Guides

The following are guidelines for pool-liner installation:

1. The pool, or the soil upon which it is placed, must be level edge to edge and graded down away from outside edges.

2. Make the pool 18 inches deep, in a configuration that suits your design.

3. Line the inside of the excavation smoothly on all sides with wet sand.

4. Rubber pool liners can be bought at garden centers and water garden suppliers. To figure the size of a liner for a pool that is 18 inches deep, add 5 feet to width and 5 feet to length. After smoothing the liner against the sand, you will have an extra 12 inches of liner to overlap the edge.

5. Fill the liner with water.

6. Install mortared or dry stone coping, or any choice of edging, to cover the top flap of the liner.

7. Add plants, snails, and a pump, for aeration. Add fish.

8. Enjoy.

Statuesque Looks

Sculpture should be integrated into the garden in a way that reflects the surroundings. For instance, a piece of sculpture will have a formal effect when used to grace an entry. Sculpture in the yard is a contrasting element. Like fountains, it should be used sparingly. Back it up with shrubbery. Relate it to a grove of trees. Set it in a bed of groundcover. Work it into the design.

A series of quarried rocks are arranged as sculpture at Brookside Gardens, Wheaton, Maryland.

A Victorian gazing ball rests on a
pedestal of three nymphs.

(Sandra Leavitt Lerner)

All sorts of objects can serve as planters—
like these old bathroom fixtures.

Green Thumb Guides

Rosemary Alexander and Anthony du Gard
Pasley, in their book *The English Gardening
School* (Weidenfeld & Nicolson, 1987), offer
ways to use the size of statuary to psychologically influence garden proportions:

◆ A large sculptural element and a smaller
   piece directly across from it make the
   sculptures appear farther apart than they
   actually are.

◆ A small statue placed on a low level
   makes its surroundings look larger.

◆ A small statue elevated appears farther
   away.

◆ Large statuary near the observer diminishes the importance of the other surroundings.

For thousands of years, urns and vases have
been used as sculptural elements. Ornate containers are probably most ornamental without
plants. But most containers manufactured
today were made to be planted, and many containers not intended for use as planters are also
being planted. There are unlimited possibilities. You have options in color, shape, size,
and material. Planters come in wood, stone,
ceramic, fiberglass, plastic, reed, brass, iron,
built-in, free-standing, sculpted, inset, painted,
new, and used. Innovative containers are buckets, shoes, tires, wheelbarrows, wood stoves,
even old bathroom fixtures.

If you are growing plants in heavy shade or
over tree roots, you might try a container on
wheels, and rotate it periodically to more
sunny locations. It's an excellent way to put
plants where you wouldn't ordinarily have
them. For plants to thrive, containers must
have drainage. Outdoors and indoors, a hole in

the bottom of the container is a must. If you closely monitor the moisture and use a generous layer of stone in the bottom of the container, you can ensure that your plants don't get wet feet. A potting mix sold at garden centers is superior to soil from the garden (although you can substitute compost for potting soil). Regular fertilizing will help container plants thrive. I prefer a water soluble, balanced fertilizer.

(Joel M. Lerner)

Almost any object can be fresh and surprising with a few flowers planted in it.

A Garden in Every Sense

Your experience in the garden goes far beyond purely visual appreciation. You experience the landscape in many ways, such as hearing wind rustle through leaves overhead, or smelling the musky odor of fallen leaves on a forest floor. The sound of rain on a roof is soothing. The crunch of snow under foot can remind you of your childhood. We experience the environment with all of our senses: sight, hearing, touch, smell, and even taste.

You can think about sight like an artist, in terms of juxtaposed colors and shapes. That's the sense you use when you choose flowering plants. But you can also think of it like a film director, "framing" views of every angle of your landscape. Check out all your views, looking as far as you can in every direction. You want to frame the beautiful views and screen the ones that are less pleasing. Trees can frame a view if they are planted to the side, or so that their foliage encroaches on but doesn't obscure the line of sight. You can also obscure an ugly view by planting trees or a hedge in front of it. One technique used famously in English gardens is to plant a hedge before a lovely sight, then cut a hole in it to reveal the view.

A keyhole-shape arch lends mystery to a garden room at Ladew Topiary Gardens, Monkton, Maryland.

Sometimes a view is best seen by means of progressive realization. A good example is the view of a house from a drive. The house is first obscured, then revealed, then obscured again, then revealed from a different angle. The last view is of the whole house. Low plantings in front of or to the sides of a view can enhance it.

Landscaping for sight also involves the use of plants for their ornamental characteristics. For example, flowers of red, yellow, and orange appear to advance toward the viewer and are quite noticeable. Gardeners can also use plants with colorful or variegated (striped, margined, or mottled) foliage for extra visual impact. Some examples are the low-growing 'Emerald 'n' gold' euonymus, with its gold-variegated leaves (12 to 15 inches) and the "silver and gold" redosier dogwood shrub, with white-variegated foliage and yellow stems in winter (about 5 feet). Japanese maples have been bred for foliage or stem color. Leaves can be red, maroon, pink, or green with many shades and styles of variegations and branch colors.

Variegated foliage can give plants extra visual impact, such as 'Emerald 'n' gold' euonymus and liriope 'Variegata.'

Autumn is the time when we notice only one ornamental feature on trees and shrubs: the color of their foliage. Here are some of the most colorful trees (colors vary according to climatic conditions):

The sugar maple offers brilliant yellow and yellow-orange fall foliage.

- Sugar maples—brilliant yellowish, orange-red
- Species Japanese maples (green in summer)—brilliant pink to orange
- Bradford pears—maroon
- Sweetgums—deep red, deep red and yellow mixed
- Hickories—brilliant yellow
- Black gums or black tupelos—shiny red
- Common dogwoods—maroon color
- Oxydendrons or Sourwoods—orange-red
- Katsuratrees—pastel

Trees aren't the only showy fall plants. There are many shrubs that qualify as important plants for their foliage:

- Winged euonymus—fiery
- Forsythia—yellowing leaves turning purple
- Crapemyrtles—reddish-bronze

◆ Nandinas (broadleaf evergreens)—red

◆ Common witchhazels—brilliant yellow

◆ Linden viburnum—rich red to maroon

Sound is usually noticed when it's a cacophony you want to screen, such as traffic, playgrounds, dogs, etc. Or when it is missing, as in the movie line, "It's too quiet out there." But adding sound, and training your ears to hear nature, will bring a new dimension to a garden. Water is the most popular method, but there are others. For example, with the slightest breeze, the thick evergreen leaves of longstalk holly make a rustling sound. Another "instrument" you might use is wind chimes. They're available in a wide range of materials and prices, including wood, ceramic, glass, and metal. My favorites are stainless steel, which make pipe organ sounds when the wind blows, and hollow wooden blocks.

Wind chimes are available in a wide range of materials and prices, including wood, ceramic, glass, and metal.

Poison Ivy!

Some people hate wind chimes, and it's a good idea not to place them where they will become part of the cacophony your neighbor is trying to shut out. The best ones are carefully tuned to sound actual notes when they are struck. If you don't have an ear for music, take along a friend with perfect pitch when you shop for chimes.

Sounds, Not Silence

Birds, insects, squirrels, frogs and "peepers," and other creatures combine with water and wind to create a symphony in the garden.

You may want to introduce some sound to your garden that is not natural, but manmade ... perhaps a Mozart sonata playing softly during an evening party. There are many kinds of outdoor speakers. You can put the speakers unobtrusively in plain sight, or disguise them with plantings. Some speakers are designed to look like rocks.

As with sound, there are pleasant and unpleasant touch experiences. Pleasurable ones can be subtle, such as the long leaves of lilyturf brushing against your ankle as it spills over onto the walkway. Or it could be the texture of a leaf that is appealing to the touch, such as Lambs-ear. Its furry, silvery foliage makes it an outstanding plant for a perennial border. Every time I see this plant in a garden, it tempts me to reach down and pet the leaves. Some plants are less pleasing and even extremely unpleasant to touch. But you may be willing to suffer the prickle of the Chinese holly because of its extremely handsome foliage or the American holly for its perfectly pyramidal evergreen form and winter berries.

A subtle pleasure of the garden is feeling the long leaves of lily-turf brushing against your ankle as it spills over onto the walkway.

Fragrance is an exciting addition to a landscape. Appreciation of fragrant plants can be traced as far back as 3000 B.C.E. in China, and 2700 B.C.E. in Egypt. Aromatic flowers and plants, and the oils extracted from them, have been used as ornament, medicine, and food, and in cultural traditions and religious rites throughout history. In the Dark Ages, other than castles and walls, the landscape was virtually devoid of garden design, yet monks continued to cultivate fragrant herb gardens for medicinal use. England carried this passion for fragrance gardens into the twentieth century, and much can be learned from them about designing the garden with a full complement of fragrances.

Hear the oohs and ahs when people catch a whiff of sweetshrub or 'Koreanspice' viburnum in bloom. On a hot summer day, an edging of herbaceous lavender, rosemary, or thyme will fill the air with a spicy, herbal bouquet. Or you might be greeted by the aroma of sweet alyssum in a window box or hanging basket by the front door. Several plants with fragrant foliage that are easy to grow, and add ornament to the garden are mint, thyme, basil, rosemary, and sweet bay.

Green Thumb Guides

Some fragrant plants:

- **Mint.** Too invasive to grow among other ornamentals, golden mint works wonderfully as a perennial container planting. Corsican mint is only half an inch tall, has a strong peppermint fragrance, and thrives in any nook and cranny you might find in the garden, including a rock wall, between patio steps, or in a knothole.

- **Thyme.** Once you experience its strong fragrance and discover the number of species available, you will want to collect them all—lemon, caraway, camphor. There are more than 400 recognized species of thyme. All can be planted in spaces between walls, walks, and patios.

The fragrance of basil is spicy-sweet and crisp.

- **Basil.** Offering the same flexibility of flavor as thyme, basil is highly valued as a culinary herb. Purple basil adds rich purple foliage to a perennial garden. Basil planted where it will spill over onto a walk emits a pleasant fragrance when bruised.

- **Rosemary.** This evergreen grows to form a mat of fragrance. It is not overly invasive. Ideal to soften the sharp line of a wall, steps, or patio, this cascading plant emits a sweet scent that will be noticed by all who pass it.

- **Sweet Bay.** This handsome shrub with deep evergreen foliage is popularly used to flavor meats and sauces. A woody shrub that fits with any type of planting, it also offers architectural value to the garden and has the added attraction of fragrance.

Tasteful Plantings

Many proud gardeners eagerly share the "fruits" of their labor with anyone kind enough to admire their handiwork. This is true of all gardeners, including annual, perennial, tree, shrub, vegetable, fruit, or herb. But a sampling from vegetable, fruit, or herb gardens usually carries a special treat with it.

The joy of vegetable gardening is sharing the fruits of your labors.

As well as stimulating your visual sense of beauty, lucky recipients will savor the flavor of the garden. The extra benefits and variations you can achieve through edible gardening are astounding. Use tomato vines to grace a walk. Train pole beans or peas onto a trellis to create privacy around a porch in summer. Strawberries make a great edible groundcover. Grow dill to soften a bare wall and cucumbers to cover a fence. Blueberry and currant bushes blend well with ornamental shrubs, and in the natural landscape, raspberries and blackberries fit beautifully. If you like nuts, plant butternut, English walnut, and Chinese chestnut, because you're probably going to plant several large shade trees anyway. Smaller fruit trees can be grown exclusively for flowering value, but if you're willing to commit to a pest- and disease-control program, you can plant one or two fruit-bearing trees.

Visitors with Wings

Among the beautiful things you can have in your garden are some that can't be planted, but can only be enticed. These are birds and butterflies. Birds are easy: They will come if you have trees. You can encourage them if you plant trees that feed them. Bird baths can be sculptural elements. Bird feeders can be selected to encourage particular kinds of birds.

Birds will come to almost any kind of foliage. Feeders like this one will attract numerous varieties.

Poison Ivy!

Bird feeders attract birds and people who like to watch birds—but they also attract rodents such as squirrels, mice, and rats. If you've been having a rodent problem, it could be caused by a bird feeder. Use plants that birds like, such as hollies, instead of feeders.

Next to water elements, the most often requested item in the garden is "something to attract butterflies." Those of you who have watched a butterfly float, dip, and drink its way through your garden understand the excitement that butterflies bring to it. The myths surrounding them are always positive expressions, such as the Native American legend that "To make a wish come true, whisper to a butterfly. Upon these wings it will be taken to heaven and granted, for they are the messengers of the great spirit."

(Sandra Leavitt Lerner)

**Purple coneflower is one plant
that attracts butterflies.**

There are more than 700 species of butterflies in the United States and Canada, and in their short life as flying insects, they visit hundreds to thousands of flowers to drink nectar and pollinate plants. They are harmless, and only one of their larvae, called caterpillars, might be considered a crop pest. The cabbage butterfly lays its eggs on young plants in the cabbage family and the larvae feed on the heads as they form. Virtually all other feeding is harmless to the plants. There are many flowers from which butterflies drink nectar, and there is a host plant on which each butterfly hatches, feeds, and pupates from egg, to caterpillar, into an adult. You should grow flowers and host plants if you want their life cycle to be self-sustaining. Of course, the first type of plants that everyone wants are the flowering ones, but without the caterpillars' habitats, you have no butterflies. It also helps to offer butterflies puddles for water and small flat rocks for sunning and relaxation.

Green Thumb Guides

How to attract butterflies:

- Get a good book and learn which butterflies frequent your area and the flowers that they prefer.
- Locate your garden in a sunny area.
- Plant nectar-producing flowers that you have seen attracting butterflies in your area.
- Single flowers (one row of petals) are more accessible to butterflies than doubles. Plant as a coordination of bloom throughout the growing season.
- Install host plants.
- Include shallow puddles for drinking and small flat rocks so they can bask in the sun.
- Don't use pesticides in or near a butterfly garden.

Here are some nectar-producing flowers that will keep butterflies occupied all summer:

- Spearmint (*Mentha spicata*)
- Verbena
- Black-eyed Susan
- Cosmos
- Butterfly bush (*Buddleia*)

Butterfly bush, or *Buddleia*, is a plant butterflies love.

- Butterfly weed or milkweed (*Aesclepias*)
- Goldenrod (*Solidago*)
- Joe-Pye weed (*Eupatorium*)
- Lantana
- Lavender (*Lavandula*)
- Purple coneflower (*Echinacea purpurea*)
- Sage (*Salvia officinalis*)

Some plants and the specific butterflies they attract:

- Daisy and aster attract the painted lady and pearly crescentspot
- Oak will host the gray hairstreak
- Plum and wild cherry play host to the coral hairstreak
- Spicebush or sassafras will provide a home to the spicebush swallowtail
- Willow, apple, and cherry are used by the viceroy and the tiger swallowtail
- Fennel, dill, parsley, and rue are preferred by the Eastern black swallowtail
- Verbena and snapdragon will host the buckeye butterfly

The Least You Need to Know

- It's your garden and your design, but holding to a few basic principles will make your design more harmonious and pleasing.
- Create the garden of your dreams with fountains, sculpture, and plants that please in all seasons.
- Think of all the senses—sight, hearing, touch, smell, and taste.
- Include attractions in your garden for creatures with fur, feathers, and wings.

In This Part

Part 4

The Hardscape How-To

Even if you won't be doing all the work yourself (after all, digging is pretty hard work!), you'll need to know how the constructed parts of your landscape, the so-called "hardscape," should be done. You should know about maximum slopes for driveways, what types of paving are available, what it means to "dry-stack" a wall, and how to set a fence post.

Some landscape projects are good for reasonably handy people—such as laying a brick or flagstone patio—and some are better left to pros—such as building decks and stairs. And everybody can do the fun stuff—placing sculpture, choosing picturesque rocks.

Finally, you'll find out how to conceal, as well as to display, things in your garden, with sheds and other storage solutions.

In This Chapter

◆ Driveways

◆ Utility lines

◆ Walkways and pathways

◆ Paving the way

A simple walkway leads from drive to door.

Chapter 13

Getting About

Driveways and walkways are part of the "hardscape," or framework of your garden. They provide ways of getting from one place to another in and through the landscape.

Besides directing vehicles and people, constructed drives and paths keep plants from being crushed or trampled. Driveways and paths can be paved, or dug out and filled with gravel or mulch. They can be simple or elaborate and can be designed to enhance your property and fit your landscape style.

An elaborate walk with steps and benches invites lingering at Meridian Hill, Washington, D.C.

Can You Dig It?

Driveways often offer the most formidable design challenge. Besides the fact that you have to figure out how to integrate a huge chunk of paving into the landscape, there are also a lot of guidelines to follow, rules dictated by law, by safety, and by common sense.

It's important to keep track of underground lines, such as the gas line indicated by this meter.

Poison Ivy!

Before you start digging on your property, you need to consider what may be below the surface. In newer construction, utilities such as cable, telephone, and power lines are often underground. But even if you live in an older area, you will have buried water and gas lines.

It's important to keep track of everything that's buried, so you don't dig anything up when installing your landscape. Before you start a project that involves any sub-surface excavation, call the supervising utility in your area (usually the power company). It's not just a good idea; the law may require notification before any digging is begun. The overseeing body will then contact all utility companies that have underground lines in your area. This is usually a completely free service. They'll dispatch a professional to mark all the lines on your property to ensure that digging doesn't disturb them. Once you've located these utilities, mark them on a piece of paper and file it with your tax plat and other property records.

And sometimes you have to deal with completely unexpected obstacles, as the following personal story demonstrates.

Four days before we settled on our home, county workers were called to check our roadway for drainage. Unrelated to their work, they discovered that one half of the semicircular driveway at the house we were about to buy had been installed without a permit. In spite of the fact that the drive had been there 14 years, county personnel responded within the hour. With road grader and dump trucks, they removed the entire nonpermitted section of driveway and, by the end of the day, had replaced it with soil, grass seed, and a curb. It would cost a few thousand dollars to post a bond and a variance to put it back again.

A driveway softened with plantings winds its way to the front of a frame Victorian house in a historic neighborhood.

An incident like this can certainly stifle your creativity. But if you take care to comply with the requirements for a permit, you are not likely to lose what you have done to enhance it aesthetically.

First, find out what your local jurisdiction requires. The jurisdiction that maintains your road, usually your city or county, owns part of your property and should be contacted before you design a new driveway or redesign an old one. The part of your yard that you don't own is called right-of-way or setback. The right-of-way isn't shown on your tax plat, but it looks like it's your property. If you're curious how much of the area in front of your house is public land, measure from the front wall to the curb and compare it with the measurement shown on your tax plat. The difference between the actual measurement and the plat is area you don't own. You often aren't permitted to build walls or plant trees on this land. The part of your driveway where you enter from the street is called the apron, and it's usually the part that's on land owned by your local government. Therefore, they can dictate how you may install that section of the drive. When you want to install a new driveway apron, you might need to submit a design and possibly a cash bond to get approval. Upon final inspection, you get your bond back.

Driving Design

To soften driveways, we try to design their lines so that they follow the contour of the land. This creates interest. Another treatment that makes driveways disappear from view is installing a raised bed to partially screen the mass of paving or by putting the driveway lower than the lawn, as long as water runs off.

(Joel M. Lerner)

A sloping driveway with formal entry posts sinks out of view of the house.

A driveway entrance that is perpendicular to the street is the safest way for your vehicle to enter a thoroughfare. (Being able to drive out front-first is also safer than backing out into the street.) Before entering traffic from your driveway, you should be able to see 300 feet in both directions on the intersecting street. Plantings and fences should never get in the way of visibility. Care should be taken when setting the grade of the driveway. The maximum ideal slope is 12 percent, but the more level the area you park on, the better. For parking or unloading passengers, try to set a slope no greater than 2 percent. You can figure percentage slope if you know how high your driveway rises and over what distance, or length of run. You divide the rise by the run. For example, if your driveway is 40 feet long and the grade rises 4 feet from the bottom to the top over a distance of 40 feet, divide 4 by 40 and you get 0.10, or a 10 percent grade.

Don't curve the driveway into the garage. You need about 12 feet of straight driveway to back out without turning the front of the car into the garage wall. Straight sections of driveway only need to be 9 feet wide, but paving it 10 feet will save the plants and help keep people on the paving. A 12-foot width is necessary where driveways curve.

Carefully designed planting beds help soften the expanse of a driveway.

For aesthetic purposes, it's nice to separate a driveway from the more ornamental gardens and lawn. That's sometimes difficult if the drive comes straight in from the street. If you can, however, consider curving it to disappear behind a grove of trees or shrubs to break up the harsh expanse. If your property is sloped, with the house banked into the hillside, bring your driveway down the hill, out of view of the front of the house and to an entry at the basement level. But remember to incorporate it with other utilitarian areas, and screen it from the garden when possible.

Unless you're a masonry contractor, you are unlikely to be able (or willing!) to install your own driveway. In some areas, driveway construction is covered under building codes, because once you cross into that apron, you're on public-owned land. You should be familiar with the requirements. Some landscape contractors are trained to install interlocking block. Whatever the material, the soil beneath is excavated and replaced with an appropriate base, which may be gravel, stone dust, reinforced concrete, or a mixture. Common driveway materials include the following:

- **Asphalt.** Hot material poured onto a prepared bed and tamped. Asphalt is extremely flexible. It needs edging, or soil packed tight to the edge, or it tends to crumble off as it ages.

- **Brick.** Individual bricks laid in mortar on a prepared base of concrete. Use only paving bricks. The mortar must be solid, to withstand the impact of vehicle traffic. The concrete should be reinforced with steel rods and poured to a depth of 4 to 5 inches.

- **Concrete.** A 4- to 6-inch-thick layer of concrete is poured over a 2- to 3-inch-high structure of steel rods, which is placed on top of a base layer of 3 to 6 inches of gravel. The concrete encases the steel rods, which is what keeps the concrete from cracking.

- **Concrete pavers.** Individual paving blocks laid on a base of crushed stone, sometimes called crusher run, ranging in size from large gravel down to sand, tamped 3 to 4 inches thick. In areas of high traffic, the bottom layer is made of 2- to 4-inch crushed stones, with a layer of gravel on top of that, and then the crusher run. This gives greater weight-bearing stability. Some pavers interlock. These can be as effective as concrete but are more ornamental.

- **Flagstone.** Individually trimmed stones mortared on a bed of concrete, as with brick. Flagstones should be at least 2 inches thick, with solid mortar beneath.

The top layer in a gravel driveway shouldn't be too thick, or it will impede traction.

Even a slight meander in a path makes it more interesting, and brings different elements into focus as you stroll along it.

- ◆ **Loose gravel.** Stones tamped into an excavated bed. The base is 2 inches of crusher run, with a top layer of an inch of ¾- to 1½-inch screened gravel. The top layer should not be too thick, or it will not provide good traction. It needs to be groomed so it doesn't develop ridges.

- ◆ **Tar and chips.** Loose stones rolled into a bed of tar. The top layer of loose gravel should not be too thick or it won't provide good traction. This gives the appearance of gravel, but it stays put.

Walk This Way

Pathways have two purposes: to speed people up and to slow them down. Before you determine the shape of a paved walkway, you must know how you want to use it. Install a pattern of circulation that encourages meandering if you're interested in admiring the garden as you walk through it. A curved line or offset sections of paving have the effect of slowing movement, causing you to notice your surroundings. This path line would be appropriate for perennial, sculpture, water, or other gardens that invite closer scrutiny than just a quick glance.

When designing a circulation line solely to accomplish chores, such as taking out trash, tending the garden, walking the dog, or getting firewood, the walkway is better designed as a straight line. This invites rapid movement and gets you from point A to point B very efficiently.

Keep in mind that curves should look as if they're supposed to be there. You can place a large plant, rock, or sculptural feature so people must walk around it.

Otherwise, human nature takes over, and people will not stay on a curved walk.

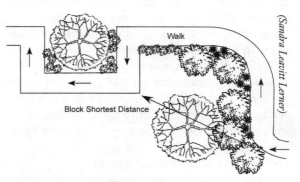

Plantings keep people from straying off a curved path.

Walks that lead to main entrances and exits should be wide. Large homes can have walkways 6 feet to 10 feet wide to fit the proportion of the building.

A wide brick walk offers a visually appealing
and appropriately proportioned
path to double entry doors.

A path 30 feet or longer should be 5 to 6 feet wide to make it fit the space more comfortably. The minimum width of a walkway is determined by basic needs. Average human shoulder width is 18 inches. Allowing an extra 6 inches, the walk should be a minimum of 24 inches wide for one person. It must be twice that wide, 48 inches, if it must accommodate people walking in two directions at the same time.

The minimum path size for people in wheelchairs is at least 6 inches wider than the vehicle, which equals 36 inches in width. However, 60 inches is enough for two-way traffic. At entries and gates, wheelchair paths should be a minimum of 32 inches wide. Another important issue for wheelchair accessibility is the grade or slope of a walk. According to the Americans With Disabilities Act, maximum grade for wheelchair accessibility on walks and ramps is 5 percent. That means a wheelchair-accessible walkway should rise or drop no more than 6 inches per each 10 feet in length. At entrances, steps, and tops of curbs, the grade should be reduced to a maximum of 2 percent.

Green Thumb Guides

For complete guidelines on accessibility for disabled individuals, call 202-514-0301 or 1-800-514-0301.

On the Surface

Texture is important on walking surfaces. A pathway must provide traction even when wet. Concrete can have a broom finish for traction; brick and flagstone should have a rough texture. Most concrete pavers that you find at home improvement and garden centers also come with a rough finish for good traction.

Concrete paving stones have a rough surface to provide traction even in the rain.

If you seal asphalt, be careful that the material you use penetrates and doesn't lie on top, giving it a slick surface. Sealants that are applied in a spray form by installers are better than those you buy and apply with a roller.

Walking surfaces should be lighted. You don't need a bright light. Very low, 15 or 20 watts, aimed onto the paving and not in your eyes, will offer lots of visibility without losing ambiance.

The decisions are what materials to use and whether to install with mortar. For do-it-yourselfers, I think a dry installation is the best, because it can be picked up and re-laid if needed. Nonetheless, before making any decision, consider the numerous materials available. There is a broad spectrum.

Fixtures under the treads of these steps provide good light.

(Bruce LaPierre, SiteLight, LD, Richmond, Virginia)

Some paths are simple: mowed grass, mulch, or gravel. Some are more elaborate: brick, flagstone, paving stones. All need to be laid on some kind of base. Concrete pavers are manufactured in numerous styles, colors, and configurations. One type locks together as they're laid and come in a variety of colors and styles that look like bricks or cobblestones. You can have concrete walks and steps poured in any color and stamped to look like flagstones, bricks, granite, cobblestones, or other materials. There is also a treatment called "exposed aggregate" that can be done with regular concrete. After it is poured, the surface is washed away to expose a stone exterior.

It's difficult to recommend one material as being the highest quality, strongest, or best value. Learn as much as you can about each before making a decision. I have a personal bias for old-fashioned mortared flagstone or brick laid on concrete. These walkways are permanent, aesthetically pleasing, and low maintenance. If a walk is designed properly, you can use any combination of masonry materials. All paths look neater, and slightly more formal, with edging. You can use your imagination when it comes to edging material: commercial wood or plastic; treated lumber; blocks partly buried; bricks on edge; staggered 4 × 4 lumber blocks; flagstones; or even boulders. While some of the epoxied or aggregate surfaces may need to be installed by professionals, a reasonably handy person can create paths in a variety of materials.

Here are some types of paths and their requirements:

Mowed Grass

Typical of an English-style garden, simple but more formal than mulch. Requires established turf, and must be maintained to keep the grass in good health so it doesn't get worn down. Obviously, not for high-traffic areas. Drains well if properly established. (Turf establishment and maintenance will be covered in the next section of this book.)

Mowed turf separates planting beds at the U.S. Botanic Garden in Washington, D.C.

Mulch

The second-simplest form of constructed path, mulch gives an informal, rustic look. It works best if it is already in a high-traffic area, so vegetation doesn't have a chance. The mulch should be deep enough to discourage growth, but not so deep it's hard to walk on. The finer the material, the deeper it can be spread. Excavate, fill partly with dirt, and tamp. Then lay landscape cloth (or even black plastic) on top of the dirt. Use some form of edging if desired, and top with mulch. Drains well but wears away and must be maintained with periodic reapplications.

Gravel

Can be formal or informal, depending on installation and material. Requires maintenance to keep it even. Use crushed gravel for stability. If you like the look of rounded stones, use crushed river gravel. Like mulch, gravel can be hard to walk on if it's too deep. Excavate to a depth of 3 or 4 inches. Place the edging, if used, first, then install landscape cloth or plastic. Cover with an inch of fine stone dust or sand, and rake it level. Use a fine hose spray to dampen material, then tamp down. Cover that with an inch or so of crushed gravel, and rake smooth.

A gravel path is inlaid with stepping stones at the U.S. Botanic Garden, Washington, D.C.

Dry-Laid Brick or Stone

Handsome treatment, can be formal or informal, depending on materials used. The purveyor will be able to tell you, based on your measurements, how much material to buy. If you have good drainage, you may be able to lay the bricks or stones on a bed of 1 to 2 inches of sand or fine stone dust. Otherwise, you will need a bottom layer of 4 inches of gravel under the sand. (The colder it gets in your area, the deeper the gravel layer should be.) Excavate to

the necessary depth and install edging. (Lay down landscape cloth or black plastic if desired. It will reduce weeding.) Pour in gravel and level. Top with sand or stone dust, dampen, and level.

A concrete aggregate path leads to an enclosed patio with dry-laid flagstones at the U.S. Botanic Garden, Washington, D.C.

Out of the Tool Shed

You can make a simple leveling tool, called a screed, by nailing two boards together, the top one wide enough to rest on the edging and the bottom one deep enough to reach the desired finish level. Pull the screed along the edging, leveling as you go.

Place the bricks or stones tightly together in the prepared bed, in the pattern of your choice, using a rubber mallet or sledgehammer to tap them into place. When all the bricks or stones are in place, top with damp sand and sweep it into the cracks between them, until it is even with the tops. Lightly spray the surface with water, so the sand settles into the joints and it drains well. May require re-sanding joints or weeding.

Bricks or Stone in Mortar

Formal or informal, depending on material, bricks or stone in mortar offer a neat, finished look. These must be installed with a slope (along the path, or from side to side) for proper drainage, and require a base of concrete at least 3 inches thick. You may need to use a bonding agent between concrete and mortar if you are covering an existing concrete slab. Dry-fit enough bricks or uniform stones to get an idea how you will place them. If you're using flag-stones that will need to be trimmed, use a brick set (a kind of chisel) and a mallet or hand sledge to score the stone, then crack it over a piece of scrap lumber. You can prepare your own concrete mix (usually 1 part portland cement, 3 parts sand) or buy a commercial mix. The purveyor should be able to give you the proper formula and tell you how much you will need.

A mortared brick pathway directs traffic to the front of a house in Washington, D.C.

To lay a flagstone or brick patio in mortar, follow these steps:

1. Prepare the mortar mixture with water until it is stiff enough to support the flagstone or brick.

2. Working a small area at a time, spread about an inch of mix on top of masonry surface where flagstone or brick is to be laid.

3. Create furrows in the mix with the edge of a mason's trowel and place the flagstone or brick on top, checking each one to ensure it is in line with the other masonry as you place it. If it isn't, tap it into place, or if necessary pick it up and scrape the mortar or add more (re-furrow) until it is right.

4. Use a wet cloth to clean each flagstone or brick as you place it.

5. When all the flagstone or brick has been placed, let the mortar set for 24 hours, then grout the joints by pressing mortar into them with a narrow trowel or using a mortar bag (a bigger version of the type of bag chefs use for icing cakes). If properly installed, the patio will drain well and require only occasional sweeping to maintain.

Installed in mortar or laid dry on a bed of gravel, stone dust or on soil, one of the methods listed above should meet your needs for circulation in your garden. You will need one of these whether you are walking or driving.

The Least You Need to Know

- Before you dig for any reason on your property, locate buried utilities.

- The challenge with driveways is to make them aesthetically pleasing (or unobtrusive), while still fulfilling all the requirements of local law and common sense.

- To create a proper path, determine its function, then choose materials to enhance your landscape design.

- Driveways and some paths need to be professionally installed, but simple walkways are suitable projects for a reasonably handy person.

In This Chapter

- ◆ Secure surroundings
- ◆ Friendly fences
- ◆ Talking about walls
- ◆ Now—how to do it

Walls and fences provide privacy, security, and screening, like this square-cut stone wall at Brookside Gardens, Wheaton, Maryland.

Chapter **14**

Round-Ups

Enclosure is one of the most important functions of the landscape. It gives human scale to the space and provides people with a sense of comfort. Fences and walls perform lots of other roles. They provide privacy, security, and screening; prevent erosion; establish style; and offer climbing and hanging space for plants as well as seating and shade for people.

Underneath It All

Under the best mortared garden walls is a solid foundation, called a footing. A footing is a continuous concrete wall poured underground below the freeze line. Structures built on an underground "wall," or footing, won't be subject to movement as soil freezes and thaws. In the Middle Atlantic states, soil can freeze down 24 to 26 inches, deeper to the west and north. So the continuous wall must be poured deeply, 24 to 30 inches. Fence posts also need to be installed deep enough to be below the level where the ground freezes, but they don't necessarily need to be set in concrete.

Footings (with the forms still in place around them) form the base of a stone and block wall.

Decks and fences are examples of structures that can be built on individual footings for the support posts. They require a fraction of the concrete a wall would require, because there's no need for a continuous underground monolith, as you would need for a perfectly plumb masonry wall. Some structures don't need footings, for example, a patio or walk. This paving doesn't need a deep foundation because it's already on the ground; it can't fall over. A shed, provided it isn't built of brick or stone, and your local government allows it, can be placed on a frame set on a crushed gravel base. If it moves, the entire platform shifts as a unit, and there is no loss of structural integrity.

Before you build anything, call your local government to learn building code specifications for structures, and any other rules and regulations that may apply. Even if you are going to hire a pro to do the work, you need to be an informed consumer.

Fence Us In

Fences mark property boundaries, keep young children and pets safely inside, protect wildlife, and provide comfort, privacy, and security. They can also be beautiful in themselves, or by screening a less-than-ideal view or feature, they can make the landscape more beautiful.

A beautiful ironwork fence at Hillwood Museum and Gardens, home of Marjorie Merriweather Post in Washington, D.C., has a brick base, and brick posts topped with pineapple finials. The posts support pyracantha.

I use the terms fence and wall interchangeably when the barriers are meant to give a sense of enclosure. They can be inviting or ominous, depending upon style. Psychologically, a low barrier (3 to 4 feet) implies privacy, but it is still inviting. A tall fence or wall (6 to 10 feet) is forbidding and says "Private."

Sweetautumn clematis tops a tall fence designed for privacy.

If you desire variation from a level fence line, an arched or dipping pattern is eye-catching. An arched pattern says private. A dipping pattern (lower in the center than at the posts) is more inviting.

A dipping pattern in the top of a fence
is tall but looks inviting.

A short, upright log fence looks appropriate behind
a statue of the Laughing Buddha in the Japanese
Garden at Hillwood Museum and Gardens.

Let It Flow

Fences should flow with the landscape. Don't let
them dominate the property. Plantings make
barriers appear less obtrusive. If you don't want
total spatial enclosure, short sections of fencing
may be enough. A section or two around a patio
or other private space may be enough to add
contrast and create an element of interest.

A fence with an arched pattern demands
privacy for its property.

The style and construction material used for a
barrier can make it look like it belongs. You
would expect to see a white wood picket fence
around a Colonial-style home or a bamboo fence
defining the boundaries of a Japanese garden.

Ornamental iron would be an expected
touch for a Spanish or New Orleans style
home, and brick for a country estate. A stone
wall wouldn't seem incongruous if it surrounded a mountain cabin or complemented
rock outcroppings.

A short run of fencing defines the edge of a property.

There is a huge range of fencing styles and materials available, custom-built or ready to install: aluminum, bamboo, board-on-board (vertical and horizontal), brick, canvas (as a windbreak on patio or deck), chain-link, louver, picket, plastic, reed, wired lath, split rail, stockade, stone, wire, woven, wrought iron, and any combination of these.

There's a type of fence for every use. A chain-link fence surrounds a dog run.

A wire fence with wood supports surrounds a space where animals can be penned.

Like most other structures, fences are subject to rules made by local jurisdictions. (Some areas even have rules about whether or not you can put up a fence.) Before doing anything, call your local government to find out maximum heights allowed for fences, and any other rules and regulations. Most jurisdictions require a building permit before fencing can be put up.

I install fence posts or walls in three ways:

◆ **Crushed gravel base.** This is the best method of do-it-yourself fence installation because it is done dry, without concrete, and can hold the fence post firmly. Wooden fences are especially susceptible to rot at ground level, and concrete can hold moisture around the post and encourage decay.

Use a post-hole digger or a shovel to dig a hole for a fence post.

The hole should be deep enough for the bottom 2 feet of the post's length.

Use a level to make sure the post
is plumb (perfectly upright).

Fill the hole with rocks that are ¾ to 1½ inches in size.

Tamp the rocks down firmly. Make sure the post is stable.

To set a wooden post, dig a hole at least 2 feet deep with a post-hole digger or auger. Place a pressure-treated 4 × 4-inch or 6 × 6-inch post into the hole. Tamp crushed gravel firmly in the hole around the post. Use a level to make the post plumb, that is, perpendicular to the ground. This method should keep the area well drained, hold the pole solidly in place, and keep it from rotting for at least 20 years, if the lumber is pressure treated.

◆ **Concrete base.** There are times when it isn't practical to use stone because it will not set the post securely enough. In this case concrete is required. It can be poured any thickness and depth depending on how securely the post needs to be set. Metal poles must be anchored in concrete because chain-link is installed to them by tightly stretching it, and only concrete withstands such pressure. The weight of wrought iron also needs permanent non-moveable concrete supports. Always use a level and set the posts plumb.

To set a post securely, put it in a
base of poured concrete.

◆ **Footing.** Masonry walls mortared together must not move or lean. They need to be perfectly plumb if they are to stand for any length of time. This is true for any mortared material. Start the wall on concrete footings, which should be poured on undisturbed soil below the freeze line. (Twenty-four inches is the average depth of footings.) Check with your county or city government for exact building codes.

Mortared masonry walls need to be perfectly plumb and set on concrete footings if they are to stand for a long time.

When professionals install a fence, they place all the posts first, then cut the cross pieces individually to fit. However, if you are working with prefabricated panels, you will need to install the posts for each section one at a time. Otherwise, you may have some surprising gaps or overlaps.

Cross pieces or panels are nailed or screwed onto the posts. Generally, these will be made of lumber, such as pine, redwood, cedar, or sometimes pressure-treated varieties. Rustic split-rail fencing, in which the cross pieces fit into slots on the posts, are often made of locust posts and oak cross-members, materials conveniently found on a rural property.

Generally, fences between the house and the front of the property must be no higher than 40 to 48 inches. This height is the maximum required for safety, because clear lines of sight are crucial in order to see pedestrians and vehicular traffic. If rear fence heights are regulated, maximum allowable heights typically range from 6 to 7 feet. Therefore, support posts should be 8 to 9 feet long (2 feet in the ground).

Wall-to-Wall Charm

There's something undeniably romantic about a walled garden. Think of *The Secret Garden*, Frances Hodgson's classic children's book (made repeatedly into screen and television movies), about a trio of children who restore a neglected rose garden, hidden behind tall brick walls and accessible only through a locked door, on an English estate. The children's delight as the garden comes back to life captures the imagination of nearly everyone who cares about plants.

Brick walls of various heights enclose a garden in the Georgetown neighborhood of Washington, D.C.

You might not be able to install a secluded garden with such high walls, but even a low wall can bring romance, enclosure, and stability to a landscape. And if the wall is low enough, you can sit on it.

Stone walls can be dry-laid if they're being used as retaining walls. If they are free-standing, they must be mortared. All brick walls need to be mortared.

"Dry-laid" stone needs no footing, though you must start slightly below ground level with a layer of gravel 2 to 3 inches deep, for leveling. Use the larger, sturdier rocks on the bottom course. Save some lighter, flat rocks for the top.

A low brick wall with a brick planting box in front of it provides a backdrop for a small pond.

Dry-stacked stone wall adds stability to the lower front corner of this house.

Walls on Retainer

Retaining walls are used to hold back soil, so they must withstand hundreds of pounds of pressure from elements pounding down on the soil. If you want to use a mortared brick or stone retaining wall, it needs a footing, rear drainage, and weep holes.

A stone retaining wall in progress has footings, rear drainage, and a weep hole (white pipe in center).

Pressure-treated 6 × 6-inch *ties*, in 6- to 8-foot lengths, are effective in retaining a bank of soil and can be installed without footings. To level ties, begin the first course on a layer of sand or stone about a foot deep in the soil. Drill and *stake* the ties with 12-inch spikes, or longer, as they are laid into place. *Batter* the wall into the bank. If the wall is more than 2 feet tall, it will need *deadman* ties.

Dry-laid rocks make good retaining walls because they don't require mortar, don't need footings, and have plenty of natural weep holes to reduce water pressure, especially if you put a layer of gravel behind them. They are easy to maintain. If a rock falls off, it can be picked up and put back without needing to replace the entire structure. Keep the rock in each course about the same size as the others on that level. Step, or batter, rocks into the bank.

Roots and Stems

A **tie** is a landscape timber or a pin used to connect objects horizontally. A **stake** is a wood or metal stick or post, often with one sharpened end, used to hold a concrete form or stacked objects in place, or as a plant support. **Batter** is the slope of a wall, a minimum of 1 inch per foot of height, from bottom to top, as it leans into a bank. In a retaining wall, a **deadman** or **sleeper** is a tie that is staked to the wall and runs perpendicular to it into the bank. The deadman is anchored to a cross piece buried 4 to 5 feet into the bank.

Plan View of Deadman Securing Tie Retaining Wall

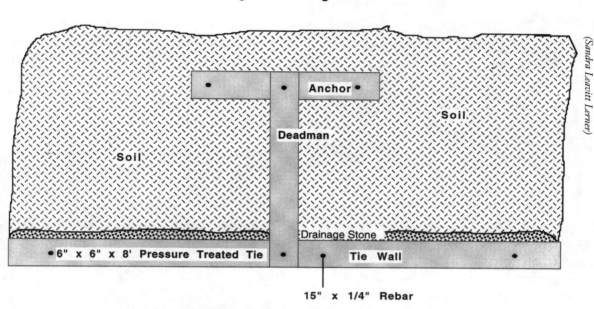

Cross section of Deadman Securing Tie Retaining Wall

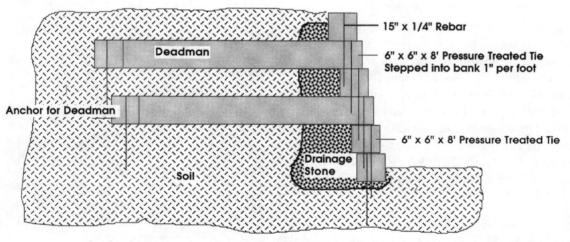

The deadman is anchored to a cross piece buried 4 to 5 feet into the bank.

(Sandra Leavitt Lerner)

Dry-laid rocks make good retaining walls, because they don't require mortar, don't need footings, and have plenty of natural weep holes.

Retaining walls can turn slopes into multi-level terraces. There are also nonstructural ways to deal with slopes, such as groundcover, rock gardens, and tree-shrub combinations. Slopes are an interesting element, but retaining walls add horizontal stability. They can also help reclaim level yard areas for sitting, croquet, or other activities requiring a flat surface.

Brick doesn't make the best retaining wall because it comes in such small units. But it is aesthetically pleasing. If you want to use brick, it needs a footing, rear drainage, and weep holes. Brick will hold up much longer if a concrete wall is poured first and battered into the bank. The concrete can be faced with brick, stone, or any material. Concrete blocks make a better retaining wall because they come in larger individual units. The blocks can be faced with brick for looks.

There are many concrete block retaining wall materials. They are built to stack and lock together, and are designed to batter automatically into the bank. These latest retaining wall systems don't require a footing; they are built dry. Because they aren't mortared, there are plenty of natural weep holes, but you should still put a layer of stone behind the wall to drain it.

Level trenches are dug in the slope to provide a flat surface for laying dry stack stones. The trenches are lines with stone dust to assist in leveling.

Concrete blocks lock together in various ways. Keystone Block retaining walls stack together on fiberglass *pins*.

Roots and Stems

A **pin** is any straight piece of wood or metal driven or passed through drilled holes to hold stacked objects in place vertically.

Soil is filled in level behind the finished retaining wall.

The blocks are designed so that each course is properly battered into the soil and gravel behind.

The final course of the wall is the series of capstones that also disguise the locking system.

The Least You Need to Know

◆ Find out the rules before you begin to build any wall or fence; you might be required to install footings, or there may be height restrictions.

◆ Fence posts can be installed in gravel or concrete, depending on the type of fencing material used.

◆ Many jurisdictions require a permit if a footing is necessary.

◆ Walls are versatile and romantic, and if used to hold back soil on slopes, can add stability (and more flat ground) to the landscape.

◆ Some methods of building walls are easy enough for homeowners to do, remembering "slow and steady wins the race."

In This Chapter

- ◆ Gimme shelter
- ◆ Gazing out, gazing in
- ◆ Siting needs
- ◆ Supporting your plants

Garden structures, like these arbors at Brookside Gardens, Wheaton, Maryland, allow us to enjoy the garden while being somewhat sheltered.

Chapter 15

Hold-Ups

Shade trellises, arbors, gazebos, pergolas … the names seem magical, but these are in fact real structures, with the slightly mysterious role of letting us live closer to nature while being sheltered from its less benign forces, such as sun and wind and rain. These shelters, whether simple or elaborate, are among the most appealing of garden enhancements, because they encourage us to spend more time in contemplation of what we, in concert with nature, have wrought.

Structurally Speaking

We have a broad spectrum of choices when it comes to choosing a garden shelter. All can be built in myriad sizes and shapes, using a wide variety of colors and materials. Essentially, any structure in the garden with beams or a roof is a shelter. They all have names, many of them derived from the rather romantic Italian or French: arbor, belvedere, bower, casino, gazebo, loggia, pergola, or portico. Or sometimes, they are called by simpler names, such as shade trellis or screened-in porch. The main distinctions are whether the structure is enclosed or open, and whether the roof is open or covered.

The following is a list of garden structures:

◆ **Enclosed garden structures.** Bower, casino, and screened-in porch denote a shelter that can serve as a summer house or guest dwelling. A bower is a rustic structure often covered with branches and vines twined together. It might be used in a woodland garden or other natural setting. The casino was introduced in Italian landscape design as a formal entry onto an estate. It was sculpturally very ornate. From the casino, which doubled as guest quarters, the visitor could enter the garden. The main house was usually located up a level on the other side of the garden. For the American-style garden shelter, the screened-in porch makes eating and relaxing outside a joy.

(Sandra Leavitt Lerner)

That all-American garden shelter, the screened-in porch, makes eating outdoors a delight.

◆ **Unenclosed solid-roof structures.** Belvedere, gazebo, loggia, and portico are open-sided structures with a solid roof for protection against the elements. The term belvedere could be applied to any garden shelter that is sited where it commands a magnificent vista. The gazebo was developed for English gardens. Its name comes from a combination of English and Latin meaning "I shall gaze," and it was built to be a retreat with a view. A loggia is a covered open area overlooking a courtyard. It is generally attached to a house. The portico is a covered promenade. It was popularly used around pools in the Moorish gardens of Spain and was decorated with mosaic tiles, carved pillars, fountains, and formal rows of shrubs.

The wood and metal Wedding Gazebo at Brookside Gardens, Wheaton, Maryland, has a stone planter as a base.

◆ **Unenclosed open-roof structures.** Arbor, pergola, and shade trellis are similar structures in that they all have an open roof. An arbor consists of open rafters or lattice overhead and is often designed as a support for vines or trained plants.

(Sandra Leavitt Lerner)

A vine-covered iron arbor in Savannah, Georgia, forms the entrance to a pedestrian bridge.

The pergola is a formal structure, generally with three walls and pillars for support along an open front. A shade trellis sometimes has one wall for screening, wind protection, or to attach to the house. It's more informal than a pergola. Any of these structures are effective with plants trained on them.

Wooden latticework forms a shade trellis over a deck in Washington, D.C.

Most garden structures these days are pre-fabricated and assembled on the site. You can also hire a licensed architect or landscape architect to design a custom shelter, and hire a contractor to build it. The professional you hire should provide you with a ready-to-build drawing of your concept.

Regardless of construction method, a garden shelter and its amenities should meet certain size requirements to ensure that it is comfortable. The most pleasant orientation is slightly elevated on a southeastern slope away from the lowest point of the property. Here are some measurements to ensure that your shelter fits human proportions:

- ◆ Total area: 50 square feet per person
- ◆ Roof: 8 feet from floor to beams, more if design requires
- ◆ Doorway: 32-inch minimum
- ◆ Table height: 29 to 31 inches
- ◆ Seating height: 17 to 20 inches
- ◆ Steps, 6-inch-tall riser, 14-inch-wide tread

Location, Location

The placement of your garden shelter depends upon usage. It's not necessary to attach it to the house, but I like to design these amenities near enough to the house for a smooth indoor/outdoor relationship. A casino, pergola, porch, or shade trellis designed to match your existing architecture will integrate the structure with your property, even if it's across the garden.

Green Thumb Guides

Some national firms to contact are Amish Country Gazebos at 1-800-700-1777, Dalton Pavilions at 1-800-532-5866, Leisure Woods, Inc. at 1-815-784-2497, and Vixen Hill Manufacturing Co. at 1-800-423-2766. Locally, check your phone book and call garden centers, home improvement contractors, outdoor furniture suppliers, or companies listed under "sheds." Check your local library for books on the subject of garden shelters. Look in such special-interest magazines as *Architectural Digest, Country Living Gardener, Fine Gardening,* and the *Better Homes and Gardens Garden, Deck & Landscape Planner.* They will have articles and display ads illustrating a variety of garden structures.

A pavilion on a lushly planted island at Brookside Gardens, Wheaton, Maryland, offers a secluded, sheltered spot.

Some garden shelters, such as a belvedere, gazebo, or bower, are most effective when completely separated from the house. One of these types should be located in a private or separate part of the garden to make you feel like you are getting away from the workaday world. The design of these structures can be completely independent of the design around your house.

A vine-covered pergola overlooks a formal garden in Northern Virginia.

Whether in close proximity or on the "lower 40," a garden shelter can give the landscape a more designed look. Often the structure doubles as a trellis for training plants, as is the case with arbors and pergolas. A separate trellis used in conjunction with the shelter can further enhance privacy and enclosure, and create more interest and beauty. Companies that handle pre-built ornamental landscape structures will usually sell or build trellises. Or you can build your own.

A free-standing trellis made of square lattice has an innovate box design.

Various trellis styles are available. They are made of pressure-treated lumber, redwood, cedar, iron, and/or plastic. They are a framework of crossed strips that form a geometric pattern. If you are training large plants that develop heavy wood, you'll need strong supports, such as steel pipe and heavy lumber. A pergola, arbor, or shade trellis might be the perfect plant support in this situation.

This house has a drab appearance prior to planting the beds and rebuilding the entry stoop.

Color has been achieved all summer with perennial black-eyed Susans, verbena, liriope, and annual sweet alyssum. Hollies add evergreen foliage and winter berries. The extended stoop expands the entry to the house.

A contemporary room added onto this Federal-style
house creates a conflicting motif. Uneven steps create an
uncomfortable circulation pattern from the rear garden
to the side entry of the house and front yard.

Another type of room has been built by removing the
contemporary addition, dividing the front yard from
the rear with a brick wall, and raising the patio level
to correct "trip" steps on the property. Spaces are left in
the flagstone for plants to soften the patio and wall.

New homes in subdivisions are often left with railings covering sliding glass doors that are elevated well above ground level. The challenge becomes how to get from the house to the garden.

Wooden decks are a logical solution to get from the house to the garden and extend the living area. Lattice panels create privacy. This patio offers a tiered effect and more space to walk among the plants.

Even this narrow space offers room for flowering trees, dwarf conifers, shrubs, and colorful perennials. Rosemary, purple sage, oregano, and lemon thyme are among the culinary plants tucked against the house wall. Ornamental flora are crapemyrtle, Montgomery blue spruce, bagatelle barberries, flying saucer coreopsis, and purple coneflowers.

This slope offers a natural spot to put a multi-level water feature. Homeowners should look for these opportunities on their properties.

Excavating for a water feature and installing a flagstone patio are integral parts of this project.

The enjoyment comes from being able to sit by the lily pond with a cascading waterfall, fish, tadpoles, waterlilies, and other aquatic plants. This feature complements the rest of the garden.

Boxwoods line the foundation of this house, which are fitting plants for Williamsburg-style homes. However, planted in this way, they accentuate the front wall instead of softening it.

All but two boxwoods, one on each side of the front door, have been transplanted to define the driveway entry. Large, sweeping beds of perennials have been added, along with a grove of river birches to meld the house with the landscape.

Nothing is more difficult to fit into the landscape than a swimming pool with a big blue cover. The objective here was to do it and maintain a view of the pasture.

A few varieties of plants used in strong repetition, such as black-eyed Susans, purple coneflowers, grasses, and crapemyrtles, have softened the pool area and enhanced the view.

This wooded hillside was cleared to accommodate a new home. The challenge was to then integrate it back into the landscape.

Almost 10,000 plants were planted to control erosion on this hillside and bring this property back into balance with nature. Waterlily star magnolias were chosen because their late bloom time keeps flower buds from freezing in early spring.

In conjunction with the other ornamental characteristics of these plants, they were also chosen for autumn hues. At the entrance pillars, leadwort was used as a groundcover for its blue flowers all summer long and maroon foliage in autumn.

This harsh expanse of flagstone is excellent for entertaining but is in need of plant material to soften its hard lines.

The fullness of the inkberry holly, silver and gold yellowtwig dogwood, lacecap hydrangea, and dwarf fothergillas create a private space around the end of this low wall.

Water adds an important element to a garden. Even this small city garden can accommodate a pond to sit by and relax.

A series of arched trellises give interest to a
garage wall forming the side of a garden.

As with all structures, the garden places must meet local building code requirements and any other jurisdictional rules. There are many ways to install these structures, including block foundation on a continuous footing, concrete pilings poured deep to act as footing, concrete pads, wooden skids made of 4 × 4-inch or 6 × 6-inch pressure-treated lumber overlaid with exterior-grade plywood for a floor. Pilings can be made of other materials, such as wood or stone, especially where the design is custom and the supports can be an integral part of the structure. Floors can be made of wood, or can be designed like a patio of brick, stone, concrete pavers, or flagstone.

The Least You Need to Know

◆ Garden structures, such as gazebos, trellises and pergolas, allow you to get closer to nature while still being somewhat sheltered from it.

◆ There's a welter of names for garden structures, but the chief distinctions are whether or not they are enclosed on the sides, and whether the roof is open or covered.

◆ Garden structures can be formal, informal, historic, or contemporary in design.

◆ Many garden structures are prefabricated; others are constructed on your site. You can use an original design when you have it built for you.

◆ A trellis is an aesthetically pleasing way to add interest in the garden, because it's a structure on which plants can grow and offers screening and flowering on the vertical plane.

In This Chapter

- ◆ Pleasant patios
- ◆ All decked out
- ◆ Playing by the rules
- ◆ Taking steps to design harmony

A deck, like this one surrounded by trees and set up for casual dining, extends your living space.

Chapter 16

Living Spaces Outdoors

Decks and patios extend your living space tremendously, especially if you can walk right out onto the deck from the dining room, living room, den, bedroom, or kitchen. Outdoor living spaces provide a place to observe nature, a place for al fresco dining, a place to entertain. There's a huge variety of styles and materials. You can easily find something that will suit your landscape and your life.

Pretty in Patios

Patios are indeed something that any reasonably handy person can create. It can even be exciting, especially if you are willing to adopt the philosophy that "Rome wasn't built in a day." The following theories and practical applications will put you one step closer to constructing the perfect patio for your garden:

◆ Site the patio in a private part of the yard with a southeastern orientation, close to the house. I have designed a lot of patios with sweeping lines, because I like the way they fit the landscape, but neither I nor anyone else should dictate what you need. Get out to see other patios. Look for ideas while you're walking through your neighborhood.

The curved sweep of a patio fits into the landscape near cutting beds at Hillwood Museum and Gardens, Washington, D.C.

◆ Summer is the best time to determine your needs. Track the number of hours and movement of the sun over your yard.

◆ Research has shown that people are most comfortable when they are 4 feet away from the next person. So ideally, a patio or deck should allow 64 square feet per person. That's about 250 square feet for a family of four.

◆ In architecture, a "golden rectangle" is considered to be the perfect shape. The ratio of its sides is 1 to 1.618, or approximately 3 to 5. Some standard patio measurements that fit this ratio are 10 by 16 feet (160 square feet), 12 by 20 (240 square feet) and 15 by 25 (375 square feet). It doesn't have to have four square corners, but the sides should have roughly those 3-to-5 proportions.

◆ Patio surfaces should always be graded so water drains away from house walls. The grade should drop at least 1 inch per 10 feet of paving. And don't block the existing drainage pattern in your yard. If the patio crosses a drainage swale, it might cut off the flow of storm water, and puddling can occur.

(Sandra Leavitt Lerner)

Golden Rectangle Reflecting a Rectangular Space in the Ratio 1:1.618. An example of this is a patio measuring 10' x 16'.

The golden rectangle, with sides in a ratio of 1 to 1.618, or approximately 3 to 5, is considered to be the perfect shape.

This mortared flagstone patio is carefully graded to slope away from the house.

The easiest type of patio for the do-it-yourselfer is one that is dry-laid, or built without mortar. It can be lifted and re-laid until you get it right. And a dry installation can be just as aesthetically pleasing and long-lived as a mortared one. The thickness of the paving material will vary, depending upon what you decide to use. Brick and most concrete pavers are 2 inches thick. Flagstone is generally 1½ inches thick. Some types of materials are more difficult to install than others, especially those that come in random sizes. The ideal would be to do a preliminary layout before final installation.

The easiest type of patio for the do-it-yourselfer to install is dry-laid stone, like this one in flagstone.

To build a dry-laid patio, dig out about 5 inches of soil. Use edging to hold the patio stones in place.

Putting the Patio in Its Place

You can build your own patio. The method, although more simplistic, can be just as rewarding as those built on concrete and set in mortar. And the best part is, if you don't like it, you can rebuild it with the same materials.

To build a dry-laid patio, follow these steps:

◆ Dig out about 5 inches of soil. The final grade should be about 1 inch above ground level.

◆ Use edging to hold the patio in place. Edging can be any material that won't decay in the ground and will hold its shape. Several options to choose from are steel, stone, pressure-treated lumber, or heavy-gauge aluminum or plastic.

◆ Spread crushed gravel in the base of your excavation. This stone layer should be a minimum of 2 to 3 inches thick to take up the seasonal movement of soil. Use crushed gravel about ¾ to 1½ inch in size.

◆ Place a layer of stone dust (very fine crushed gravel) 1½ inches thick on top of the coarse gravel as a leveling agent. The gravel and the stone dust are available in bulk or by the bag. If you tell the supplier your patio measurements and how thick you're laying the gravel base, they will help you calculate how many cubic feet, yards, or tons you'll need.

Spread crushed gravel in the base of your excavation and top it with fine stone dust.

◆ Slide a board, or screed, across the stone dust at a set height to create a flat surface. Number 15 roofing felt, available at home improvement centers, can be placed on top of the stone dust for added strength. This works well with some materials, such as bricks, where the individual units are small. Finally, lay your paving material on top.

◆ Use a 2-foot to 4-foot-long bubble-type level as you lay the paving. Then you'll be fairly well assured that the finished product will appear level.

The bubble in the level will tell you that the stones are fairly level, but will still drain.

The joints (points where bricks, flagstones or other pavers touch) should be as close together as possible when laid dry. If there are openings, sweep fine stone dust between the joints to fill in all of the spaces.

Place the stones as close together as possible. When all the stones are in place, sweep fine stone dust into cracks.

Once your work is done, plant a shade tree on the southwestern side. Make up a pitcher of lemonade, and spend a relaxing day lazing in your new outdoor living space.

When the patio is finished, surround it with plantings and trees and enjoy.

Deck Details

Decks are the most versatile types of structures to put in the landscape. I've designed many brick and stone patios because decks didn't match the architecture of the house, but masonry must be laid on level ground and drained. With decks, location doesn't matter. I have designed them on hillsides, over tree roots, in barren deserts, and built them into almost every soil, sand, loam, or clay.

(Sandra Leavitt Lerner)

With decks, location doesn't matter. This one, in progress, is on the edge of a steep hillside.

By the nature of their construction, decks are raised above ground level. Spaces between planks allow rain to flow through, so drainage isn't a problem. Taller decks also stand above any possible cold air sinks, which form in low spots when we get an arctic blast. This will extend the useful season of a deck. And if possible, design your deck with a southeastern orientation to capture the morning sun.

Because wood is a natural substance, it fits harmoniously into any natural or informal setting. It has texture and design, which makes it aesthetically appealing. And decks provide year-round enjoyment.

Make your deck interesting. You can design it as a two-tiered structure, one level to eat on and the other for relaxing. It can be installed in conjunction with a patio. Located a few steps above brick, flagstone, or other masonry paving, the deck will enclose and add privacy. If you plant flowers, shrubs, and trees on and around the deck, the garden will have interest on two levels. Even if it's only slightly elevated, a deck offers a wonderful view of plantings below.

A deck covered by a shade trellis
is decorated for fall.

Even if it's only slightly elevated, a deck offers a
wonderful view of plantings below.

Before you build, or hire someone to do it, get to know all you can about decks. Doing this during the design and drafting stages will keep you from exposing yourself to unknown

hazards or having to break up, cut down, and/or hide your mistakes. Decks can be more susceptible to wind lift, warping, and rotting than other forms of paving. Setting the footings, connecting all the pieces, and attaching it to the house correctly are all crucial, so much so that you're required by your county to get a building permit to construct a deck. Lumberyards and home improvement centers are your best sources for obtaining a complete supply of deck-building materials and information. Some offer regular classes on deck building.

The wood to buy for outdoor structures should be pressure-treated lumber, to make it resistant to rot. Treated wood will resist insect invasion for many years.

Poison Ivy!

Handle pressure-treated lumber carefully. It remains pest-free because it has been treated with the arsenic compound chromated copper arsenate (CCA). You'll recognize it by its green hue. However, after December 30, 2003, all pressure-treated wood for decks, playgrounds, and typical residential uses (such as for decks), will be treated with copper azole, recycled copper combined with an organic fungicide (no arsenic, no chromium). Precautions should be taken when working with pressure-treated materials. Wear a dust mask to avoid inhaling toxic sawdust. Wear gloves when handling it for prolonged periods of time. Don't burn the scraps.

Privacy Issues

Your greatest design challenge will be creating privacy for tall decks, such as those at a second-story level or over walk-out basements. In these cases, I like to work with vines and lattice, or plant several fast-growing evergreen trees like Eastern white pines or Norway spruces. Another method of screening high decks is using tall, low branching trees such as beeches, birches, columnar maples, or English oaks. You can purchase them small or at the size you need, depending on your budget. These deciduous trees will have leaves for shade and privacy when you need them in summer.

Vines of pink-flowering Montana clematis cascade over a lattice, providing screening for a deck.

Putting planters on the deck can give you some interest and while it may not be total, there is implied screening. If you want to plant containers with shrubs and trees that will ride out the winter, choose plants that are hardy to Zone 3 or Zone 4 (−20 to −40 degrees Fahrenheit). Several plants I use are Siberian pea shrubs, hedge maples, burning bushes, and Northern bayberries. The best time to plant them is in spring.

Fall-flowering Sweetautumn clematis blooms on a fence, screening the lower level of a deck, where a bench and a container provide some implied screening.

Another deck issue is what to do underneath. If it's low, 3 to 4 feet tall, lattice or other panels will screen the bare ground. If you attach the screening with hinges, you can use the area for storage. For decks 7 feet tall and taller, use a shade-tolerant groundcover, such as sweetbox or creeping lily-turf. Consider turning the area into a shaded sitting section with pavers, a couple of swinging chairs bolted into the deck above, a birdbath, and other site amenities.

A hanging swing turns the area under a deck into a shady spot for bird-watching or reading.

Tips on Deck

Here are a few tips on deck construction that will save you time and money:

◆ Use only Number 1 grade or clear lumber for decking, or else knotholes will detract from the look of the deck as it weathers. Pressure-treated lumber in these grades might be a special-order item, but if you can afford it, buy it. In the long run, it will pay off.

◆ Lay the planks tightly against one another. The spaces you see between decking planks usually form as the lumber weathers and shrinks. If you leave spaces between the planks when laying them, the joints will become too large during the weathering process.

(Sandra Leavitt Lerner)

Planks should be laid together tightly.
As they weather, spaces will develop between them.

◆ Kiln-dried lumber is the least likely to shrink and warp. It will hold a more finished appearance after installation.

Schedule permitting, an experienced deck builder can usually secure the necessary clearances and construct one within a week.

Ups and Downs

For landscape design unity, build stairs of the same material as the walk, deck, or patio. The measurements are different than a typical indoor flight of steps. Movement outside has a different flow. The most comfortable width for steps in the landscape is at least 3 feet, with a riser height of 6 inches and a tread depth of 14 inches. (I prefer widths of about 42 inches.) Masons may want to build risers higher, but they're not landscape designers. The steps will never be as comfortable if you make them higher and with treads of less than 14 inches.

For landscape unity, steps should be made of the
same material as an adjacent walk, patio, or deck.

Green Thumb Guides

Note that steps and stairs *always* have exactly the same measurements from one to the other for their entire length. That means that every step has exactly the same rise and exactly the same tread width as every other step. You may be tempted, when building steps yourself, to fiddle with the measurements, but don't do it. If one step is even a little bit off, it will cause people to trip every single time they use it, even if they know it's there.

Steps always have exactly the same measurements from one to the other for their entire length, so they do not cause people to trip.

A staircase from one deck level to another is divided into two runs of 10 steps and 8 steps by a landing. Comfort is also aided by a double railing.

Never have stairs in the dark. Always top light them for safety. Also, for safety and comfort, don't build a single stair in the landscape; it's a trip step. Always install a 32-inch-high railing with more than five steps. And never have more than ten steps without a landing.

I once compromised the "10 steps" rule by installing 11, but came up with a design solution that made them comfortable. A landing would have stood out like a sore thumb, so, in the name of art, we opted for continuity and built the stairs in a single flight. To make it safer and help soften the visual impact, I designed a curved stairway and partially enclosed the stairs with walls.

Steps in the landscape can be beautiful and inviting. Consider mixing materials to make them visually more interesting. You could, for instance, make the steps of a concrete aggregate material and line them with brick. You could make the steps of flagstone and line them with boulders. Steps can be made more interesting and softened with plantings on one or both sides.

All of these rules and suggestions are meant to be guidelines. Regardless of whether you are building a Versailles or a postage-stamp-size piece of paradise, any good mason or landscape designer will tell you that rules are not "set in stone." They often have to be modified to make the structure fit the landscape.

Where there was no room for a landing, a run of 11 steps is softened
by a curve and made safer by partial enclosure with walls.

Flagstone-topped stone steps from a lawn to an
upper garden are beautiful and visually interesting
in themselves, and are softened with plantings.

The Least You Need to Know

- ◆ Properly sited, patios can offer private
  and appealing extended living space
  within the beauty of the garden.

- ◆ Without drainage, paved areas can have
  standing water causing moss and algae to
  make a slippery and unusable surface.

- ◆ Decks are among the most versatile of
  structures, because they can be built at
  any level, over any terrain.

- ◆ Well-designed, properly proportioned
  stairs and steps in the garden can be
  inviting as well as useful.

In This Chapter

- ◆ Outdoor décor
- ◆ Water for everywhere
- ◆ Odds and urns
- ◆ Rock on

Nasturtiums spill from an unusual ceramic garden container.

Chapter **17**

Just for Fun

For some people, the best thing about owning a house is the opportunity to decorate it. Every paint color, every carpet, every piece of furniture is carefully chosen. And every object, from the dishes in the cabinets to the books on the shelves, the pictures on the walls, and the small decorative objects on the tables is lovingly picked for the place it will occupy. The house truly reflects its inhabitants. Gardens benefit from the same careful choosing of decorative objects.

Furnishing the Garden

There's a wide range of objects to place in the landscape, from fountains to containers to sculpture. And there are found elements as well, especially rocks. In Chinese and Japanese gardens, rocks held a symbolic place, representing mountains. All these decorative elements provide contrast and points of interest in the garden.

They may be made of fiberglass, metal, ceramic, stone, or concrete. Styles run from simple to elaborate, from rustic to formal. Even the water has style: It can be a mere bubble, a trickle, a spray, or a torrent. Prices vary with material and complexity. The simplest self-contained units are easy for a handy person to install. Or you can hire a specialist to design and install a fountain just for you.

When you are building a fountain, experiment with water delivery to achieve a certain stream or flow. Alter the shape of the outlet pipe to change the effect. Move the pipe around to try different angles of flow over the surface of the fountain.

Wooden containers house palm trees in an elaborate setting at the U.S. Botanic Garden, Washington, D.C.

A small, sunny fish pond sports a tiny spray fountain, and the dark color of the liner makes it look bottomless.

Altering the nozzle at the end of the pipe and the force of water can change the appearance of a fountain.

The best plan for a home landscape is to keep the water elements simple. Few of us live in Versailles-style palaces. If you dominate your landscape with water features or sprays shooting in all directions, you risk losing the beauty of the feature. Keep in mind that the moving water of fountains is not conducive to the growth of aquatic plants. They grow better in pools.

Pooled Resources

Make sure you place a pool in a sunny area so plants and fish thrive. It should also not be located in a place where it will collect a lot of leaves and other yard debris.

If you add exotic flowering plants to your pool, you can double the aesthetic benefits. All pools need a healthy natural balance. That is, shade from aquatic plants, the cleaning action of snails, and the aeration of a pump. Then you can install fish, especially koi, or Japanese carp, which can be trained to swim over and eat out of your hand. Watching and caring for fish can provide hours of entertainment and besides, it's good for you.

Building a pool can be a simple task. Today you can buy pre-formed fiberglass liners, or dig a hole and install a liner. Here are some guidelines for liner installation:

- The pool must be level and graded down away from outside edges.
- The depth should be 18 to 24 inches, in a configuration that fits your design.
- When you have dug out the soil, put wet sand into the excavation. Smooth all sides of the hole with it.
- Place a plastic pool liner over the sand. (These liners can be bought at garden centers and water-garden suppliers.) To figure the size of a liner for a pool that is 18 inches deep, add 5 feet to the width and 5 feet to the length. After you smooth the liner over the sand, you will have a 12-inch flap to overlap the edge.

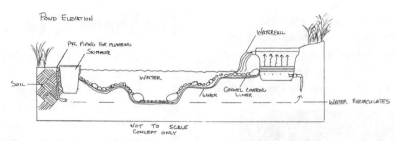

Elevation of a pool shows liner, gravel covering, and mechanics.

(Sandra Leavitt Lerner)

◆ Fill the liner with water.

◆ Cover the top flap of the liner with mortared or dry stone coping, or any choice of edging.

◆ Purchase plants (which grow in containers under the water), snails, and a pump. Add fish.

A pump recirculates the water in this tiny lined pool but is arranged so it appears as water flowing from a spring.

Poison Ivy!

If you stock your pond with expensive koi, be prepared to protect them. One gardener I know came out one early morning to find a great blue heron standing in her tiny backyard pool, happily breakfasting on one of her prize carp. The birds and the other wildlife, unlike the fish, are usually protected by law. One idea might be a wooden frame with chicken wire laid over the pool when you're not around.

Content with Containers

For thousands of years, urns and vases have been used as sculptural elements in the landscape. Ornate containers are probably most ornamental without plants. But most containers manufactured today are made to be planted, and many containers not intended for use as planters are also being planted.

A traditional terra cotta planter rests beside a bench in a garden in suburban Maryland.

There are unlimited possibilities. You have options in color, shape, size, and material. Planters come in wood, stone, clay and ceramic, fiberglass, plastic, reed, brass, and iron. They may be built-in, free-standing, sculpted, inset, painted, new, and used. Innovative containers are buckets, shoes, tires, wheelbarrows, wood stoves, even old bath fixtures. (If you are growing plants in heavy shade or over tree roots, you might try a container on wheels, and rotate it periodically to more sunny locations. It's an excellent way to put plants where you wouldn't ordinarily have them.)

An old iron implement makes an innovative free-standing planter.

For plantings to thrive, their containers must have drainage. As with gardens, drainage is the most important consideration for the health of your plants. Outdoors and indoors, a hole in the bottom of the container is a must. If you closely monitor the moisture and use a generous layer of stone in the bottom of the container, you can ensure that your plants don't get wet feet. Any potting mix sold at garden centers is superior to soil from the garden, although you can substitute compost for potting mix. Regular fertilizing will help plants thrive.

The Shape of Things

When crews were cleaning out weeds and underbrush from a property I was landscaping, they came across some large, rusting pieces of metal. They would have tossed these things out as junk, but the owners of the garden saw something appealing in the shapes and colors. So they kept them, and now an old bumper, complete with license plate, hangs on a slab of plywood, and an old auto differential will be planted amid black Mexican garden stones. The former trash has become sculptural treasure.

Old metal car parts have a sculptural look against plywood slabs and black Mexican beach pebbles.

You may not be "lucky" enough to find interesting-looking auto parts in your yard, but if you look around, you can find all sorts of objects that have sculptural qualities. Old garden containers, such as watering cans, have a pleasing shape and can double as planters. Pieces of driftwood; old stumps or bits of log; architectural pieces such as grates, columns, capitals, and decorative fragments; even old manhole covers can provide contrast and a bit of spark in the garden.

Of course, you can always buy a piece of real sculpture and place it artistically in the garden.

A statue of the mythological figure Pan peers out from under the branches of a tree at Ladew Topiary Gardens, Monkton, Maryland.

I'm not a fan of the overly precious statues sometimes sold at garden centers and in cute catalogs. But a carefully chosen piece, properly placed, can be a real gem in your garden. Among the most striking objects I've seen are rocks carved into rough-textured but perfect balls. In fact, rocks of all sorts have become so popular they deserve a section of their own.

Rocks Rule

I don't know if it's the native-gardening sentiment sweeping the nation or the popularity of constructing homes on mountainsides, but my clients are requesting more frequently these days that I design rockscapes for their properties. Whatever the reason, rocks have really caught on for the garden, so much so that they are being sold in ordinary garden centers. Of course, if you have too many natural rocks in your soil, you may not think they're as much picturesque as they are a nuisance. But maybe

you should consider setting up a roadside stand to sell them to people whose gardens are bare of these interesting natural objects.

Natural rock outcroppings are a desirable feature in the garden.

Large rocks or stones are among the easiest sculptural elements to incorporate into gardens when you want a designed, natural look. They can be "planted" at any time of the year, even in the dead of winter, and they require no maintenance.

There are a few rules for using them, however. Specimen rocks should always look like they belong, as if they are part of the natural surroundings. Therefore, repetition is an important design principle. In the mountains, this is a given. But if you have only one natural rock outcropping in the yard, bring more onsite to set stone as the theme. Except for the glacial strewn look, most rocks appear in the landscape because they had no place to go, typically trapped by the soil. Make your rockscape appear as though its stones are jutting out of the earth, simulating the outcropped look. Work to make them complement the plantings so the rocks look like they belong.

To achieve a natural appearance, vary stone sizes and spread them throughout the beds. Don't use too many, two to three in a bed at most. You aren't building a garden of rocks, you're accenting your landscape. Arrange them in a random fashion.

(Peter C. Benjamin)

Rocks used as sculptural elements in the garden should look like part of the natural surroundings.

A large rock, carefully placed next to a small deck, was chosen for its pink and white color.

Rocks do have one distinct disadvantage for the home landscaper: They're heavy. Stones can weigh 100 pounds or more per cubic foot. Smooth, flat rocks that make natural seats in the garden could weigh a couple tons. If you're planning to place big rocks, you'll need equipment. Placement is so important that the person you work with must be patient. When I order rocks for a client's landscape, they're usually delivered in a truck that includes a self-contained crane and a highly experienced operator to lift and place them. Because of the cost and care required to move them, rocks can be expensive.

Even though you shouldn't lift them, you can still hand-pick rocks from quarries and stone yards. Some companies have showrooms where they import and display rocks from other parts of the country. Native rocks fit the natural look and are less expensive than rocks from elsewhere. Some companies give you a hard hat and allow you to pick what you want from the quarry. It helps to know the dimensions that you are looking for by measuring the space that you hope to fill with the stone. Be as particular at picking stones as you are when choosing plants, looking at color, texture, shape, and size.

The effort and expense of transporting and placing elements weighing several tons can limit the use of ornamental rocks in the landscape. However, nature has produced lava rock, and modern technology has stepped in with artificial rocks that look authentic. Both weigh a great deal less and are easier to transport.

Lava rock, a very porous volcanic material, is significantly lighter than other stone and is available in a number of colors: blacks, browns, russets, and grays. They are available at stone suppliers and garden centers, but they don't fit the native garden theme. They do, however, fit other types of natural gardens, including Japanese.

Most synthetic rocks are composites of several materials, primarily colored fiberglass. A person could single-handedly lift a piece of artificial rock that would weigh 6 tons if it were real stone. Ersatz rocks are being used more often and are becoming more available.

There are a lot of ways stones can enhance landscapes. Be innovative. I've seen Stonehenge-type designs with 6-foot-tall rocks sticking up out of the ground. Such a staggered wall of huge rock slabs can be used in gardens for partial screening and dramatic effect.

You can plant rocks in the soil as steps. Use big flat ones arranged in a comfortable fashion up or down a slope. Keep them level, all treads the same (ideally about 14 inches wide or wider) and risers fairly equivalent to one another and not higher than 6 inches.

Rock is the perfect enhancement for water features. Stone coping around a natural water feature such as a lily pond fits the rockscaping theme. Other features to install in a water garden are stone fountains bubbling up or falling down over rocks. Stone can be used to imply a riverbed and at the same time hold a drainage swale. Covering the soil surface with a consistent aggregate material such as rounded river gravel will provide an effective and ornamental drainage medium. Mix varying sized larger rocks for a natural stream design. Aggregate mulch gives a Southwestern feel to a garden, especially when mixed with sand, larger rocks, and cacti. Make sure the area is well drained.

Water from a fountain cascades over pebbles placed in a compass rose pattern.

(Peter C. Benjamin)

Stone can be used to imply a riverbed and at the same time hold a drainage swale. This rock swale is in New Mexico.

Because smaller, loose stones come in a kaleidoscope of colors, grays, tans, pinks, blues, blacks, and more, and are available in a range of sizes, from "pea" to 4 inches, an extremely ornamental use is to create a formal Italian pebble garden, such as the one at Dumbarton Oaks in the Georgetown neighborhood of Washington, D.C. Use colorful crushed or rounded gravel for a variety of appearances. Set the stones in mortar, or simply lay them in steel or aluminum frames. Another effective technique used in pebble gardens is to place under a layer of water 4 to 8 inches deep from a running fountain. You're limited only by your imagination.

A fountain with a mosaic pattern in pebbles is the centerpiece in an elaborate patterned garden.

The Least You Need to Know

◆ Furnishing your garden with a carefully chosen array of decorative elements, from fountains and pools to sculpture and rocks, will put your personal stamp on the landscape.

◆ Besides being beautiful, fountains add the pleasant sound of water to the garden.

◆ Ornamental containers, formal or informal, rustic or modern, created or found, give style and interest to a garden.

◆ Artistic or simply "found," sculptural elements provide spark and contrast in the landscape.

◆ When it comes to natural objects that both anchor and spice up a garden design, rocks rule.

In This Chapter

- ◆ Store it away
- ◆ Be original with your organizers
- ◆ Protecting plants
- ◆ Greenhouses for the green life

A simple, neat storage shed is tucked away behind plants at
Brookside Gardens, Wheaton, Maryland.

Chapter **18**

Nurture and Store

Not every garden will have the need or the space for it, and not every gardener will have the equipment or the desire, but two things that can greatly enhance enjoyment of the garden are structures to store materials and equipment, and a place to nurture new plant growth and to protect tender plants. What's needed are storehouses and greenhouses.

Store It Away

As you work on your landscape plans, I want you to look ahead and anticipate your storage needs. If you consider them while you design your patio and garden, you'll be able to install the necessary storage as a part of the whole and not as an afterthought. You may find the need to store landscape maintenance and recreational equipment, tools, lawn and garden supplies, or almost anything else that requires protection from the elements or, for aesthetic reasons, must be kept out of view.

One approach is to conceal unsightly areas with a shed. For example, if you already have a space that you wish to shield from view, such as one that is used for trash cans, a heat pump, gas meter, or other utility, use a storage shed as a screen by positioning it to hide such unsightly areas.

You might use an ornate storage building to create spatial enclosure, to separate a rear garden from a front garden, or to define a small space. Put a small sitting area and some flowers around it to tie it into your landscape design as an ornamental feature. Build a storage shed to look like a cottage, a play-house, a rustic log cabin, or whatever fits with your design. If your storage shed is a pleasant-looking structure, a building resembling a springhouse, for example, locate it to the rear of the garden. It could be planted with shrubs and perennials and serve as a focal point that you can see from other parts of your landscape.

(Joel M. Lerner)

A former playhouse has become a storage shed now that the children who used it have grown up and gone.

Store and More

You can use a shed for triple duty: for storage, to screen, and to shade your air-conditioning unit or heat pump. This will block the view of these units plus help you save money on utility bills by shielding them from the sun's rays. Shading your heat pump can save you as much as 3 percent on your utility bills.

Prefabricated storage sheds range in size from 4 feet by 6 feet to 12 feet by 12 feet and larger. However, these utilitarian structures may not be very showy, and to emphasize the beauty and serenity of your garden, you might want to hide them in some way. Screen the area with a row of evergreens or a border of mixed flowering plants.

A prefabricated shed holds tools and lawn and garden equipment.

You can also set a purely utilitarian shed, or tool house, in a service area that you might also use for a dog run, gas grill, firewood, compost pile, or other utility purposes. I have seen people use a shed as a doghouse, and even install air-conditioning.

A couple very lucky dogs share this dog run and air-conditioned doghouse in suburban Virginia.

Out of Sight

You might also include some camouflaged storage in your plantings. Build a compartment under a bench or padded outdoor hassock. Mass large shrubs or small trees around it, and orient the seating toward a pleasant view. A storage container could be tucked away and out of sight, surrounded by plants or under seating, but very functional to store gardening tools or other outdoor utensils. It just needs to be waterproof.

A small bin built under a deck provides storage for garden equipment.

You can store items just by hanging them on a fence. Use an evergreen shrub to screen a storage rack. I designed a storage area once by simply attaching tool holders onto a section of fence behind a mature tree trunk. Hooks were attached to hold a variety of tools, and the 36-inch diameter tree trunk screened them from easy view. You can use different kinds of hooks or large galvanized nails on a fence to hold tools. Some tools rust, of course, and wooden handles will check and split as they weather, so my preference is usually to store them in a dry area whenever possible.

There are other utilitarian features in your landscape that can provide storage space. Build storage cabinets under the benches of your deck. A potting shed or a covered outdoor bar for entertaining can also offer covered storage.

A wooden wall made out of 2×2-inch horizontal lumber screens the space between steps and a wall that will be used for garden storage.

Going for the Green

Cold storage for vegetables and plants evolved out of the necessities of life, particularly on the farm, but it can still serve a practical purpose. Use underground cold storage to hold winter vegetables such as potatoes and turnips. It can be as simple as a basement room, or it may be a separate underground stone or wood structure. The latter will give historic as well as utilitarian value to a rustic, rural design style.

Sometimes you'll need to store growing plants. You may have some living material that you didn't get around to installing. To store plants over a season, we heel them in. This means putting the plant in a shady location, throwing mulch around its base and keeping it moist. Most plants that are fully hardy will overwinter well that way. You can also create a shelter for the plants by stapling burlap onto 2 × 2-inch stakes tall enough to shield the plants from prevailing winds.

To protect plants from winter, cover them with mulch and keep them moist.

If you have extremely cold conditions, or if you like to grow plants that are less cold-hardy than your plant hardiness zone allows, you may want a more elaborate system of protection.

A greenhouse, sometimes called a hothouse, enables you to grow anything you want to all year-round. You can grow vegetables, flowers, shrubs, and trees, from seeds or cuttings, if you wish. You can raise exotic flora from warmer zones. You can plant the containers on your patio with figs, bananas, and other tropicals. Many people think of a greenhouse as a building separate from their main house. It is in some cases, but not all.

Greenhouses come in myriad sizes and shapes, using a wide variety of colors and materials. One style can have a very different climate than another. I have seen greenhouses created inside solaria no larger than a bay window. They can be something as simple as a sunroom, enclosed swimming pool, or indoor patio. Almost any controlled environment can serve as a hothouse.

If you want a traditional greenhouse, you can have one built, or you might be lucky enough to find a specialist who rescues and restores old greenhouses. These can be pricey, however, costing as much as a small house. If you do not wish to spend so much money but want a greenhouse on your property, there are prefabricated units for much less. Some of these are designed to attach to a house so the house wall serves as one of the walls for the greenhouse.

A homeowner can use a greenhouse to grow and keep many different kinds of plants.

A greenhouse at Brookside Gardens, Wheaton, Maryland, is used to grow plants used in the conservatory and outdoor garden spaces.

The Panes of It All

Though their frames may be wood or metal, the window parts of greenhouses are made of glass, polyethylene, polycarbonate, or fiberglass. They can be transparent or translucent depending on the location of the structure and the season. Glass is preferred by far, and it should be glazed, meaning to have a finish applied, and tempered to make it harder. Fiberglass, polyethylene, or polycarbonate are also used when cost is a factor. It will reduce the price considerably and you can find these types of greenhouses starting at about $1,500.

The floor of the greenhouse should be a liberal layer of gravel for drainage with wood or other raised walks for a dry walking surface. Finer greenhouses have concrete or other masonry surfaces for more permanence than wood. Floor drains and proper drainage are carefully designed and installed to control irrigation runoff.

Greenhouses require a built-in drainage system to prevent flooding.

Airing It Out

Ventilation is crucial to plant health and is achieved by the exchange of outside air through vents, windows, and fans. They can be regulated automatically depending on outside wind, rain, and, primarily, temperature. (It can get hot in a greenhouse, hot enough to twist metal. If you have ever left anything plastic in a car in summer, you know how hot it can get under glass.)

Air circulation is also critical inside the greenhouse. You want humidity, molecules of water suspended in the air, but not condensation, large droplets of water hanging on surfaces, including plants and tools. Whether vents are open or not, condensation shouldn't form on the windows or plants; it promotes disease. Internal circulating fans will mimic wind and evaporate water on surfaces.

Depending on the surrounding trees and other structures, a greenhouse may require some method of shading the windows during the hottest periods. Usually this is done with simple shades, but a removable paint will serve the same purpose in a glass greenhouse.

Bring on the Heat

Because greenhouses are meant to protect plants from winter, you will also need a heat source during the colder months. Whether you heat with oil, gas, or electricity, this dries plants and makes it necessary to add humidity to the atmosphere. You can use a humidifier to supplement moisture in winter.

Irrigation of plants depends entirely on what you are growing. There are tubes that will drip the water onto the planting medium in whatever way you want it delivered, by spray or dripping directly into the soil. Or you could simply use a hose for delivery.

Irrigation in a greenhouse is necessary and achieved in various ways such as overhead sprinklers, driplines, or hoses.

Just as there is a choice of watering, you have a choice of supplemental lighting. You might consider grow lights in a greenhouse a contradiction in terms. But there are times when you might want them, such as to extend the growth period so a tropical plant can fruit or flower when days get shorter. Or you might just need to supplement a low-light situation. (Try to site your greenhouse so this isn't necessary.) Various types of light sources and methods of mounting are used. Hotter bulbs must be placed farther away from plants or they will burn the leaves.

Benches are an important tool for holding pots and keeping everything drained, watered, and at a comfortable working height. You will find these and all the other furnishings and accessories through the same companies offering greenhouses.

Potting benches, where plants rest, are an important part of greenhouse equipment.

A less expensive way to protect your plants is using a cold frame. With an old window and some bricks, blocks, or rocks you can make one, or they, too, are available commercially. Sometimes cold frames, when heated from below by composting manure or electrical cables, are referred to as hotbeds. They were used for hundreds of years to propagate and protect tender seedlings and rooted cuttings.

The Least You Need to Know

- Storage sheds for tools, maintenance equipment, and garden and other outdoor materials such as sports equipment, are necessary for many properties.
- Innovative thought to your storage can result in it serving as screening, or can be designed to look like an old-fashioned building such as a springhouse.
- Plants can be protected in winter by heeling in (mulching) or by surrounding them with burlap around stakes.
- If you want to grow any plant, any time, you will need a greenhouse.
- Greenhouses can be simple or elaborate, costing as little as $1,500 or up to tens of thousands of dollars.

Green Thumb Guides

Here are some companies that offer prefabricated, inexpensive options for greenhouses, cold frames, and other supplies:

- Turner Greenhouses, 1-800-672-4770, www.turnergreenhouses.com.
- Strong-Tie GardenHouse, 1-800-999-5099.
- Gardener's Supply, 1-800-427-3363, www.gardeners.com.
- Charley's Greenhouse Supply, 1-800-322-4707, www.charleysgreenhouse.com.
- Sundance Supply, 1-800-776-2534, www.sundancesupply.com/index2.html.
- Janco Greenhouses, 301-498-5700, www.jancoinc.com.
- For more information see the Hobby Greenhouse Association website at www.hobbygreenhouse.org, or check out cold frames and greenhouse growing at gardening.about.com/homegarden/gardening/cs/msub43/index.html.

In This Part

Part 5

The Softscape How-To

Once you have the structure of your landscape in place, you can begin to cover your living canvas with green stuff and flowers. You can paint with a broad brush—a swath of lawn, a patch of groundcover, a fence covered in vines—or with the tiniest touches of individual flowers and plants. You can plant trees and hedges to define and enclose spaces, and to create comfort and mystery. You can find a perfect plant for every need and niche, for every sense and season, for every purse.

Then, when your landscape is beginning to take shape, you'll learn how to take care of it so that as it gives you pleasure and purpose, you can give it the nips and tucks and turns and touches it needs at the proper times. A garden is an ongoing activity, interactive in the best sense. For every small service you provide, it will reward you many, many times over.

In This Chapter

- ◆ Lovely lawns, great grasses
- ◆ Maintaining control
- ◆ Covering all grounds
- ◆ Reaching for the sky

Lawns help control erosion and dust, improve soil and water quality, dissipate heat and noise, reduce glare, decrease noxious pests, reduce the risk of fire, and offer space for recreation.

Chapter 19

From the Ground Up

Few things in the landscape are more admired than a lovely lawn. Lawns help control erosion and dust, improve soil and water quality, dissipate heat and noise, reduce glare, decrease noxious pests, lower your fire hazard, and are used for recreation and aesthetics. It's true that grass "paints" a pretty, uniform, green look on the landscape, even if it's just a tiny patch. However, there are other ways to cover expanses. When you think about getting out a large paintbrush for your property, think also about groundcovers and vines.

The Goodness of Grass

The grass family includes grains that feed two thirds of the world's population. It also gives us corn-on-the-cob, popcorn, and cereal. Grasses are planted ornamentally for arching leaves and a showy inflorescence. Bamboo is a grass, without which panda bears couldn't survive. And palm trees are grasses. So when you're planting the lawn, incredible as it may sound, the seeds you are using are related to coconuts.

Lawn grass, also called turfgrass, has been used by humans for more than a thousand years, and contributes a great deal toward a healthy environment. Just 2,500 square feet of it will produce enough oxygen for a family of four. Grasses are great for just about everything but the common cold.

Incredible as it may sound, the grass you cut on your lawn is a relative of the palm tree.

In spite of the numerous plants within the grass family, few are suited to being used as turf. Lawn grasses are rather specialized plants. They must tolerate regular cutting at heights of 1 to 4 inches, be perennial, stay green most of the year, and grow into a tight carpet that will withstand foot traffic. You should keep in mind that these peculiarities mean that large swaths of grass can require heavy maintenance to keep them green and lush, and are impossible to keep healthy in a drought.

Lawn grasses must tolerate regular mowing. This is a reel mower.

Grasses that fit these criteria have been divided into two types, warm season and cool season. Warm-season grasses are brown in winter and don't begin growing until average temperatures are above 60 degrees Fahrenheit. In fact, they love it when it's hotter. They aren't shade tolerant, but when growing well, they form dense mats that have a carpetlike texture. Plant Hardiness Zone 6 is on the northern cusp of viability for warm-season grasses.

Warm-season grasses don't begin growing until average temperatures are above 60 degrees Fahrenheit. They turn brown in winter in most temperate parts of the country.

Cool-season grasses are the opposite of warm. They stay green during cool temperatures and turn brown during drought and heat. Some will stay green through the winter. Cool-season grasses are more suitable for Zones 6 and below. They hold their chlorophyll longer and withstand winters better.

Cool-season grasses are the opposite of warm. They stay green during cool temperatures and turn brown during drought and heat.

Pick a cool-season grass seed by choosing between two styles, the tall fescues or fine-leafed types, such as bluegrasses, fine fescues, and perennial ryes. I suggest a blend of several compact-growing tall fescues or a mix of fine-textured grasses for overseeding your lawn (see the following lists). What you choose depends on your needs and desires. Tall fescues are wear-tolerant, disease-resistant, and tolerate being mowed at 3 to 4 inches in height. Fine-textured bluegrass, fine fescue, and/or perennial rye are more prone to disease but softer to the eye and to the touch. They can be mowed as low as 2½ inches and still maintain their lush appearance.

Turf's Up!

Timing is the secret to caring for your lawn. And going into fall is perfect for establishing and maintaining it. The practices are simple. Check your pH with a soil test through your county Cooperative Extension Service. They will tell you how to adjust the pH if needed. While you're waiting for the results, add the other ingredients for a healthy lawn, which are aeration, compost, nutrition, seed, and moisture:

◆ Aerate with a machine called a plug aerator that you get from an equipment rental company. The spikes that aerate must be hollow and take plugs of soil with each penetration. Because you have to rent the machine for half a day, go over the lawn three or four times, more if possible. Never aerate when the lawn is wet. Don't use an aerator with solid tines. They allow penetration of water and nutrients but don't aerate. Solid tines actually compact the soil by pushing it together.

The hollow spikes of the plug aerator pick up small plugs of soil with each penetration.

◆ Condition the soil with compost that is fine-textured enough to fill the aeration holes in the lawn. Sprinkle it about half an inch thick over the holes, making sure it doesn't cover healthy growing turf. Your own compost is the best material to use. If you need to buy some, get Compro. You help the environment because you'll be using composted sewage sludge, and it is the perfect texture and pH for sprinkling onto your lawn. You might use as many as 5 bags of Compro per 1,000 square feet of turf if your lawn has a lot of bare areas, and as few as 1 or 2 per 1,000 if you already have a thick lawn.

Sprinkle compost about half an inch thick over the holes, making sure it doesn't cover healthy growing turf.

◆ Your lawn should be fertilized three times during the growing season, in April, September, and October. If you can do it only once a year, September is the prime month to add nutrients. Cool-season grasses can use high-nitrogen fertilizer in fall, because their leaves and roots grow vigorously between then and winter. Fertilize with a drop spreader or broadcast spreader. Use Greenview Green Power Lawn Fertilizer 30-4-4, Lofts Lawn Food 28-3-8, or a comparable product at the recommended rate shown on the bag. Read the label. Get a fertilizer that is 40 to 50 percent organic with a percentage of slow-release or water insoluble nitrogen (WIN).

Your lawn should be fertilized three times during the growing season, in April, September, and October.

◆ Overseed the lawn with 3 to 4 pounds per 1,000 square feet of a blend of compact-growing tall fescues, such as Compact Blend, Confederate, or another blend of three or more seed varieties. For a finer-textured Kentucky bluegrass/fine fescue/perennial rye mix, try Blue Ribbon Shade for light shade (five to six hours of sun), or use Scotts All Purpose, Proscape Superior Sun and Shade, or other named mix. Do not buy generic seed; use a named variety.

Overseed the lawn with 3 to 4 pounds per 1,000 square feet of a blend of compact-growing tall fescues.

◆ After you aerate and spread the compost, fertilizer, and seed, ensure proper distribution of these amendments and break up the soil plugs taken from the holes in your lawn. Do this by walking an upside-down wire rake over the surface. And remember, lawns need five hours or more of direct sunlight to flourish.

Break up the soil plugs taken from the holes in the lawn and mix in the seed, fertilizer, and compost by walking an upside-down wire rake over the surface.

Along with the sun, all of these lawn-care practices must also be combined with water. Without it, nothing grows. To be sure your newly aerated and amended lawn is moist enough, irrigate with 1 inch of water. If dryness persists, sprinkle the area with a quarter-inch of water when the surface appears dry. Measure depth of watering by placing a container under the sprinkler and catching it.

Measure depth of watering by placing a container under the sprinkler and catching it.

Green Thumb Guides

How do you know if your lawn is as healthy as it should be? If it looks good, it's healthy. Or you could get scientific and count the blades. There are approximately 564,536,500 blades of grass in an acre of healthy turf. While you're counting, think about the many environmental benefits that it offers, and how its close cousins could end world hunger.

Staying Green

Once your lawn is planted and growing, maintaining it becomes a primary task. If you don't want to do the work yourself, there is an entire industry of lawn-treatment professionals who are trained to keep turfgrass healthy.

Lawn-treatment companies typically offer six- or seven-step programs that include several fertilizings, herbicide for pre-emerging weeds, post-emergent weed control, fungicide, lawn insecticide, and lime, if necessary. All applications are timed to be performed when they're most effective. As mandated by the Federal Insecticide, Fungicide and Rodenticide Act (FIFRA)

passed in 1972, and reauthorized periodically, anyone who applies lawn-care products for a living must be licensed to handle the articles they're spraying and spreading. Every state has licensing requirements for performing lawn treatments. In most cases, the states have adopted laws that are stricter than the federal ones. Licenses are vigorously enforced, so you may wish to check out the company's record first with the appropriate licensing agency. Ask to see an applicator's photo identification, which is required to be carried at all times.

Oddly enough, you, the homeowner, are the only unlicensed individual who may legally apply pesticides to your lawn. But, if you're found to have used a material in a manner other than that shown on labeled instructions, it's illegal. You could be cited and fined, as well as be responsible for damage.

Let Grasses Reign

Herbicides, especially the types for pre-emerging lawn weeds, are most effective used as a preventive control. Unless you checked for the reddish-brown inflorescence and seed heads on crabgrass the previous autumn, you won't know there's a problem until it's too late. If there's crabgrass, its seeds will invade every space in the soil and grow profusely the following year.

Therefore, particularly if you haven't done it in the past, the time to apply pre-emergent herbicides for spring-germinating annual grasses, primarily crabgrass, is mid-March to early April. It's often applied in combination with fertilizer. If you prefer not to spread an herbicide, even a pre-emergent, until it's absolutely necessary, a lawn-care professional can monitor your lawn through the season and advise you.

The time to check for crabgrass is in the fall, when it is in flower.

The time to apply pre-emergent herbicides for spring-germinating annual grasses, primarily crabgrass, is mid-March to early April.

Post-emergent weed control is also often spread with fertilizer in May. It'll be easy to tell if the lawn needs that treatment. There are dozens of broadleaf weeds that can invade it. Fertilizer isn't necessary in May unless you need the post-emergent weed killer that comes with it. If you don't see a problem with the weeds, you might skip this application.

It's good to see natural and organically based materials being offered by a growing number of companies. It's another option and keeps consciousness high for the natural landscape. Natural or synthetic forms of fertilizer offer very similar nutrients and benefits to the lawn. But the slower-release materials are somewhat better for the environment because they don't wash through the soil as quickly. The organic materials are usually the slowest-release. If it's available, have your technician use a fertilizer that's at least 40 to 50 percent organic with a percentage of slow-release or water-insoluble nitrogen (WIN). He or she can also check your pH with a soil test and adjust it if needed.

Green Thumb Guides

You may want to pull select weeds by hand—because, amazingly, some of them have culinary value. Dandelions, for example, when young and tender, are at their best for making wine and salads. If you use them for food, you might not have enough in your lawn and might have to get permission to harvest the neighborhood lawns.

Despise dandelions in the yard? Use them in salads or for making wine.

Chicory roots can be pulverized to make a coffee substitute. You can eat purslane. The red fleshy stems, thick succulent leaves, and small yellow flowers of this prostrate grower can be eaten in a salad or cooked like spinach, but do not eat the root of purslane.

The stems, leaves, and small yellow flowers of purslane can be eaten in a salad or cooked like spinach as long as there are no chemicals on your lawn. Be sure not to eat the roots.

Before you eat any weed, be sure to get a positive identification from a garden center, plant clinic, or a Cooperative Extension Service. If you plan to eat weeds, do not use herbicides or insecticides.

The best weed control is to have thick, healthy turfgrass through proper mowing, fertilizing, and watering. Some reasons for severe weed problems can be foot traffic, pets, rocks, low organic content, shade, or other cultural conditions. You can correct most of these problems by aerating or tilling the soil, amending the area with a layer of compost, and keeping foot traffic from compacting the soil. Of course, some lawn weeds will always be present.

Green Thumb Guides

For more detailed advice on herbicides, call one of the following organizations:

◆ RISE, Responsible Industry for Sound Environment, 202-872-3860

◆ Professional Lawn Care Association, 770-977-5222

◆ EPA, Environmental Protection Agency, 202-260-2090

◆ Cooperative Extension Service in your region

Covering the Grounds

If planting and maintaining a lawn is not your idea of garden fun, you can still cover a lot of ground, and benefit the soil, with another kind of groundcover. Like turfgrass, groundcovers can help control erosion and dust, improve soil quality, dissipate heat and noise, and reduce glare.

Groundcovers, like this pachysandra, can help control erosion and dust, improve soil quality, dissipate heat and noise, and reduce glare.

Raindrop splash is the number one cause of soil erosion, and groundcovers alleviate this problem. In addition, groundcover plantings are one of the most aesthetically pleasing ways to save your landscape.

Liriope spicata makes an unusual and elegant groundcover, used here along with regular turf.

Some situations where groundcovers help are as masses of flowering green carpets in areas impossible to mow, islands of lush evergreen foliage that grows in shade where lawn won't, and meadows of wildflowers on acreage where mowing would leave time for little else.

On acreage where mowing would leave time for little else, a wildflower meadow covers the ground beautifully.

Plants ranging from 4 inches to 4 feet in height that will mass together to form a mat make useful groundcover. Most groundcovers suited for residential properties are planted as rooted cuttings or seedlings. They are more labor intensive to install than spreading seed, but many of the most desirable groundcovers would take far too long to grow from a sprout. They may not even produce seed, like English ivy.

English ivy is happy to climb or crawl. Here it's used as a groundcover and to cover a fence.

Cover the Possibilities

Choose groundcovers that have multiple seasons of interest. As long as the site is prepared and designed correctly, a lush, virtually maintenance-free carpet of plants will grow. If chosen properly, they can offer fragrance, flowers, berries, fall color, and are a natural controller of competing weeds. Any vigorous low-growing plant that persists year after year is an excellent candidate. Keep your eyes open for possibilities.

Siting the Situation

When preparing a site, add organic material in the form of compost, which usually isn't sufficient in most soils. It must be added in advance of planting because plants will grow together, and there is no longer an opportunity to dig it into the soil. Then follow this plan:

1. Test the soil. Contact your county Cooperative Extension Service for testing information.

2. In April, spray glyphosate (Roundup, Finale, or Kleeraway) to control weeds or grass when present and actively growing.

3. At least 10 days after last spraying with glyphosate, cultivate composted organic material (1- to 2-inch layer) and amendments (from test) into top 4 to 6 inches of soil.

4. Level area, and plant groundcover after incorporating compost.

5. Mulch with 2 to 3 inches of aged shredded hardwood bark for weed control and moisture holding.

6. When establishing plantings, water thoroughly at time of planting and during dry periods. Weed as necessary.

Green Thumb Guides

Here are some of my favorite groundcovers. Purchase them as plants, not seeds:

Use the following for full to partial sun:

◆ **Arnold dwarf creeping forsythia.** Any soil; excellent bank cover; spring flower; sometimes good fall color. Plant 3 or more feet apart.

◆ **Bergenia.** Well-drained humus; will take shade; pink flowers just above foliage in spring; bronze fall color; perennial. Plant 12 inches apart.

◆ **Compact andorra juniper.** Most soils; low-massing shrubs to 18 inches; turning light purple to plum in winter; evergreen. Plant 3 feet apart.

◆ **Flowering groundcover roses.** Most soils; low-growing, long-blooming rose; available in white, red, and pink; may wish to cut back at end of season. Plant 3 feet apart.

◆ **Plumbago.** Moist well-drained soil; protected or eastern sun is best; deep blue flower all summer; red fall color; cut back spring. Plant 8 inches apart. (The groundcover plumbago is not a true plumbago. The botanical name of the groundcover is *Ceratostigma plumbaginoides*.

The violet-blue flowers of plumbago give way in fall to bright orange-red and red foliage.

◆ **St. John's-wort.** Any soil; blue-green foliage; invasive rhizome habit; may wish to contain; yellow flowers in summer; deciduous sub-shrub. Plant 2 feet apart.

◆ **Snow-in-Summer.** Any soil; silvery-green foliage; dense, low grower; white flower spring and early summer; perennial. Plant 12 inches apart.

◆ **Weeping willowleaf cotoneaster.** Moist, well-drained soil; vigorous prostrate shrub; maroon fall color; red berries into winter. Plant 3 feet apart.

Use the following for partial to heavy shade:

◆ **Creeping lily-turf.** Any soil; green 12-inch-long evergreen grassy foliage; available with white variegation; excellent hedge against erosion in sun or shade. Plant 12 inches apart.

◆ **English Ivy.** Moist, well-drained humus; lush deep evergreen foliage; many leaf textures and color variegations available; vine on structures. Plant 8 inches apart.

◆ **Pachysandra.** Moist, well-drained humus; evergreen; handsome new growth; white spike flower in spring; easy to transplant. Plant 8 inches apart.

◆ **Periwinkle.** Moist, well-drained humus; blue or white flowers in spring; fine-textured deep green; variegated cultivars available; evergreen. Plant 8 inches apart.

◆ **Sweetbox.** Moist, well-drained humus; handsome dark green foliage; fragrant flowers; evergreen low shrub; slow to establish. Plant 2 feet apart.

◆ **Wintercreeper.** Moist, well-drained humus; red margin on leaves; maroon fall coloration; evergreen; vigorous grower. Plant 8 inches apart.

Installing groundcover requires planting a lot of pieces. Depending on the size of the root ball, professionals often use a soil auger with drill, a digging bar, or a post hole digger to dig holes faster. Of primary importance is ensuring that the plant's roots are firmly anchored in the soil.

When you're installing groundcover, use a digging tool, such as this digging bar, to make the holes faster.

The groundcover pachysandra spreads through underground plant stems (here pulled up for display).

Lantana spreads by stolons, horizontal branches that produce new plants from buds.

Use the following information to figure how many plants you'll need to cover the area you are planting:

- Planting 8 inches apart, install 150 plants per 100 square feet.
- Planting 12 inches apart, install 100 plants per 100 square feet.
- Planting 18 inches apart, install 45 plants per 100 square feet.
- Planting 2 feet apart, install 25 plants per 100 square feet.
- Planting 3 feet apart, install 11 plants per 100 square feet.

Many groundcovers spread by rhizomes (underground plant stems that produce new plants) and stolons (horizontal branches that produce new plants from buds), and may become invasive.

Check with growers or garden center personnel. You may wish to contain vigorous growing groundcovers with edging. Some plants may require pruning once or twice a year to keep them in bounds. You can look forward to a diminishing workload of weeding and mulching as the plants grow together over a period of two to five years.

Bean There, Vine That

If the "ground" you need to cover happens to be vertical, there are plants happy to help you reach for the sky. Ever wonder why the magic seeds in the fairy tale "Jack and the Beanstalk" were beans? Because it was the logical choice for a storyteller who needed a fast-growing vine that, planted at night, would grow "right up into the very sky" by morning. While there are no magic beans that have such a growth habit, some of these members of the pea family grow 20 to 30 feet in one season.

Turfgrass and groundcovers use the ground for support, but all vines need a trellis. Loosely defined, a trellis is an ornamental arrangement of sticks, rods, or poles, crossed to form a lattice that can support a plant. You can train vines onto almost any structure, including a deck, porch, shed, pergola, house wall, pole, wire fence, or arbor. The types of climbers you are training determines how you should attach them to the trellis.

The following are ways that plants climb:

◆ **Aerial roots.** Ivy and trumpet vine have aerial roots that will attach to any solid wall without training. If you plant ivy or trumpet vine on a trellis with an open framework, you must tie it to the supports until it self-attaches. (These aerial roots are also called adventitious roots, because these hairlike plant structures will develop roots if they touch the ground.)

◆ **Twining.** As some plants come into contact with other objects, they twine around them. Clematis, morning-glory, honeysuckle, or wisteria will train themselves onto anything. The greatest challenge is keeping them under control.

◆ **Tendrils.** Plants such as the grape have spiral, springlike stems called tendrils that curl around wires and other narrow supports. Tendrils of beans and peas grow from leaf stems and curl around wires and poles in the same way grapevines do. They'll train themselves up a pole, onto an arbor or over lattice. Boston ivy has modified connectors at the end of each tendril called discs that attach to the structure.

Clematis jackmanii climbs up a two-panel black metal trellis, used here to screen outdoor utility boxes.

Wisteria is a climbing plant that will train itself onto anything.

Air Shrubs

Shrubs that aren't natural climbers can also be trained on trellises. The best shrub is a vigorous grower with a gangly habit that will take hard pruning and dependably renew itself. Rose and pyracantha are shrubs that can be trained as climbers. Pruning keeps them tight against the trellis and full of flowers, fruits, or berries. The shrubs you choose to train should have interesting leaf color, berries, flowers, branching habits, or other outstanding characteristics.

Trellising plants and keeping them narrow are excellent approaches for tight spaces. The practice of training shrubs and trees on trellises is called espalier. It was developed by the French as an intensive gardening practice to stimulate fruit production in a small area. You can achieve almost any branching pattern, from fishbone or fan-shape to training your surname across the front of your home.

A simplified description of *espalier* is to develop branch structure by training stems in the direction you want them to grow. Often this means pruning the front and rear growing branches, and leaving only the desired side branches. For a plant on an overhead structure, cut shoots that are growing too high or too low to keep the plant on the arbor. Leave stems with two or three buds coming off the side branches so there are buds to produce flowers and fruit. The time to prune depends on the use of a plant. Most should flower or fruit before pruning.

Roots and Stems

Espalier is an ornamental tree or shrub that is trained to grow in a flat plane, as fastened against a wall. Espaliers could be simple, in which a shrub growing more or less naturally is pinned to a wall for effect. Or they could be extensive and their patterns quite elaborate, with interlacing branches and forms.

A variegated dogwood is espaliered, trained to grow against a stone wall at Brookside Gardens, Wheaton, Maryland.

Supporting Players

Install one of these supports for your vines and climbers:

◆ **Rods.** Galvanized pipes or rebar (reinforcing rods) can be set 2 feet apart in concrete on the ground and extended to the eaves of the house or garden shelter. Wires can be strung across the bars, creating a ladder effect if plants need it.

◆ **Wire Mesh.** Plastic-coated or galvanized reinforcing wire can be attached to a fence or wall. Mesh that comes in 6-by-6-inch squares works well. It gives you something to tie onto and works for plants with tendrils and those with the twining habit. If you attach wire to a wooden structure, avoid holding moisture against the wood by leaving an air space between wall and mesh.

◆ **Lattice.** Many styles are sold at garden centers, lumberyards, and building suppliers. Built from wood, plastic, fiberglass, metal, and combinations thereof, they are a framework of crossed strips that usually form a geometric pattern such as a fan, diamond, ladder, or other variation. If plants develop heavy wood, they will need strong supports such as steel pipe and heavy lumber.

◆ **Walls and Fences.** A natural spot for trellising plants, especially on a small property, is a wall or fence. Some vines will attach themselves without training. To cover fences with greenery, make sure the wood is pressure-treated. Otherwise, plantings should be placed on supports a few inches away. English and Baltic ivy are thought by some to deteriorate mortar on masonry walls. You may wish to use a trellis in front of the masonry for ivy.

These roses climbing up brick posts were planted for Marjorie Merriweather Post at her home in Washington, D.C., now Hillwood Museum and Gardens.

Green Thumb Guides

The following vines are favorites of mine:

◆ **Virginia creeper.** Fast grower in sun or shade that will cover walls in a season or two. Green summer foliage is excellent background for a water feature, sculpture, or planting. Fall color is an outstanding red.

Virginia creeper, here growing with clematis, is a fast grower that can cover a fence or wall in a season or two.

◆ **Clematis.** The red, purple, pink, or white 5- to 6-inch flowers of the jackman clematis and the fact that it blooms all season, late spring into fall, are reasons to choose this vine. The Montana or anemone clematis grows vigorously to cascade over a fence or wall and is covered with white flowers in May. Another is sweetautumn clematis. It will run rampant over any plant or structure in its way but doesn't need a heavy support. The lacy, white, fragrant flowers open in fall.

◆ **Climbing rose.** One that was given to me several years ago is planted between two buildings in about six hours of light and has totally taken care of itself. It is called "aloha." Look for disease-resistant varieties.

◆ **Everlasting or perennial sweet pea.** Flowers of deep pink to purple, summer and fall, is a good reason to grow this fully hardy vine, which will cover a 6-foot trellis in a season.

◆ **Japanese wisteria.** Woody twining deciduous vine has lavender, fragrant flowers in spring, followed by long pods. This vine is especially pleasing in full bloom, trained on pillars, a deck, stair railings, or other structures. Needs heavy supports, like pipe or lumber. Training is a must, because it grows strong woody stems around everything it touches.

◆ **Kolomikta actinidia.** Woody twining vine that is fully hardy and should be grown on a strong structure. It has striking white, red, and green variegated leaves. Excellent over an arbor at an entry to the garden. (If you have a male and a female of this plant, the vines may produce kiwi fruit.)

◆ **Morning-glory.** Try any of these free-flowering annuals in full sun. They will self-sow and come back annually. Color range is broad, including red, blue, lavender, pink, and white. This twining plant will grow on any trellis and is easily controlled because it dies annually.

Morning-glory vines will grow on any trellis and are easily controlled because they die annually. They come in a wide range of colors.

◆ **Purple lablab or hyacinth bean.** Fast-growing vine that starts from seed. Annual. Deep pink flowers and red pods of this tendril climber are outstanding. Grow in a planter on narrow stakes, a wire fence, or lattice in full sun. Bean can be eaten. Let some go to seed. Save and grow next year. Dig into the soil when it dies at the end of the season.

Purple lablab is an outstanding climber that has deep pink flowers and red pods.

I don't know of any vines that are magic, but vines that have flowers or fruit, grow vigorously, attract beneficial insects to the garden, and offer a unique sculptural element in the landscape can be pretty magical to a gardener.

The Least You Need to Know

◆ Lawns help control erosion and dust, improve soil and water quality, dissipate heat and noise, reduce glare, decrease noxious pests, lower your fire hazard, and are used for recreation and aesthetics.

◆ Nurturing your lawn to keep it thick and control weeds is all but a national pastime.

◆ If you don't want the high-maintenance aspect of a lawn, use another type of groundcover to fill up an expanse.

◆ Sometimes a landscape needs to "cover" vertical ground, and for that there are vines and climbing shrubs that may also offer fruit or flowers.

◆ Espalier of plants and training vines can be accomplished in many different fashions, both formal and informal.

In This Chapter

- ◆ Greenery overarching
- ◆ The latest in caring for trees
- ◆ Shrubbing up
- ◆ Hedging options

Trees, chosen carefully for size, flower, berry, and fall color, will give instant shape and character to your landscape.

Chapter 20

Greenery Above

Trees are almost always the first plants to be installed on a property, because they're usually the slowest elements to establish and attain maximum ornamental value. But if you choose your trees carefully, you will give instant shape and character to your landscape. Trees and shrubs are important to consider for size, flower, berry, and fall color, as well as form. And they make perfect backgrounds for perennial borders and accents for the house or other large structures. (With the exception of vines, all woody landscape plants are referred to as trees and shrubs.)

Branching Out

Before you plant any tree, develop a concept. Choosing the shape of your trees and shrubs is an important design decision.

Green Thumb Guides

The following are tree shapes:

- **Vase.** These are smaller at the bottom, spreading uniformly outward at the top (for example, winged euonymus or mock-oranges that haven't been pruned).

This mature purple-leafed crabapple has a vase shape.

- **Globose.** As the name suggests, these are round (for example, winterberry hollies or sugar maples).

- **Fan.** These arch out from the base (for example, Chinese witchhazels or zelkova trees).

- **Pyramidal.** Uniformly wider at the bottom than the top (for example, blue spruce or Christmas tree fir).

The baldcypress starts out sharply pyramidal, but as it matures it softens into a more rounded shape.

Don't select a plant simply because you know its name. Think about all the ornamental characteristics you want. Install a tree or shrub that will have the leaf, flower, shape, and other characteristics you're looking for. Take your criteria to a nursery or garden center where a professional can help you put it all together.

Nothing better emphasizes the importance of developing a design in advance than tree placement. Trees come in many sizes, and this will be your first consideration in selecting one.

You should also keep in mind that large trees create shade. When you're landscaping with big trees, whether you or someone from a previous generation started them, your job is to create a garden that will thrive in low light.

No plant will grow in complete shade. You have to find plants that thrive in partial sun. There are many that tolerate low light conditions, as long as you're not trying to plant them in a woody mass of roots belonging to the trees above. Design shade plants toward the tree's dripline, or outer branch spread, to ensure enough light and less root competition. If you need shade-tolerant shrubs, ask for them while you're at the garden center.

The curved edge of the planting bed, visible lower left, follows the dripline of the tree.

Amend the soil deeply with compost when planting your trees and shrubs. Incorporate it into as wide an area as possible, digging 3 inches of compost laid on the surface into the top 12 to 15 inches of soil. To fertilize in spring or fall, broadcast fertilizer over the roots. Consider that the root zone covers a little wider area than the canopy, or dripline, of the tree. Spread 5-10-5 or 5-10-10 granular general-purpose fertilizer. Broadcast it according to the product's instruction on the bag.

Tree Happy

Don't plant in a monoculture, which means installing only one species. Variety is the spice of life. This is a tip that applies to city planners as well as home gardeners. For example, the United States was well populated with American elms, one of the most regal specimens of large trees, with its tall arching cathedral-like habit. The National Capitol Mall in Washington and many of the main streets throughout the United States were lined with magnificent specimens. Unfortunately, most of these trees have been lost to Dutch elm disease. Blights tend to strike selectively—you may have a problem such as gypsy moths, Dutch elm disease, oak blight, chestnut blight, or pear thrips. If you mix varieties, you'll never lose your whole stand of trees or shrubs.

Avoid giving the appearance of a one-of-each collection. A way to do this is to mass small trees together, for example, three dogwoods or three crapemyrtles. Then change varieties to several eastern redbuds or hawthorns. Next, group some crabapples in another part of the garden. The same guidelines can be used for shrubs. You don't need to repeat the same shrubs everywhere.

A grouping of three small trees, in this case crapemyrtles, give cohesion to a brick-paved garden.

Green Thumb Guides

"The golden section" is a theory of plant placement that has determined the best way to locate plants or beds. It dictates that you should install plants about two thirds of the distance from the house to the street, or from one side of the lot to the other. The best composition is never dead center. You always want to offset your plantings slightly, perhaps a bed on one side, a shade tree on the other.

Here are some steps for planting trees:

1. When you ready the site for growing a tree, till the soil 4 to 8 feet in diameter, or as widely as you have room for, and 12 inches deep, or the depth of the root ball. The planting medium should consist of the original native soil with a 2- to 3-inch layer of leaf mold or other compost dug in.

The planting medium should consist of the original native soil with a 2- to 3-inch layer of leaf mold or other compost dug in.

This ensures that the tree will be placed in a well-drained medium and that its roots will grow to a depth of 12 to 18 inches and not run across the surface of the soil as they mature.

2. Dig the planting hole.

Dig the planting hole deep enough that at least three quarters to two thirds of the root ball will be underground.

3. Find the tree's root collar, which is a noticeable flare in the trunk at the base of the bark. The roots grow horizontally underground from this point. The flare must be above ground. Place the ball so that the root collar is several inches above the existing soil line, and set it on undisturbed or packed soil so it doesn't settle.

When you're planting a tree, it's important to locate the tree's root collar, which is a noticeable flare in the trunk at the base of the bark.

Don't mulch against that flare or let any soil pile against it more than an inch or two, or it could rot the bark, increase susceptibility to disease and insects, and interrupt nutrient circulation.

4. Place the tree so that the best side is facing in the direction that you want it. Be sure that it is perpendicular and resting on firm soil. Fill the hole about a third of the way, enough to support the root ball.

5. Remove any ropes or fabric if possible. Otherwise, pull back and fold down burlap from the top third or more of the ball. If the tree was in an open wire basket, leave it on.

6. Fill the hole the rest of the way with a soil amended with compost. Form a soil dam around the edges of the root ball to hold in water.

A soil dam around the edges of the root ball will help keep water in place.

7. Water your tree immediately and thoroughly. Keep it watered weekly if there is not enough rain to keep the new plant moist.

8. Mulch with ornamental bark for aesthetics and to hold moisture, being careful not to cover the root collar. Use 2 inches of a compost or leaf mold that will hold moisture and protect the roots through winter.

Ornamental bark mulch makes the newly planted tree look better and will help hold in moisture.

Poison Ivy!

If your lawn has roots running across it that frequently cause people to trip, it's the result of improper site preparation. The roots are growing to the surface because that's the only place for them to find a moist, aerated, well-drained environment. Preparing properly when planting is the only remedy, otherwise roots can stick out of the ground 3 inches or more.

You can also get large trees in containers, up to a 25-gallon size. When you plant a container tree, remove it completely from the pot and make vertical cuts down the roots in three or four places around the ball. This will encourage it to grow into the surrounding soil. You can get bare-root trees, too. They don't come in as mature a size as balled and burlapped trees, but the price is right. You typically find them through mail order.

When you plant a container tree, remove it completely from the pot and make vertical cuts down the roots in three or four places around the ball.

Bare roots should be planted by spreading them over a mound of amended soil tamped firm with a shovel or some other tool. The mound of soil should be high enough so that the tree's root collar will be above ground. Backfill the rest of the hole using the amended soil on site. Using the native soil helps trees adapt to their new surroundings. Form a basin around the edge of the root ball to catch rain and irrigation water. Don't fertilize while backfilling. Add a variety of growth stimulants, such as humic acid, fish emulsion, kelp, or vitamins instead.

Less Prunes for the New

Do less pruning on newly planted trees. Old guidelines advised pruning to compensate for roots that were cut in transplanting. However, it is now believed that cutting the roots shocks the tree enough, and that you should prune no more than 15 percent of the branches at the time of planting.

If You Must Stake

If you must stake trees, use tree stakes from a garden center. Wire the tree on three sides to keep it from blowing to one side or the other. Use rubber hose to protect the bark from the wire. Don't stake or wire trees into place unless necessary. Research shows that they establish better if their tops are allowed to blow in the wind without being staked and wired.

Save the Trees

Like the dinosaurs, trees are slow to adapt to inhospitable environments, such as changes in air and climate. It's impossible for them to survive paving, trenching for utilities, and clear cutting. We have to learn trees' needs to help them cope with modern society.

A tree's vascular system runs from its tiniest root hairs, which absorb nutrients, minerals, and water, up along the trunk, just under the bark, to the leaves, which act as lungs. This circulation system is a tree's lifeline. Impeding the flow at any point affects its health and vigor. That's what happens when too many insects chew roots, leaves, or bark. It's what funguses do when rotting feeder roots and stems. Bark damage from mowers and heavy equipment crushing roots also severely impacts or kills a tree.

When insects infest a tree and chew too many of the leaves, they interfere with the tree's vascular lifeline. Excessive damage can kill the tree.

Lawn has been shown to be fairly incompatible with trees. As trees mature, you should yield to their canopy, and pull the grass back to the full sun areas of the yard. Lawn, as well as the annual planting of flowers, keeps the tree's important feeder roots from developing. Let fallen leaves lie. A tree's leaves are its own best fertilizer, so let them lie to decay, except where they're smothering the lawn or ornamental plantings. Use your mower to grind leaves to speed up decomposition. Check for rocks and branches before mowing.

Mature trees are generally incompatible with lawn grasses.

A large tree may not be as much in the way as you think. The trunk may be incorporated into a deck or patio design.

Or Don't Save Them ...

It's a question I get all the time: "Should I cut down a large, mature tree on my property?" Some homeowners feel guilty cutting a venerable, massive, old woody plant.

Others fear its size and insist on removal to reduce the risk of it falling on them. I have mixed emotions. One way to answer this is by asking other questions:

◆ **Is it causing structural damage?** A tree planted too close to the house could lift the walk, rot the eaves and drop juicy purple berries at the entry that are then tracked through the house. Weigh the damage or inconvenience it can cause with the value of having it there, and think about ways you can alleviate the problem with the least impact to the tree.

◆ **Is it making the property difficult to use?** Try to include the tree in your plans. The trunk can be incorporated into a deck or patio design.

◆ **Can tree removal positively impact the space?** If healthier and more desirable species will be planted in place of the one that was removed, it can be good for the environment.

◆ **Is it economically feasible?** Get a price for removal from a tree company and you might decide that the tree has earned the right to stay.

◆ **Is it legal?** Some communities have codes, codicils, laws, or other controls on what trees are permitted to be cut. You might be required to get a permit to cut on your property. Always check with your local jurisdiction before cutting down any trees.

◆ **Are you emotionally attached?** A tree planted to mark a special occasion may have an emotional value that overrides its ornamental value.

When it is time to cut a tree, have it taken down by a company that is insured and can supply you with references from satisfied clients. When the tree is cut, plant the stump with vines, and a multitude of birds will thank you. You can also have the trunk carved into a sculpture or a garden bench.

You Want a Shrubbery?

What's the difference between trees and shrubs? Generally, shrubs grow full to the ground with multiple stems, while tree branches elevate to show a single trunk.

Shrubs, like these roses, grow full to the ground with multiple stems.

However, it's not quite that simple. Woody plants can be low to the ground and still be considered trees, such as sargents crabapples, or they can be tall and be called shrubs, like common witchhazels. Many plant species are comprised of both trees and shrubs. For example, the majority of maples are trees, yet amur or hedge maples are generally used as shrubs. Bloodtwig and redosier dogwoods are grown as shrubs, and common and kousa dogwoods are trees. What you use depends on your design intent and how they are pruned. Crapemyrtles or butterfly bushes, for example, could be perennials, shrubs, or trees, depending on whether they are cut down annually, sheared, or have their lower limbs elevated to expose mature trunks.

Shrubs are woody plants; that is, ones whose branches or stems usually live all winter and form bark. Evergreen or deciduous, they grow new leaves and stems in spring directly from their branches, as opposed to leafing out from the roots like herbaceous perennials. They are generally used as low screening (such as to hide the exposed foundation of a house) or for ornamental purposes (such as a focal point at the corner of a property).

But shrubs are far more than short trees. They come in almost endless varieties and have an enormous range of attributes. It's worthwhile to search for specific plants for your specific needs.

One client of mine wanted shrubs across the front of his property—a distance of more than a hundred feet from one corner to the other. He wanted the plants to be deer-resistant, perform in wet sites, and tolerate heat and humidity. In addition, he didn't want the plants to spread too rapidly (as do photinias, evergreen members of the rose family), or invade other areas of the garden from seed (as does the hibiscus-related rose-of-Sharon). He also didn't want them to clash with the house when in bloom (as would magenta azaleas against red brick). Amazingly, we found plants that answered all these needs.

Here are some of our choices:

◆ Cherrylaurels were our first pick, especially a hybrid called Otto Luyken. They mass together fairly dependably, have plush-looking foliage and fragrant white spring flowers, and will soften the foundation of a home year-round.

Cherrylaurels mass together fairly dependably and have plush-looking foliage and fragrant white spring flowers.

◆ Southern bayberry, an evergreen native shrub, especially one called Hiwassee. Its waxy berries, which are used in the production of bayberry candles, remain ornamental through winter. When new growth develops in spring, it emits a "bayberry candle" odor.

◆ Inkberry holly, another versatile native, is a fully hardy evergreen that's more graceful looking than most hollies. It has small leaves, prefers moist sites, and can be grown with little pruning. Plant it in masses or group several with other broadleaf evergreens.

Inkberry holly is a tough evergreen that's more graceful looking than most hollies.

◆ 'Dragon Lady' hollies are the perfect vertical elements. They offer shiny, deep green foliage, a handsome spiked leaf, and pyramidal form, with big red berries in winter. They grow 10 to 15 feet in height and only spread 6 to 7 feet. They're a focal point year-round.

Before we could plant anything, however, we had to improve drainage by adding compost to the entire planting area. This prevented any chance of having individual planting holes that wouldn't drain. We laid compost 2 to 3 inches thick over the surface and tilled it deeply into the soil. Because plants were being installed against a house, we also made sure that the surface was graded so that it directed water away from the structure.

Hedging Your Landscape Bets

Other than fences, hedges are the most common solution for creating privacy in residential landscape design. Hedges are shrubs planted in a row so that they'll grow together and form a dense barrier to act as a screening element. And evergreen shrubs offer year-round enclosure.

Shrubs sheared into tightly clipped geometric shapes become an architectural element. But why install plants to create an architectural barrier? With patience, if you site evergreens properly, they'll be ornamental, low maintenance, and offer year-round screening without looking like a wall or fence.

Evergreen boxwoods offer a soft, billowing look that provides screening without the edges of a wall or fence.

After finding an evergreen that you like, ascertain at the garden center its mature size and growth habit. Even hedge plants must be installed far enough apart to get fairly mature before growing together. Plant them so a screen will form in four to seven years. Then they'll develop into an aesthetically pleasing form that will be effective and easy to maintain. Don't try to achieve complete enclosure in one growing season.

Calling All Conifers

Many evergreen, needle-bearing trees are conifers. Common ones are firs, pines, and spruces. They usually grow tall with a pyramidal, Christmas-tree-shape branched full to the ground. They must be planted in full sun, in order to mature to maximum fullness and size. I'll often design spruces and firs in groupings to screen the winter wind and enhance privacy.

A group of newly planted Norway spruce, background right, will grow up to screen a tennis court.

One exception to the pyramidal habit of most conifers is Japanese black pine, which has a handsome sweeping, windblown look. Design these windswept specimens for use in a Japanese-style garden or en masse as a windbreak. They are a dependable conifer for your garden and are known to be tolerant of salt air, so they'll also perform well planted near the ocean.

A less formal way to screen without need for a hedge is to place large evergreens in groupings, massing three to five of the same species together. Or stagger them in a random pattern, such as three or four broadleaf evergreens or conifers strategically placed to screen the items necessary and yet appear to be located in a hit-or-miss fashion. I call it a "planned randomness" method of planting. Evergreens can create a parklike setting when planted in this fashion, especially conifers.

Broader Interests

I generally find broadleaf evergreen trees and shrubs more interesting than conifers because they have flowers and berries or other showy fruits. Some of these shrubs make excellent hedges.

Shrubs that will mass together as dependable broadleaf evergreen hedges are hollies, common boxwoods, and cherrylaurels. Osmanthus will also create a formidable barrier visually and for security, as well as offering flowers and fragrance. But you must give each plant room to develop.

This fortune's osmanthus hedge creates a formidable barrier visually and for security, as well as offering fragrance and flower.

Several broadleaf evergreens get large enough to qualify more as trees than hedging plants. These can be installed in random strategic locations. English, American, and Foster's hollies are valuable broadleaf evergreen trees with deep green foliage, berries, and a handsome pyramidal form. Install them in groupings or individually as large screens.

These 'Dragon Lady' hollies, planted to form a hedge, have sharp spikes that make a formidable barrier.

One of these plants can make a great accent for a planting bed and double as a screen. Several of them will grow into a handsome grouping. Proper spacing is crucial to the health of the plants. They're living, growing entities. Plant larger evergreen trees at least 10 to 15 feet apart, farther for southern magnolias.

The Least You Need to Know

◆ If you choose your trees carefully, you will give instant shape and character to your landscape.

◆ Think of the future when planting by careful site preparation and where the branches will be growing in 10 to 15 years.

◆ Shrubs are generally used as low screening (such as to hide the exposed foundation of a house) or for ornamental purposes (such as a focal point at the corner of a property).

◆ Security can be greatly enhanced using barrier plantings, especially using shrubs that have thorns and thick growth.

◆ Hedges are shrubs planted in a row so that they'll grow together and form a dense barrier to act as a screening element.

In This Chapter

- ◆ Lights, color, texture, action!
- ◆ All along the borders
- ◆ Bright bulbs going on
- ◆ Gorgeous grasses
- ◆ Herbs for happiness

In this lushly planted garden, lavender, on the left, softens the look
of a stone wall. Purple dome asters, center left, echo the color of
the lavender, while hardy begonias, along the house at right, offer the
contrast of pink flowers and broad foliage.

Chapter 21

Bright Spots

When you've established the larger outlines of your landscape with paths, walls, fences, sheds and ornamental structures, fountains, sculpture, lawns, and major trees and shrubs, it is time for what most people consider the real "garden" part of gardening: planting flowers. Flowers are the icing on the cake, the lace on the collar, the highlights in the painting. They have practical purposes, defining shapes and contributing texture and contrast to the garden. They also have purely fun aspects, offering color, change, and whimsy. Today perhaps more than ever, there is an enormous array of plant materials to choose from. And thanks partly to the popularity of native plants and the informality of the New American Garden style, the types of plants within that array are more varied. It is time to get out your paintbrush and touch your landscape with color.

The ABPs

Flowering herbaceous plants are roughly grouped according to their longevity. They are …

- ◆ **Annuals.** Plants that last only one growing season and then die.
- ◆ **Biennials.** Plants that display foliage the first year, flower profusely the second, then go to seed and die at the end of their second season.
- ◆ **Perennials.** Plants that die back after each season, but then return the next year.

Begonias, in front, and salvia, in center
of bed, are annuals.

Hostas, right foreground, phlox, center, and grasses,
center background, are perennials.

Some examples of annuals are most of the colorful plants you see in trays at garden centers, such as petunias and impatiens. Biennials include foxgloves, hollyhocks, and pansies. Perennials are those lovely English-border type plants, such as peonies, black-eyed Susans, purple coneflowers, hostas, lilies, columbines, poppies, and primroses.

The plant world is not so simple, of course. Plants are also grouped according to their method of generation: seeds, bulbs, rhizomes, or roots. Climate also plays a role. Some plants that are perennials in temperate climate are only annuals under harsher conditions. Pansies, for instance, may winter over in milder climates. Some varieties of a particular plant are perennials, such as the salvias 'May Night' or 'Blue Hills,' and other varieties of the same plant are annuals,

such as the salvia blue Victoria. (Some of the most common garden flowers, such as roses, azaleas, and lilacs, have woody stems and are considered shrubs.) In addition, there are herbs, ferns, and grasses, some of which are perennials and some of which are annuals.

Every plant has its benefits and its disadvantages. When you are considering what flowers to plant, think like a landscape designer and ask yourself what you want the plants to do for you. Do you want riotous color, instant gratification, maximum flexibility? Plant annuals or biennials. If you want low maintenance, reliable reappearance year after year, and care as much about texture as color, perennials are for you. Of course, you can always mix the types. And if you plan carefully, you can arrange it so there is always something colorful and interesting going on in your garden, even in winter.

Whatever you decide to plant, methods of installation are similar. Prepare the site with ample compost. Dig a hole slightly larger than the roots. Make sure there's good soil contact. Tamp the plant in to make sure it's stable. The main difference between annuals and other herbaceous counterparts is that annuals need regular watering throughout the growing season.

Life on the Border

One of the most common, and most striking, uses of flowers is in borders. Borders are wide planting beds that surround or outline a property or structure. Planted borders enclose lawns, woods, patios, swimming pools, gazebos, and many other features in the landscape. Think of the landscaped border as a picture frame. And the flowering type of frame is the most frequently used today. The line of the frame doesn't have to be straight. Although I've seen some very ornate straight-lined borders, my preference is for sweeping bed lines. Because plants do not naturally grow square, a curve often fits their growth habits better.

The showiest landscaped borders are created using a combination of plants, mixing and matching them to get just the right blend. Borders shouldn't be made too narrow. They should be at least 7 to 15 feet wide so they'll accommodate a mix of plants. And since you're planting a variety of flora together in the same beds, you can coordinate the plants' ornamental characteristics to achieve year-round interest. In general, borders contain tall plants, including shrubs, at the back, and shorter plants at the front. This is called sequencing.

Evergreens form a backdrop for a perennial bed.

Trees, Too

Include trees, at least one here or there, like Stewartia for summer flower, fall color, and interesting lacy bark; white fringetree to serve up spring fragrance; and Japanese maple, an aristocrat of small trees, for its clean, open growth habit and fine-textured leaves. Trees are necessary for enhancing the overhead plane of your landscaped border.

(Sandra Leavitt Lerner)

Purple blossoms, right foreground, mounded yellow flowers, center, spiky liatris, and frilly foliage on pink cosmos are some of the plants in a wide flowering border. Deciduous and evergreen shrubs form the background.

Background shrubs could be lilacs that produce fragrant flowers in early spring ahead of most perennials. Another deciduous background shrub for the flowering border is winged euonymus. Its foliage turns a brilliant red in autumn at a time when many perennials have lost their luster. This euonymus, called burning bush, also looks good with ornamental grasses. A few of them will make wonderful additions to the planted border. Two that I like are Maiden Japanese silver grass and 'Karl Forster's' feather reed grass. Both grow about 4 to 6 feet tall and shouldn't need staking if grown in full sun.

To extend the season, add 'Arnold Promise' witchhazel for outstanding fall colors and yellow flowers in winter. Two or three plants of each variety are always better than one. One good companion shrub for witchhazels is viburnum. Hybrids of linden viburnum, such as 'Erie' or 'Iroquois,' are covered with white flowers in spring and red berries in summer. In the fall, the viburnum leaves turn burgundy and will superbly compliment the yellow-orange autumn foliage of the witchhazels.

Stewartia offers summer flower, fall color, and interesting lacy bark, in the border or as a specimen.

Witchhazel exhibits outstanding fall colors and yellow flowers in winter.

Perennial Favorites

The most common plants requested for flowering borders are perennials. They provide most of the show from June to September. Low ones can be planted to the front and they can be installed to get progressively taller as they grow to the center and back of the border.

Along a sweeping bedline, if you are sequencing plants by height, try low perennials such as candytufts and Japanese painted ferns. Or try sweet Williams, carnations, and other dianthus to the front. In the center, plant medium-height perennials such as peonies, lilies, astilbes, bleeding hearts, and 'Autumn Joy' sedums. To the rear, among the taller shrubs, place perennials such as liatris, ironweed, asters, boltonia, or snakeroot.

You can keep your border informal, but in a studied way, by placing each plant in groupings rather than broadcasting them in a shotgun method. But keep the arrangement informal and natural so they look like they sprouted where nature sowed them.

Groupings of perennials in a bed at the U.S. National Arboretum in Washington, D.C., have an informal, natural look that butterflies love.

Many perennials can be grown in the flowering border for their interesting foliage, such as hostas with showy variegated leaves and artemisias for their soft, flowing, fragrant silver foliage. 'Autumn Joy' sedums also display attractive foliage throughout the season and have red flowers in fall.

Autumn-flowering sedums also display attractive foliage throughout the season and have red flowers in fall.

The feathery spikes of Russian sage add an informal touch to a border.

Bulbs can also add to the border. Since most bulbs will not hold their foliage throughout the season, grow them with perennials to mask the yellowing foliage. Some interesting combinations are astilbes coming up as daffodils are fading, hostas growing to replace the leaves of tulips, or lilies as a filler for roses.

Planting Informality

For an informal-looking border, use plants with a more open growth habit. Some examples are Japanese anemones, Russian sages, purple coneflowers, and yarrows. A very informal arrangement can be achieved by planting one species of perennial and letting it naturalize in a free-spreading fashion. Black-eyed Susans colonize very well that way. Astilbes in a shadier location give the same shrubby, massing effect. I've seen columbines seed themselves into colonies in cool, protected sites.

As plantings grow together, you will find that your quest for the consummate landscaped border is an ongoing process. Be patient. The creation of a flowering border is an art, not a science. It takes time. As a rule of thumb, I advise that it takes three to five years for perennials simply to mature. And it takes at least a decade for your garden to become a work of art. By then, you'll have developed other ideas and will want to fine-tune them further. Be willing to take something out, or move it to another place in your garden.

Bully for Bulbs

Spring-flowering bulbs can be planted until Thanksgiving or later, even into January in warmer zones.

I use the term "bulb" generically, as many horticulturists do, to refer to a variety of plants with specialized roots for storing food. But all thick or fleshy rooted plants aren't true bulbs. They could actually be corms, rhizomes, tubers, or bulbs depending on their exact physiology. True bulbs consist of a leaf or flower bud encased in food-storage layers called scales.

You can plant bulbs in forests, fields, flower beds, and containers, as long as they'll get six hours of sun every day. Keep containers in a garage until mid-March. Trees overhead won't rob sunlight from early bulbs if they have died down, or *seasoned*, before the onset of heavy shade.

Roots and Stems

When a bulb **seasons**, it stores enough food for the next year, and the leaves turn brown or yellow and begin to fade away.

(Sandra Leavitt Lerner)

A drift of white daffodils enlivens
a hillside garden bed.

Signs of Spring

The earliest spring-flowering bulbs emerge
through the snow, such as snowdrops and
glory-of-the-snow. Some can be planted in your
lawn and will season in time to be cut down
with the first mowing in spring, to return the
same time next year. These include crocuses
and early daffodils, such as the February-
blooming 'Rijnveld's Early Sensation.'

If you're planting into a lawn, drop a handful of compost into each hole. The plants will
appreciate it, even though only tulips don't
produce enough food on their own and truly
need supplemental feeding. Bulbs like a balanced fertilizer, such as 9-9-6 Bulb Booster or
equivalent material spread at a rate of 2 pounds
per 100 square feet. It can be incorporated
when tilling the soil.

Or you can fertilize the bulb beds naturally
by coating the soil surface with bone meal, cottonseed meal, and hardwood ashes. Spread
each one at a rate of 5 to 10 pounds per 100
square feet; then dig it in with your organic
material. You can find bone meal and cottonseed meal at your local garden center. Take
wood ash from your fireplace.

Bulbs are most effective in the landscape
when they're used in drifts or waves of the
same color. Always buy multiples of 8 to 10 or
more of each variety. A hundred is usually ten
times better, if you have the room! If you like
to mix colors that all bloom at the same time,
sprinkle them evenly for the best effect.

(Sandra Leavitt Lerner)

Bulbs are more effective when planted in groups,
like these successive drifts of red and yellow tulips
at Hershey Gardens in Hershey, Pennsylvania.

Planting bulbs, whether a few or a lot, can be
a labor-intensive task. There are a variety of
tools on the market that might make things
easier. There are specialized bulb-planting hand
tools that push straight down into the soil and
remove a plug at the proper depth. Or there are
various size augers that fit on a $\frac{1}{2}$-inch electric
drill. (Hold the drill firmly, but don't lean on it;
you're not drilling iron.) In case the auger hooks
into a root, it'll help if the drill has a reverse.

A bulb-planting tool makes putting bulbs in the
ground much easier.

Using a bulb-planting tool will help if you are planting a lot of bulbs.

Plant bulbs approximately three times as deep as the height of the bulb.

Toss a handful of compost on top of the bulb before filling each hole with soil.

Bestowing Bulbs

Use bulb size as a depth gauge, and plant them approximately three times as deep as the height of the bulb. For example, if a tulip bulb is 2 inches high, plant it 6 inches deep. For corms and true bulbs, place the pointed side up and the flatter side down. Water when planting. Don't overwater. Bulbs don't like wet feet.

Planting Ideas

Here are some common spring-flowering bulbs:

◆ **Crocuses.** These small, early blooming corms can be planted in mixed colors. I prefer grouping the same varieties together, and like to use a hybrid that has a multi-colored flower, such as 'Blue Pearl' with soft blue flowers and a bronzy-yellow base. Crocuses come in hues of purple, blue, yellow, or white. They'll naturalize to come back for many years.

◆ **Snowdrops.** These white-flowering bulbs will be the easiest to grow and fastest to naturalize and fill an area, even in your woodland garden. I consider them the harbingers of spring because of their early bloom.

◆ **Glory-of-the-snows.** The brilliant blue flowers that appear around the same time as snowdrops have 6 to 10 flowers on each plant. For best results, site these true bulbs in full eastern sun with afternoon shade. They're also a good lawn bulb.

◆ **Crown Imperial.** The yellow, orange, white, or checkered colored flowers from May into June are most unusual. The bulb is planted on its side at a depth of three times its width. Their roots are repugnant enough to be a repellent to moles, voles, rabbits, and other critters. Flowering stems can be up to 3 feet tall. Try an American native, 'Vancouver Island,' with burgundy-brown drooping bell-shape flowers on 10- to 12-inch stems.

Grass Roots

Ornamental grasses are closely related to the kinds of grasses we mow, but have striking shapes, and some have beautiful, plumelike flower clusters. Ornamental grasses fit well planted next to perennials such as daylilies, black-eyed Susans, bleeding hearts, Shasta daisies, hostas, and astilbes, to give just a very few examples.

Most ornamental grasses are also perennials and used in design as much for the architectural effect of their foliage as for their flowers. Such flowers are referred to as "inflorescence," which is actually the arrangement of their flowering parts on the stems. Some have an outstanding inflorescence, such as Japanese silver grass (available from 4 to 12 feet tall), and 'Karl Forster's' feather reed grass (4 to 5 feet tall), and fountain grass (2 to 3 feet tall).

Fountain grass has pale, fuzzy flowers, called inflorescence, at the end of drooping stems.

I prefer to use sweeps of color. The foliage can be red like purpurascens Japanese silver feather grass or Japanese bloodgrass, a low, slow-spreading species. Or it can be yellow as you'll find with golden hakone grass. A white variegation occurs on ribbon grass and various sedges. Golden speckles and other patterns are possible on the leaves of zebra or stricta Japanese silver grasses, which grow 6 to 8 feet tall.

Some ornamental grasses are shade-tolerant, but most need full sun. Sedges and hakone grasses are shade-tolerant and showy, but range only from 1 to 2 feet in height.

Golden yellow hakone grasses are shade-tolerant and showy, ranging from 1 to 2 feet in height.

Grasses in Their Places

All of these relatives of the lawn have a somewhat specialized place in the garden. Don't use them as shrubbery, because they don't have the same architecture as a woody plant. They lose structure as the leaves die and fall apart. By late winter, usually what you see is dead grass. Cut them down when the winter wind starts to knock them apart.

Some bigger, heavier varieties, such as most species of Japanese silver grasses, may be knocked down before the winter winds begin and need to be tied together and staked to retain ornamental value. One grass that is very self-supportive is maiden grass, also called

'Gracillimus' Japanese silver grass. It doesn't flower dependably but is worth growing for its 5- to 6-foot-tall upright growth habit that it will hold late into winter.

Maiden grass has an extremely graceful and self-supportive shape.

I recommend to my clients that they use ornamental grasses in conjunction with flowering shrubs and other perennials. They make an excellent accent or focal point within a mixed-perennial, deciduous-shrub border.

Grasses' striking texture makes them ideal in combination with flowering shrubs and other perennials.

Grasses thrive in organic, well-drained soil and don't need regular fertilizing. The only maintenance is annual renewal when their leaves are dead. Then you cut them to the ground and grind them for your compost. You may use electric shears or a hand hedge-trimmer to cut them back. Not surprisingly, some can be tough. If you can, mow with a lawn mower on its maximum height setting or try a scythe or a machete. Do your cutting before they start their annual growth.

Poison Ivy!

Be wary of plants with extremely vigorous growth habits, like bamboo, a woody grass, or those that produce prolific seed, because they can take over a garden in short order and overrun your other plantings. And they'll also become your neighbor's plants within a year or two. If you want them for their ornamental qualities, plant them in containers. Or plant a clump-forming bamboo, such as *Fargesia nitida*, a noninvasive species.

Hello, Herb

The term "herb" literally means any plant with foliage that dies back to the ground every year. That means perennials, annuals, and bulbs are, technically, all herbs. However, through common use, herbs have come to be defined as plants that alter the flavor of food, display medicinal qualities, possess toxic substances, or exude fragrance. Contrary to their definition, they can be of a woody nature, such as rosemary, germander, bay leaves, or lavender, and might not die to the ground annually.

Along with their value as tinctures, salves, sachets, and seasonings, many of these plants have ornamental value in the landscape. So, why not get a two-for-one deal and design with herbs, be they culinary, medicinal, or fragrant?

There are several that are excellent in the rose garden, especially when used with hybrid tea roses, which are valued mainly for their repeat blooms. Hybrid tea roses offer little in the way of foliar interest. Therefore, the blue-green, sweet-smelling foliage of lavender or the silvery, fragrant leaves of artemesia or santolina are perfect with the reds, yellows, pinks, mauves, or other floral colors that'll appear on the roses throughout the growing season. The flowers of these herbs are also small and subtle enough that they don't compete with roses.

Herbs, like these in the culinary garden at the U.S. National Arboretum, Washington, D.C., have ornamental value as well.

Two desirable lavenders to plant are Hidcote or the more compact-growing baby blue. Their showy, fragrant, blue-green foliage, deep blue flowers, and compact habits make them good for both massing and edging. Plant about 18 inches apart. They'll hold foliage into winter. This is a drought-tolerant woody sub-shrub that grows about 18 inches tall and wide. Once you experience the relaxing effect their tiny leaves and flowers can have when bruised in your fingertips, lavender will be impossible to

walk past without taking a pinch. The flowers can be cut and dried for sachets. In conjunction with its calming effect, it has been used in pillows to get rid of headaches.

Artemesias are medieval herbs and a wonderful addition to most gardens. The ornate types aren't used medicinally any longer and the only culinary one, French tarragon, isn't ornate, but is a good flavoring for chicken, vinegar, or herb butter. Other artemesias are grown for their fragrant silvery foliage but shouldn't be eaten. Install 'powis castle' artemesia, which grows about 2 to 4 feet in height, or 'silver brocade,' which grows 6 to 8 inches tall and forms a low mat.

Artemesias such as 'Powis castle' are planted for their fragrant, silver foliage, though they're not edible.

The silvery foliage and stems of the medieval medicinal herb gray santolina have a strong lavender fragrance and a soft fine-textured appearance. It's a low shrub that grows 18 inches high and wide and can be sheared into a low edging plant or allowed to sprawl over the bed and spill onto the paving. It certainly smells good if someone brushes or bruises it when walking past.

A couple of prostrate herbs for planting in the joints of your patio, so you can bruise the foliage and get the fragrance from the plantings, are: low, mat-forming Corsican mints, and woolly thyme, a low spreading thyme that's happy in the stone dust joints of your path, even in as little as five or six hours of sunlight. I also like to plant them into pockets of soil in unmortared rock retaining walls.

A perennial herb for edging your flower borders is tricolor sage, with soft leaves of mixed green, white, and pink foliage. For one color to unify the garden, plant purple or golden sage. All are excellent culinary herbs, and it doesn't take many leaves for flavor. Or try the annual purple basil for an ornamental eye-catcher. Green basil has more flavor but is less showy. Plant enough of it in the sunny, well-drained areas of your garden to clip its foliage for pesto.

Green basil is loved for its spicy, peppery flavor.

Some plants that have been used for their landscape design value for years are also known to have medicinal properties. *Echinacea* or purple coneflower is used for preventing the common cold and will lift your spirits another way when you see it flowering in summer in your perennial border.

> **Green Thumb Guides**
>
> The following are herbal recommendations:
>
> Foster, Steven. *101 Medicinal Herbs.* Interweave Press, 1998. Showing many ornamental plants suitable for perennial herb borders, it would round out any ornamental herb library. This book also has excellent color photography.
>
> Keville, Kathi. *Herbs: An Illustrated Encyclopedia.* Friedman/Fairfax, 1999. Loaded with suggestions of ornamental and edible plants, it's a most thorough compilation of information about herbs that are also candidates for landscape design.
>
> Rosenfeld, Richard. *American Horticultural Society Herb Gardens.* DK Publishing, 1999. This handbook approaches herbs from the perspective of landscape design and has excellent visuals.

The Least You Need to Know

- Flowers are the highlights in the painting of landscape design, offering practical purposes (such as defining shapes and contributing texture and contrast to the garden), and purely fun aspects (such as color, change, and whimsy).

- One of the most common, and most striking, uses of flowers is in borders, wide planting beds that surround or outline a property or structure.

- You can plant bulbs in forests, fields, flower beds, and containers, as long as they'll get six hours of sun every day.

- Most ornamental grasses are also perennials and are used in design as much for the architectural effect of their foliage as for their flowers.

- Along with their value as tinctures, salves, sachets, and seasonings, many herbs—such as lavender, woolly thyme, basil, and sage—have ornamental value in the landscape.

In This Chapter

- ◆ Snow or no (December, January, February)
- ◆ Spring ahead (March, April, May)
- ◆ Bloomin' season (June, July, August)
- ◆ Cleanup time (September, October, November)

Maintaining your landscape in tip-top shape involves some work, but you will be amply rewarded in beauty and usefulness.

Chapter **22**

Training and Maintaining

I said early on in this book that there's no such thing as a no-maintenance garden. Everything needs maintenance: our bodies, houses, automobiles, appliances, and computers. The landscape is no different. But I hope you now see how many wonderful functions your landscape can perform for you, from providing privacy and comfort to offering relaxation and recreation; you'll want to keep it in tip-top form all year-round. It's hard but rewarding work. And every task you finish will give you a sense of satisfaction and make your garden enjoyment all the more complete.

'Tis Always the Season

Landscape maintenance tasks tend to be heaviest in spring and early summer, when you are preparing the gardens for the growing season, and in the fall, when you are preparing them for winter. Early spring, early summer, and late fall are the big months for garden work. (The exact month varies by what part of the country you are in, being earlier in the south and later in the north.) Early in the year, maintenance includes clipping, cutting, digging, edging, elevating, grading, hauling, manicuring, mowing, planting, pruning, raking, skimming, spraying, spreading, and transplanting. In fall, it's cutting back, pruning, mulching, lifting, composting, protecting, raking, and cleaning up. The rest of the year, jobs are simpler, with weeding, watering, and mowing leading the list.

Always think design when doing any activity in the garden. Design is the aesthetically pleasing part of landscaping, and it's what gets you into the garden in the first place. But timing is everything, and there are some basic horticultural practices that you need to perform at certain times of the year to keep your garden growing while you're working on its design.

Snow Jobs (Early Year)

This is the stuff that gets rid of cabin fever. It gets you out in the garden at a time when most people are still inside huddled by the fireplace looking forward to spring.

Selective Shrubbery

At the turn of the year, and very early in the year, even if, in cooler climates, there is snow on the ground, there are some tasks you need to be doing.

If you have overgrown azaleas, rhododendrons, yews, and boxwoods and wish to turn them back into full small shrubs, this is the time to do it. Once you figure out the complete scheme for your garden, you can even transplant them to other locations.

If you have overgrown broadleaf evergreens and want to turn them back into full small shrubs, late in the year is the time to do it.

These evergreens deliver their most vigorous growth in spring. Even if you cut a 6- or 7-foot-tall plant back to 18 inches in height and the stems are an inch or two thick, new leaves will grow back through the bark of the plant. But only if they are cut back hard between January and March 15, *before spring growth begins*.

This is called renewal pruning, and is used only where plants are overgrown and have lost ornamental value. By following these pruning suggestions, you sacrifice the current year's flowers on azaleas and rhododendrons, but most grow back in a season as full, small shrubs.

Plants that don't need hard renewal pruning should be cut after blooming. And then you selectively cut the branches to leave at least two thirds of the plant's foliage.

An Early Snack

January, February, and March are the months you should also fertilize your azaleas, rhododendrons, hollies, and dogwoods. (Keep in mind these tasks come early in this period in warmer climates and later in the period in cooler climes.)

To fertilize, broadcast 1 pound per 100 square feet of an organically based fertilizer for acid-loving plants, and lay a generous amount of compost into the bed over their roots. You can fertilize trees and deciduous shrubs by spreading 1 pound of a 5-10-5 fertilizer over the roots of the plants. A tree or shrub's root zone is roughly in line with the spread of the top growth on the plant. Laying fertilizer over the surface of the soil now affords it the opportunity to work its way into the soil in time for peak spring growth.

You can find the root zone of a tree or shrub by tracing the outermost reach of the leaf canopy. In this case, shade helps locate the leaf spread.

In warmer climates or in mild winters, spring bulbs may be appearing about this time. Fertilize them as they emerge with a general-purpose 5-10-5 fertilizer or a designated bulb food, which is especially good for tulips and will also offer a boost to hyacinths, grape hyacinths, and daffodils.

If you want to fertilize the bulb bed the natural way, top dress around the base of the bulbs with bonemeal, cottonseed meal, and wood ash. You can find bonemeal and cottonseed meal at your local garden center, and wood ash in your fireplace. Because none of these offers a full spectrum of nutrients, it is best to combine all three materials and broadcast this natural mix over the bulb beds.

Really Clean Up

After fertilizing your trees, shrubs, and bulbs, give your compost pile a turn. Throw on a couple shovels of topsoil and sprinkle with water to really speed up the organisms.

Cut back your ornamental grasses that stood all winter and are probably starting to fall apart about now. And if you're itching to start your lawn mower, cut back the lily-turf and mondo-grass. Set the mower height to 3¹/₂ or 4 inches and mow last year's leaves before new growth begins.

If you really want to get a jump on spring, do a cleanup. Take the leaves out of the shrubs, and pull the winter weeds. There are a lot of winter-germinating weeds, with such charming old-fashioned names as chickweed, speedwell, henbit, peppergrass, shepherd's purse, and yellow rocket. Regardless of their names, pull them now, before they become thousands of weeds. And don't put this year's debris into last year's compost pile. Start another one to be ready next year.

Over the winter, throw a couple shovels of topsoil in your compost and sprinkle with water to really speed up the organisms. Give the whole pile a turn.

Ampelopsis is an invasive vining weed that needs to be pulled out of trees and dug from the ground before the spring growing season.

If you didn't seed the lawn last fall, don't wait until spring. On a beautiful dry day, clean up the lawn with a wire rake. Rake over the entire area, exposing soil where no grass is growing.

Then overseed in February or March with a blend of dwarf tall fescue at 3 pounds per 1,000 square feet. There are hundreds of blends available, to fit every situation of sun or shade.

You can plant grass seed late in the year. Rake the entire lawn to expose soil where no grass is growing.

This is also the last opportunity of the season to do a clean-out pruning of your deciduous trees (including deciduous conifers such as dawn redwood and baldcypress) while you can still see branch structure. Prune inside crossing branches, dead wood, and lower limbs.

When you're pruning lower limbs, they may be too thick to use clippers or hand pruners. Use a pruning saw, and begin by making two or three cuts through the bark underneath.

After cutting the bark underneath, cut the limb off from the top. Leave the branch collar, or flare, where the limb joined the tree.

Don't top the tree, and don't leave half branches or stubs. Prune to a crossing branch or to the trunk. Leave the one-quarter- to one-half-inch flare that you will see at the base of the branch you cut. Research has shown that the flare, called the branch collar, is where the scar tissue forms that heals the cut.

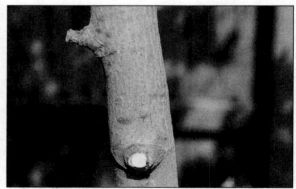

The light circle at the bottom center shows where a branch has been properly pruned to the branch collar. The older pruning, above left, is incorrect.

When pruning a deciduous tree, cut the branch back to the trunk, sparing only the branch collar. Don't leave stubs.

Seeds, for Starters

Start your annual flower and vegetable seeds no later than March. Purchase the most disease-resistant varieties. Resistance is designated by letters listed on the package. The more resistance the better. Most plants will be resistant only to one or two of these diseases because they are only susceptible to those. What to look for on seed packets are A (alternaria), ANTH (anthracnose), ALS (angular leaf spot), DM (downy mildew), F1 or F2 (fusarium wilt), PM (powdery mildew), T or TMV (tobacco mosaic virus), and V (verticillium wilt).

It's also time to take cuttings from the geranium, impatiens, begonia, or other annuals you dug up and brought inside for winter. Cut green shoots that are about 4 to 5 inches long, dip in a rooting hormone, like RooTone, and place in wet perlite, a lightweight aggregate available at your local garden center. Keep the perlite wet while rooting the cuttings. In mid-April, plant rooted cuttings in potting soil. Grow in good light. Grow lights are a good addition to the sun if you don't have a bright room. The first of May, plant the rooted annuals in your garden.

Harbingers (Spring)

Now it's time to get back into the swing of things and start typical spring maintenance. Pruning properly at this time of the year is what will keep your plants trim throughout the growing season.

Fading Flowers

As flowers fade on spring-blooming shrubs, in March, April, and May, it's time to switch from cleanup and weeding mode to pruning. As a general rule, you may prune most shrubs just after they finish flowering. Many have their own special requirements so they can achieve maximum ornamental value.

Several plants that have finished or are almost finished flowering at this time of year are deciduous shrubs such as forsythias, floweringquinces, dwarf fothergillas, Korean-spice viburnums, bridalwreath spireas, and pussy willows. A few broadleaf evergreens whose flowers have faded are Japanese pieris and early azaleas.

Pruning for Pleasing

Forsythias in full sun are vigorous growing shrubs. I recommend cutting them back annually, right after they flower. Prune them down to 12 to 18 inches in height. Don't prune them again this year, and they'll grow long, arching woody stems that will have profuse golden blooms covering them next spring. Exceptions to this pruning rule are if the forsythias are growing in shade or being used for screening. In shade, they'll grow with a more open habit and stay small enough to be manageable without much pruning. For forsythias to have ornamental value as a screening shrub, they should be cut down to about 3 to 4 feet now and not pruned again until after flowering next year.

Floweringquinces have dependable displays of red, scarlet, magenta, or orange flowers every year and small apple-looking fruits that can be used to make a jelly. If sited so they can spread 4 to 5 feet, they'll grow for five years or longer without need for pruning. But if yours has gotten so thick that you see more wood than flower and greenery, cut it back to about 12 to 18 inches tall after the blossoms fade this year.

Poison Ivy! _____

Always wear heavy leather gloves to prune sharp or thorny plants and handle thorny trimmings.

Select Cuts

Dwarf fothergillas seldom need pruning if sited in partial shade and planted at least 5 feet apart. These disease-free members of the witchhazel family offer several seasons of interest, so if it's necessary to prune them back, do it now in order to get the most from their fragrant, fuzzy flowers in early spring and orange-red autumn leaves. Pruning should be done selectively, cutting only the branches that are growing where the plant has become too large of a mass. Cut the widest-spreading and tallest stems so the shrub will fit its space. Prune to a bud or just above a crossing branch.

Pruning guidelines for Koreanspice viburnums are the same as for fothergillas. Shape selectively, pruning the stems that are growing too high or wide. Because the scented blooms are its main ornamental attribute, do the pruning soon to encourage maximum growth and flowering next spring.

Prune woody plants selectively. This aucuba is encroaching onto the space in front of a door.

Trim the out-of-place branch back to a bud or just above a crossing branch.

Selectively pruned shrubs have a neat appearance and stay where they belong.

Old-fashioned bridalwreath spirea will often bloom again if you shear off the blossoms as they fade. Pussy willows can be cut back anytime, and as hard as you want. Because they make a rather weak-wooded tree, they should be maintained as shrubs. In early spring, the soft, furry male flowers, called catkins, offer the main ornamental value of this plant. Prune them back to 3 feet now, so you'll have a good supply of pussy willow stems for your flower arrangements next spring.

Broad(leaf)ly Speaking

You only need to do corrective or touch up pruning to broadleaf evergreens. If ones that have already flowered, like Japanese pieris, the P.J.M. hybrid rhododendrons, and early azaleas, are performing just as you want them to, don't prune them except to cut off branches that are too tall or in the way of other plants. If planted in a well-drained site, rich in compost, Japanese pieris is one of the most vigorous growing of the early spring-blooming evergreens. Where a plant has grown too tall or wide, you can cut it rather hard. Prune it selectively, removing individual branches one at a time, shaping the shrub as you go. Cut the branch just above a point where another one joins it, or prune to a cluster of leaves. Now is the time to do it, because this shrub forms its buds for next year's flowers on the new stems and leaves that develop during this growing season.

The dwarf P.J.M. rhododendron seldom needs any pruning. It is a compact shrub that grows to about 5 feet tall and wide. But if it was installed too close to other plantings, this is the perfect time to prune it to correct an errant stem or balance the shape of the plant. This is all the pruning it should ever need.

Japanese pieris needs a well-drained site, rich in compost. It's one of the most vigorous growing of the early spring-blooming evergreens.

Early blooming azaleas that have finished flowering now can be corrected for form. Cut the branches that are growing where you don't want them. Always prune them selectively just after flowering to ensure the fullest flush of flowers next year.

Berry Good

An exception to the "prune after flowering" rule is when you want the flowers to develop into berries. Viburnums, hollies, and pyracanthas are examples of these. Viburnum berries are sought after by birds, and holly berries are in demand for ornamentation and as food for birds. Pyracanthas develop outstanding, ornamental clusters of red or orange berries in fall. Do light pruning that won't adversely affect the berrying ability of these shrubs, or you can prune hard but sacrifice the fruit for a year.

Pyracantha develops outstanding, ornamental clusters of red or orange berries in fall.

If a hedge has no flowering value, like this dwarf winged euonymus, it can be sheared any time during summer.

Bursts Abloom (Summer)

The expression "this is not an exact science" couldn't relate to any discipline more than landscaping. What you do, and exactly when you do it, depends on geographic location, including your elevation, proximity to water, and many other factors such as whether you are in Maine or Missouri. Your flowers will bloom at different times. The timing we offer is meant to be used as a general guideline.

Touch-Ups

In summer, June, July, and August are the times to do touch-up pruning to plants such as later-blooming azaleas. They and many plants just need light pruning to be kept in shape. When pruning at this season, always leave at least two thirds of a plant's branches.

A long hedge might require shearing; if so, do it no more than once a year, usually after flowering. If a hedge has no flowering value, shear it anytime during the summer. The exceptions are coniferous hedges, pines, spruces, cedars, or firs, for example, which should not be pruned. (It's possible to slow or halt growth of some conifers by trimming new growth, but in general, they should be sited where they can reach mature size without the need for pruning.)

Bulb Behavior

Daffodils will come back for years without any attention. They don't need transplanting, but they're quite forgiving and could be dug and replanted to a new location as soon as the foliage fades. If you wish to dig them, do it before the leaves decay or you may not be able to find them until next spring.

Hybrid tulips are not as adaptable as daffodils. After foliage browns, they must be dug and placed in a dry area with good air circulation for a warming period of three to four weeks. Then clean and divide the small tulip bulbs that have formed. Those over an inch in diameter will probably flower next year. After the warming period, store in a cool, dry place for the next few months and replant in the beginning of November. Tulip bulbs don't supply all of their own nutrients, so plant them with a balanced fertilizer formulated specifically for bulbs at a rate of 1 to 2 pounds per 100 square feet. (Some species of tulips will reliably renew themselves yearly, but their flowers are not as showy.)

Putting the Pinch On

Weed your garden as you cut back the bulbs. You can also pinch off the tops of your hardy chrysanthemums to make them fuller at blooming time. These can be fertilized now and again next month with a granular 5-10-5 nutrient sprinkled around each plant.

Pinch off the tops of hardy chrysanthemums in late spring and early summer for vigorous blooms in fall.

Fertilize container plants through the growing season with water-soluble fertilizer. Mix according to labeled directions and fertilize every other watering. For plantings to thrive outside in containers, they must also have adequate drainage. As in gardens, drainage is the most important consideration for the health of your plants. A hole in the bottom of the container is a must, and use a generous layer of stone, to insure that plants don't stand in water.

To keep even moisture on vegetables and annuals, begin watering now. Once a week isn't too much. If it doesn't rain for a week, you should also water plantings, trees, shrubs, and perennials installed in the past year or two. Soak the base of each plant enough to saturate 6 to 7 inches. Check depth with a screwdriver or wooden dowel. The implement will push easily through wet soil. The point at which you hit resistance is where the moisture ends.

No matter what material your plant containers are made of, it's important that they have at least one drainage hole in the bottom.

Plants Now

This time of year is also a fine time for planting, as long as the plant is already out of the ground in a container or a root ball covered with burlap, and as long as you have a way to irrigate. For the best planting medium, prepare wide areas of existing soil with 2 to 3 inches of compost dug into the top 10 inches of soil. Bring soil up to top of roots, and fashion a saucer shape to catch water at the ball. Remember to water the plantings during hot, dry periods into fall. (For how to plant a tree, see Chapter 20.)

Summer is a good time to plant trees that are already out of the ground, in containers, or in burlap. Plant high, with about 10 to 20 percent of the root ball above the soil line.

Even if you can't dig it in, the best possible treatment for your plants is compost to lighten their soil, make it more fertile, and give better moisture retention, aeration, and drainage. Lay 1 to 2 inches of compost over your beds. Get it from your yard or use leaf compost. If possible, lightly cultivate the compost into the soil. Nature will do the rest. (Call your Cooperative Extension Service to inquire about programs that offer these soil amendments.)

Numerous perennials are making their show now, including achilleas, coreopsis, daylilies, purple coneflowers, carnations, lilies, liatris, evening primroses, verbenas, and many others. So be sure to enjoy the landscape while performing your summer gardening activities.

Green Thumb Guides

Water is essential to all life, and nothing has a greater impact on plants. Its effects can be quite dramatic. The addition of water can create a lawn in a matter of days. The lack of it can keep grass from growing for months and cause plants to shrivel and die overnight. As the temperatures climb into the torrid range, evaporation increases tremendously. Without a soaking rain a couple times a week, supplemental watering is crucial, especially for annuals, vegetables, or newly planted trees and shrubs.

While excessive amounts of water can cause problems such as flooding, erosion, and root-rot diseases, drought or insufficient irrigation has ruined many more home garden plants than too much water.

Consider your irrigation needs early in your design and installation process. This is much more efficient than retrofitting after all the plants are in. If you're not getting an irrigation system, hand watering or a lawn sprinkler, like those found at home and garden centers and hardware stores, works fine.

There are two basic methods of irrigation, drip and spray (applies to both above-ground and underground systems). I recommend the use of drip line in most cases when you need to irrigate. A drip line is plastic hose with small holes or pores that release water at a set rate evenly along the entire line. This waters your plants slowly and thoroughly, with no waste, because it saturates the soil and doesn't evaporate into the air or flow away from the plants. It can be installed in the soil or just under the mulch.

For lawns, use a spray or sprinkler. This method can also be used, but not as efficiently, for trees and shrubs. When you use spray-type irrigation, including sprinklers that attach to your garden hose, give trees and shrubs about an inch of water once or twice a week. Measure this by placing a glass or other measuring device in the area of spray. Run the spray until 1 inch of water is collected in the glass. This will soak the ground you are watering to a depth of 6 to 8 inches, depending on the texture of the soil.

When you use spray-type irrigation, including sprinklers that attach to your garden hose, give trees and shrubs about an inch of water once or twice a week.

To avoid excess evaporation, do not water on windy days or during the hottest time of the day. This is particularly relevant when using spray systems. Water in the morning so plant leaves will dry by evening. This greatly diminishes the risk of fungus problems on your plants. (In drought conditions, local jurisdictions may impose watering rules that contradict these guidelines. It's important for plants to get water, whatever time it is.)

In-ground systems are a pleasure, but require a higher level of maintenance. The main problem occurs because of poor records, so that the lines are accidentally cut by an unknowing new homeowner or landscaper. If you install an underground irrigation system, make a map of it; attach it to the plat of your house, and make sure it is transferred to subsequent owners.

Falling into the Season (Fall)

For many, this is the most pleasant time to get into the garden. Brisk winds are stimulating and autumn colors awe-inspiring. And it's a good thing, because there is still much to do in the landscape.

It's Never Over

And just when you thought the yard work was all over but the leaf raking—along come September, October, and November. These are great months to evaluate your landscape for what worked and what didn't, for what changes you might want to make, and to get the gardens ready to flourish next season.

> ### Green Thumb Guides
>
> Depending on where you live in North America, September in the northern states or mountains, October across the middle of the country, or November in southern climes is the most important month to ensure that your plants stay healthy year-round. Attention to the landscape in October is the stuff that your neighbor's property is made of. The one that you gawk at in spring and say, "why doesn't my place look like that?" It's always because the neighbor thought about the landscape before spring—the October before.
>
>
>
> **Great spring and summer gardens begin the year before, with superior maintenance work in October.**

October is the time to make topsoil. Topsoil is subsoil with organic material (compost) added. It takes nature about 100 years or more to make 1 inch of it. But you can make topsoil in a day, by mixing compost into your lawn and planting beds. Spread compost 2 inches thick over the flowerbeds, and dig it into the top 10 to 12 inches of soil. Then add another 2 inches on top as a protective layer of mulch.

This time of year, mulch is not for aesthetics and weed control as in spring. It's for frost protection and moisture holding. So don't rake the leaves out of the beds, unless they're covering a winter-flowering plant, such as winter jasmine, lenten rose, or vernal witchhazel, or smothering evergreen groundcovers that need light in winter.

Making Mulch of It

There are several sources for compost. You can buy it, pick it up for free (if your locality offers such a service), or make it. If you didn't make a compost pile in the spring, your only option now is to buy it. But you can get a head start on next year by starting your mulch pile now with fall debris. It's free, nutrient-rich, made right on your premises, and good for the environment.

Follow these simple steps:

1. Put organic material into a bin or a pile that is about 3 to 4 feet square and in full sun. Do not add diseased plants or meat scraps.

2. Arrange materials in alternating layers— a 6-inch layer of leaves and twigs, then a 6-inch layer of grass, weeds, and other herbaceous materials. Fill a bucket three-quarters full of soil and sprinkle over the layers of leaves and grass. Continue this process to a maximum height of 4 feet.

3. Keep the pile moist. Turn every 5 to 6 weeks, and it will be ready by May.

Tip: Make your compost bin out of stacked bales of straw, and they will decompose into rich compost in a couple of years.

Give It Air

To enrich the soil under your lawn, aerate it with a plug aerator (you can rent one). Go over the lawn with the aerator three or four times. Then spread compost with a broadcast spreader or shovel. Sprinkle it so that the compost gets down into the aeration holes, but not so much that it covers the blades of grass.

Mow any leaves on the lawn into tiny particles. They help fertilize. If the leaves become too thick to mow, take them to the compost pile or they'll mat together and kill the grass underneath. Also keep heavy accumulations of leaves off the lawn so that you can continue mowing until the lawn stops growing (usually in November or December for cool-season grasses). This also greatly reduces the chance of having snow mold or other winter fungus-related lawn diseases.

Happily Ever After

Many perennials are happiest when they are moved, divided, and planted in the fall, unless they are in bloom. Asters, Boltonias, New York ironweed, 'Autumn joy sedums,' and chrysanthemums are a few of the perennials that can wait until November or even March to be divided. But fall planting of most perennials gives the garden a head start in spring. It's an especially big boost for peonies, irises, and Oriental poppies. Remember the difference compost makes, and, of course, always water when planting.

You can also get a jump on spring if you transplant and plant deciduous shrubs and trees (plants that lose their leaves) in October.

Give the garden a head start by planting hardy perennials in fall.

The Root of Pruning

The best step before digging a tree or shrub is to *root prune* it a year in advance.

Roots and Stems

Root pruning is trimming the roots of a tree or shrub 6 to 12 inches deep around the trunk or stems of the plant and far enough away to cut roots that will easily regrow.

Root prune this fall to transplant trees or shrubs next fall. The tool for this, as well as for transplanting, dividing, and doing many other tasks in the garden, is a square, straight-edged garden or nursery spade.

The way to root prune is to measure out from the trunk or center of a plant 18 to 24 inches, depending on the diameter of the trunk. Following a circle around the trunk, slice down deeply with the spade at a very slight angle toward the root ball. Don't pry the roots, just slice down cleanly and lift the spade straight out of the soil. Follow all the way around the circle that was marked, cutting through all the roots of the plant as deeply as possible.

In the past 30 years, I've moved a lot of woody plants with no root pruning. In the land-scape business, we don't generally have the lux-ury of coming onto the site a year in advance. You can try transplanting without root pruning; we've had few losses. Or root prune now and put it on your calendar to move the plant next fall. (*Note:* The more mature the plant, the less the success rate for transplanting.)

Start digging 18 to 24 inches from the trunk of the tree. The exact size depends on the trunk diameter. Slice down deeply, cutting through roots all the way around the base of the plant.

Before transplanting a tree or shrub, like this dwarf Japanese maple, gather the branches and anchor a rope in some of the sturdiest ones.

Dig down 6 to 8 inches, then begin slicing underneath the roots all the way around the tree, lifting it evenly as you go.

Gently bind the branches of the tree or shrub to be transplanted so it will be easier to dig underneath.

When the tree is dug out, lift it onto a piece of plastic, landscape fabric, or burlap to move it where it will be replanted. Remove fabric for planting.

Making the Move

Relocate shrubs and trees as their foliage drops or stops growing. They should have excellent soil moisture, but it shouldn't be too wet or muddy. Don't dig if the soil sticks together when you try to crumble it in your hand.

To transplant, do the following:

1. Come several inches outside the circle you cut last year when root-pruning.

2. Slice down deeply, cutting through the roots all the way around the base of the plant.

3. Dig away the soil where you are standing, on the outside of the root ball. Dig down about 6 to 8 inches and then slice underneath the roots. Do this all the way around the plant to form a ball.

4. Start lifting the plant from underneath, raising it evenly on all sides with the nursery spade. (*Note:* The size of the ball is determined by plant size. Some can be large, others quite small.)

5. Details are offered in Chapter 20 for moving your tree or shrub to a new location and how to plant it.

If you're lucky, you may get a few weeks to relax between the end of this season's garden activities and next season's. It's time to work on your garden plans, to refine your landscape design, and to study the plant catalogs arriving in the mail for ideas. Some gardeners are dismayed when the arrival of true winter keeps them indoors. The better designed your landscape is, the more enjoyment you get out of being in it and benefiting from it, the more likely you are to join these ranks. Meanwhile, rest assured of this: No matter how anxious you are to get into the garden, your plants are even more anxious to get out of the ground and start growing again.

The Least You Need to Know

◆ Landscape maintenance tasks tend to be heaviest in spring and early summer, when you are preparing the gardens for the growing season, and in the fall, when you are preparing them for winter, but there is always something to do, even with snow on the ground.

◆ As flowers fade on spring-blooming shrubs, in March, April, and May, it's time to switch from cleanup and weeding mode to pruning, once most shrubs have finished flowering.

◆ During the summer months, you'll be busy in the garden trimming, caring for spent bulbs, feeding, and watering, but don't get too caught up to enjoy the summer perennial flower show.

◆ Late in the year is the time to evaluate your landscape for what worked and what didn't, for what changes you might want to make, and to get the gardens ready to flourish next season.

Glossary

amend   To add nutrients, compost, or other materials to improve soil structure.

annuals   Plants that don't grow back after freezing, so must be planted every year, including flowers, herbs, and grasses.

batter   The slope of a wall, stepped in a minimum of 1 inch per foot of height, from bottom to top, as it leans into a bank.

biennials   Plants that grow foliage the first year, then flower, then go to seed the second year and decline or die, with new plants often springing up from the seeds.

canopy   In the landscape, this is the covering usually created by shade trees or overhead structures.

compost   Decaying organic material, such as leaves and other landscape debris, used as fertilizer for plants.

deciduous   Plants that lose their leaves annually in autumn.

elevation   A scale drawing of a section of a structure or landscape as seen from eye level.

espalier   An ornamental tree or shrub that is trained to grow on a flat plane, as fastened against a wall.

evergreen   Plants that hold green foliage year-round. Leaves are renewed on a regular basis, but older foliage falls while new growth stays green.

excavating   Removing soil by digging or scooping out.

fan   Arching out from the base (examples: Chinese witchhazels or zelkova trees).

garden (*verb*)   To cultivate a private plot of land with flowers, vegetables, and fruits.

globose   Round (examples: boxwoods or common horsechestnuts).

grading   Altering the surface of the land, especially its contours.

hardscape   The walks, patios, sheds, arbors, trellises, pools, and other structural elements of the landscape.

herbaceous plant   A seed-producing annual, biennial, or perennial that does not develop persistent woody tissue but dies down at the end of a growing season.

horizon   The apparent intersection of earth and sky, or of skyline and sky.

hydrology   The science that deals with the occurrence, circulation, distribution, and properties of the waters of the earth.

knot   A complex, compact, interlacing pattern of plantings in a garden bed.

landscape (*verb*)   To improve or adorn a plot of land by contouring and planting shrubs or trees.

mulch   A covering of protective material, usually organic, around plants to prevent moisture evaporation and root freezing, and to control weeds.

overhead   A view down on an object or set of objects as from a height.

parterre   A garden in which beds and paths are designed to form a pattern.

percolate   To drain or seep through a porous substance or filter.

perennials   Plants that come up year after year, including trees, shrubs, bulbs, grasses, ferns, and flowers.

perspective   A rendering of objects in depth, as viewed with normal binocular vision.

pH   Comes from (p)otential of (H)ydrogen, measures the acidity or alkalinity of a solution, with neutral being 7 and higher numbers indicating greater alkalinity and lower numbers greater acidity.

pin   Any straight piece of wood or metal driven or passed through drilled or preformed holes to hold stacked objects in place vertically.

pyramidal   Uniformly wider at the bottom than the top, growing to a point displaying a Christmas tree form (examples: blue spruce, Douglasfir).

root pruning   Trimming the roots of a tree or shrub 6 to 12 inches deep around the trunk or stems of the plant and far enough away to cut roots that will easily regrow.

season   For a bulb to store enough food for the next year, at which time the leaves turn brown or yellow and begin to fade away.

sleeper or **deadman**   In a retaining wall, a tie that is staked to the wall and runs perpendicular to it into the bank. The deadman is anchored to a cross piece buried 4 to 5 feet into the bank.

softscape   The trees, shrubs, foliage, and flowers in a landscape.

stake   A wood or metal stick or post, often with one sharpened end, used to hold a concrete form or stacked objects in place, or as a plant support.

tie   A landscape timber, or a pin used to connect objects horizontally.

variegated   Having discrete markings of different colors.

vase   Smaller at the bottom, spreading uniformly outward at the top (examples: winged euonymus or mockoranges that haven't been pruned).

xeriscape (*ZEER-is-cape*)   Landscape design for dry conditions.

Appendix **B**

Tools and Devices

Every job in the landscape is easier if you have the proper tools. In fact, without the right tools, these tasks would be ridiculously difficult to perform. It's important to get good tools. If you buy quality tools and take care of them, they will last a long time, maybe as long as the garden or the gardener! Fortunately, most of the tools needed in the landscape are hand tools, so they are less expensive than power tools.

In fact, probably the only power tool considered essential is a lawn mower, and that's only if you have a lawn. Here are some of the tools I use and recommend.

Mowers

Gasoline (two- and four-cycle), electric (cord or battery), and people-powered mowers are available at lawn and garden equipment dealers or hardware stores. All mowers cut grass, but your choices are mind-boggling. The type of mower should be determined by the size of your property, and your penchant for exercise and bipedal locomotion.

Any brand of gasoline-powered mower will give good service for years. Keep the blade sharp, change the oil, and clean the air filter every 20 to 25 hours of operation. Change the spark plug every 100 hours. Lubricate wheels with #2 multipurpose lithium grease, if they have fittings. Don't mow over rocks or heavy surface roots, and winterize it according to manufacturer recommendations. Two-cycle engines burn a mixture of gas and oil. They don't require oil changes.

Electric mowers get their power from a house outlet or a rechargeable onboard battery. They are low maintenance. All you need to do is keep the blade sharp. In the case of AC-powered units, purchase a long enough extension cord to reach the outermost boundaries of your lawn, and be very, very careful not to run over it.

For those of you who favor the old-fashioned way, new versions of the reel-type push mower do an excellent job if a lawn is mowed regularly. A reel-type mower is fun and easy to use, and you don't have to winterize it. Just keep the blades sharp and shoot a little WD-40 lubricant onto the cutting surface and axle shafts every few weeks.

Reel-type push mower.

Poison Ivy!

In your first days of mowing after winter, be very careful of rocks, cans, wires, and any other debris that might have collected. And always mow in long pants and sturdy shoes.

The more features a mower offers (e.g., grass catcher, self-propelled, ride-on, easy-adjust variable heights, multiple-speed gear box, etc.), the more expensive and, candidly, the more opportunity for problems. I prefer basic mowers with the emphasis on safety (e.g., toe guard, rear deflector, extended discharge chute, lower rpm, automatic shut-off whenever your hands leave the mower, etc.).

Spreaders and Sprayers

The tools for applying lawn and garden nutrients are spreaders and sprayers. The only way to assure accuracy and even distribution of dry fertilizer, weed killer, or insect control is to use a drop spreader (which drops material through holes in the bottom of a hopper) and measure the quantity of material spread. A broadcast spreader throws material 6 to 10 feet in a circular pattern, and should not be used for weed killer or insecticide because of the inaccuracy of the spread. But it's perfect for grass seed, lime, gypsum, fertilizer, fine-textured compost, and even ice-melting salts in winter.

Broadcast spreader.

Sprayer tanks are used to apply liquid nutrients and pesticides. I prefer a two-gallon plastic pump sprayer. It's lightweight to carry, and plastic is noncorrosive. Keep two sprayers, one for total brush killer, the other for lawn weeds, fertilizer, and insecticide. Always clean sprayers and spreaders after every use. If it wasn't done last time you used them, you probably need new ones because most landscape treatment chemicals are extremely corrosive.

Pump sprayer.

Manual hedge shears.

Electric hedge shears.

Pruners

There are all kinds of clipping-type pruning tools, but hand pruners that you can hold in one hand are best. Anvil pruners have a single blade that cuts onto a flat surface set into the jaw of the pruner; by-pass pruners cut like scissors. Long-handled lopping shears, which cut by either an anvil or by-pass method, will cut thicker tree limbs and shrub stems than hand pruners. Some pruners ratchet down onto branches and cut with little effort. These are good for people with limited movement or a weak grip.

The only other pruner you need is a saw. There are folding pruning saws that cut branches up to 3 or 4 inches thick.

If you cut more than an occasional branch that is 3 or 4 inches in diameter, I recommend a bow saw. Get one with a comfortable grip that efficiently cuts from branch- to firewood-sized timber.

An optional pruning tool is a hedge shear. Shrubs on some properties have to be sheared because of the type or spacing of the plants. A good-quality pair of scissors-type hand shears works fine, once you learn the rhythm of using them. If you have a lot of shearing to do, you might be happier with electric hedge shears.

Winter months are the time to do a lot of pruning. Before cool weather arrives, pruning tools probably need sharpening and oiling. Give them a shot of oil on the pivot point; clean them, and sharpen their blades. To sharpen, I prefer a sharpening stone or a fine-textured, flat metal file. Use it to remove burrs and sharpen the bevel. Don't sharpen a pruner razor thin or change the angle of the bevel on the blade, or it'll lose its edge too quickly. And don't remove deep nicks in the blade, just little ones. This will greatly extend the blade life. This is all you need to do to maintain by-pass pruners, which are the ones that cut like scissors and are my preference.

To get wooden handles in shape and reduce the chance for splinters, sand them with a fine sand paper and rub in a mixture of linseed oil and kerosene. Dilute the linseed with enough kerosene to thin it so that it soaks into the wood. All your wooden tool handles will last a lot longer and are a pleasure to use after being oiled. Be sure to do it outdoors or in a well-ventilated tool shed.

Digging Tools

My favorite multipurpose digging tool that needs virtually no maintenance is an all-steel or steel-reinforced, straight-edge garden or nursery spade with a 27-inch handle with a D-shape grip.

Garden spade.

It's extremely useful. Several tasks it has made easier for me are transplanting trees and shrubs, dividing perennials, manicuring a bed edge, skimming sod, and weeding. I prefer one with a heavy steel digging blade, because it's built to withstand slamming through rocks and roots. The tool for digging a hole or turning soil is called a round-point spading shovel. I prefer one with a 48-inch handle.

Round-point spading shovel.

If you must dig holes or a trench, especially through rocks and tree roots, you'll want a mattock, a cutter or pickax type head with a 36-inch handle. It's also an excellent tool for planting bulbs and perennials.

Mattock.

Ready the digging part of your shovel by honing it to remove burrs, nicks, and dullness, using a fine-textured, flat metal file. Leave the shovel edge somewhat blunt or thick at the end so you won't wear the edge down too quickly digging into rocky soil. But it should still be sharp enough to dig through smaller tree roots. Replace broken handles now. Some are worth replacing; others aren't. A good-quality tool is worth the effort of pounding, burning, drilling, or otherwise removing the handle and soaking, slamming, and attaching a new one. An inexpensive one isn't worth the effort.

Raking and Tossing Tools

No tool collection is complete without a leaf rake, and, if you have a compost pile, a pitchfork. You need a leaf rake to clean up yard debris, a shovel to dig in the garden, and a pitchfork to turn the compost pile and spread mulch. Tools to perform these chores should also be of high quality if they are to last the life of your garden. I prefer a spring steel wire rake for leaves as opposed to its polypropylene or bamboo counterparts.

Hard steel rake.

A pitchfork is your most practical tool for turning a compost pile, spreading mulch, or lifting tangles of yard debris. Buy a heavy-duty 5- or 6-tine manure fork with a 54-inch handle.

Leaf rake.

You will also need a hard steel garden rake for raking rocks, leveling bare soil, readying a tilled vegetable garden or lawn area, spreading stone dust or gravel for walkways, and other heavy-duty jobs in the garden.

Pitchfork.

Optional Tools

Other recommended options for the fully outfitted landscape gardener are a coarse-textured push broom, a flat scoop shovel, and a wheelbarrow or lawn cart. These make gardening easier, although I've used a household broom, a dust pan, and plastic tarpaulin almost as effectively.

Flat scoop shovel.

Push broom.

Wheelbarrow.

Plants

The following plants are listed by botanical name, common name, plant hardiness zone, light preference, and notes for use.

The designations of sun, shade, and part shade are only general guidelines that indicate where a plant tends to grow best. Actually, all plants need sun to grow and their preference for shade often stems from the fact that they need a cooler environment. Some plants will grow in full sun if located in cooler climates or soil higher in organic material, but need shade if heat, humidity, and poor soil are the existing conditions. With that said, here are the number of hours of sun often accepted for each designation: full sun = eight hours or more; part shade = five to eight hours; shade = five hours or less.

Shade Trees over 40 Feet

Acer rubrum, Red Maple, 3–9, sun. Excellent fall color.

Acer saccharum 'Endowment,' Columnar Sugar Maple, 3–8, sun. Excellent fall color, not for cities.

Acer platanoides 'Crimson King,' Crimson King Norway Maple, 3–7, sun. Crimson foliage all summer.

Aesculus hippocastanum, Common Horsechestnut, 3–7, sun. Flowers, best for large spaces.

Fraxinus pennsylvanica, Green Ash, 3–9, sun. For tough-to-grow areas, especially Midwest.

Gymnocladus dioicus, Kentucky Coffeetree, 3–8, sun. Interesting large-space tree.

Ginkgo biloba, Ginkgo, 3–8, sun. Good city tree and fall color.

Liquidambar styraciflua, Sweetgum, 6–9, sun. Wide conical shape, maroon fall color.

Liriodendron tulipifera, Tulip Tree, 5–9, sun.
Large tree to 100 feet, tulip-looking flowers.

Quercus coccinea, Scarlet Oak, 4–9, sun.
Dark green in summer, scarlet fall color.

Quercus alba, White Oak, 5–9, sun.
Native to eastern North America.
Spreading habit, peeling bark.

Quercus palustris, Pin Oak, 4–8, sun. Nice
pyramidal habit, residential landscape.

Quercus phellos, Willow Oak, 5–9, sun.
Clean, good lawn tree.

Foliage detail of Red Oak.

Quercus rubra, Red Oak, 4–8, sun.
Fast-growing shade tree.

Tilia cordata, Littleleaf Linden, 3–7, sun.
Can prune into hedge.

Zelkova serrata, Japanese Zelkova, 5–8, sun. Elm substitute, fall color.

Small Flowering Specimen Trees Under 40 Feet

Acer griseum, Paperbark Maple, 5–7, sun. Fall color, attractive peeling bark.

Acer palmatum 'Kamagata,' Dwarf Japanese Maple, 5–8, sun. Dwarf plant, delicate appearance.

Acer palmatum 'Sango-kaku,' Coralbark Japanese Maple, 5–8, sun. Bark turns orange-red in winter.

Acer palmatum 'Seiryu,' Upright Cutleaf Japanese Maple, 5–8, sun. Upright habit with fine cut foliage.

Aralia spinosa, Devil's-Walkingstick, 4–9, sun. Pollution-tolerant, thorny.

Amelanchier arborea, Downy Serviceberry, 4–9, sun. White flowers, fall color.

Betula nigra, River Birch, 4–9, sun. Large birch, borer resistant.

Cercis canadensis, Eastern Redbud, 4–9, part sun. Flowers early, good in natural setting.

Cornus mas, Corneliancherry Dogwood, 4–8, part sun. Early flower, mass together.

Cornus florida, Flowering Dogwood, 6–9, part sun. Patio tree.

Magnolia virginiana, Sweetbay Magnolia, 5–9, part sun. Fragrant flowers, good in wet areas.

Cornus kousa, Kousa Dogwood, 5–8, sun. Good near house.

Malus floribunda, Flowering Crabapple, 3–8, sun. Flowers, many growth habits.

Detail of flowering crabapple fruit.

Lagerstroemia hybrid, Crapemyrtle, 7–9, sun. Specimen for bark, blooms all summer.

Detail of bark of Crapemyrtle.

Parrotia persica, Persian Parrotia, 4–8, sun. Pest-free.

Detail of bark of Persian Parrotia.

Pyrus calleryana 'Bradford,' Bradford Pear, 4–8, sun. Flower, dense habit, shiny leaf.

Prunus subhirtella 'Pendula,' Weeping Higan Cherry, 4–8, sun. Graceful, single pink flowers.

Stewartia pseudocamellia, Japanese Stewartia, 5–8, part sun. Good flower, bark, and fall color.

Styrax japonicus, Japanese Snowbell, 5–8, sun. White bell-shaped flowers, patio or entry tree.

Styrax japonicus 'Carillon,' Weeping Japanese Snowbell, 5–8, sun. Weeping, diminutive size, slow growth habit.

Styrax obassia, Fragrant Snowbell, 5–8, sun. Large, white, fragrant flowers, large 3- to 8-inch leaves.

Evergreen Trees and Conifers over 15 Feet

Cedrus atlantica 'Glauca Pendula,' Weeping Blue Atlas Cedar, 6–9, sun. Blue needles, drooping, curtainlike branches.

Cedrus deodora, Deodar Cedar, 7–8, sun. Graceful branching, can be pruned.

Chamaecyparis nootkatensis, Alaska Falsecypress, 5–8, sun. Conical habit, weeping branches.

Chamaecyparis obtusa 'Cripsii,' Golden Hinoki Falsecypress, 5–8, sun. Whorled, upright habit, gold foliage.

Chamaecyparis obtusa, Hinoki Falsecypress, 5–8, sun. Whorled, upright habit, dark green specimen.

Ilex aquifolium 'Aureo marginata,' Gold Margined English Holly, 6–9, sun. Berries, specimen, gold-margined leaves.

Ilex opaca, American Holly, 5–9, sun or part shade. Winter berries, native, shade-tolerant.

Magnolia grandiflora, Southern Magnolia, 7–9, sun. Large leaf, large fragrant flowers, wide habit.

Ilex x attenuata 'Fosteri,' Foster's Holly, 6–9, sun. Pyramidal habit, heavy fruit in winter.

Metasequoia glyptostroboides, Dawn Redwood, 4–8, sun. Deciduous conifer, fast-growing for large areas.

Picea abies 'Pendula,' Weeping Norway Spruce, 3–7, sun. Upright trunk with graceful weeping habit.

Picea pungens f. glauca, Colorado Blue Spruce, 3–7, sun. Stiff habit, blue needles, handsome form.

Picea glauca 'Conica,' Dwarf Alberta Spruce, 2–6, sun. Hardy specimen, slow growth, 15 feet in 25 years.

Detail of blue spruce needles.

Pinus cembra, Swiss Stone Pine, 3–7, sun. Handsome bluish foliage, full habit, slow growth.

Pinus wallichiana, Himalayan Pine, 5–7, sun. Long graceful needles, habit like white pine.

Pinus nigra, Austrian Pine, 3–7, sun. Specimen for cold, windy locations.

Detail of Himalayan cone and needles.

Quercus virginiana 'Darlingtonii,'
Darlington Live Oak, 7–10, sun. Specimen
tree, hybrid hardier than species.

Taxodium distichum, Common Baldcypress,
4–11, sun. Deciduous conifer, specimen
fall color.

Sciadopitys verticillata, Japanese
Umbrella-pine, 5–7, sun. Fleshy needles,
unusual texture, specimen.

Detail of Baldcypress cone and needles.

Tsuga canadensis, Canadian Hemlock, 3–7, part shade. Graceful, excellent hedge, very shade-tolerant.

Tsuga canadensis 'Sargentii,' Sargent's Canadian Hemlock, 3–7, part shade. Graceful, weeping specimen, shade tolerant.

Evergreen Shrubs 5 Feet to 25 Feet

Abelia x *grandiflora,* Glossy Abelia, 6–9, sun or part shade. Fragrant, flowers all summer, attracts pollinators.

Aucuba japonica, Japanese Aucuba, 7–10, shade. Variegated leaf available, tolerant of dense shade.

Buxus microphylla, Littleleaf Boxwood, 6–9, sun or shade. Hedge, formal garden.

Buxus sempervirens 'Suffruticosa,' English Boxwood, 5–8, sun or shade. Hedge, specimen.

Camellia x 'Frost Princess,' Frost Princess Camellia, 7–9, part shade. Flowers in late fall, specimen, hardy Camellia.

Chamaecyparis obtusa 'Nana Gracillis,' Dwarf Hinoki Falsecypress, 5–8, sun. Smaller than species, whorled growth.

Chamaecyparis pisifera 'Filifera Aurea,' Goldthread Falsecypress, 5–8, sun. Yellow threadlike leaves, full rounded habit.

Elaeagnus pungens, Fragrant Elaeagnus, 6–9, shade. Green with silver under leaves, fragrant fall flowers.

Ilex cornuta 'Rotunda,' Rotunda Chinese Holly, 7–9, sun. Excellent barrier hedge, thorny textured foliage.

Euonymus fortunii 'Emerald n'Gold,' Emerald and Gold Euonymus, 5–9, part shade or shade. Variegated, low-growing.

Ilex crenata 'Sky Pencil,' Sky Pencil Japanese Holly, 5–6, sun. Good narrow vertical habit, 1 foot wide, 8 feet tall.

Euonymus japonica 'Greenspire,' Greenspire Euonymus, 5–9, part shade or shade. Deep green columnar, small leaf.

Ilex crenata 'Helleri,' Helleri Holly, 5–6, sun. Low, slow-growing horizontal branching habit.

Ilex x *meserveae* 'Blue Maid,' Blue Maid Holly, 5–7, sun or part shade. Low-growing hedge holly, good berries.

Ilex x *aquipernyi* 'Dragon Lady,' Dragon Lady Holly, 6–9 sun. Narrow upright habit, deer-resistant, berries.

Juniperus chinensis 'Corcocor Emerald Sentinal,' Corcocor Redcedar, 4–9, sun. Deep green, full, disease-resistant.

Nandina domestica, Heavenly Bamboo, 6–9, sun or shade. Foliage red spring and fall, berry clusters through winter.

Nerium oleander, Oleander, 8–10, sun. Showy flower, pollution-tolerant, all parts poisonous.

Detail of berry and leaf of Nandina.

Osmanthus heterophyllus 'Goshiki,' Goshiki Osmanthus, 7–9, sun or part shade. Hedge or specimen, marble-colored leaf.

Photinia serrulata, Chinese Photinia, 6–9, sun or part shade. New growth red, needs shearing or large area.

Pieris japonica, Japanese Pieris, 5–7, part shade. Beautiful flower, specimen.

Pittosporum tobira, Japanese Pittosporum, 8, sun or shade. Good massing shrub, showy foliage, foundation plant.

Detail of Pittosporum foliage.

Prunus laurocerasus 'Schipkaensis,' Schip Cherrylaurel, 6–8, sun, part shade. Hedge, mass, fragrant flower.

Viburnum rhytidophyllum, Leatherleaf Viburnum, 5–7, part shade. Large leaf, rhododendron companion, screen.

Deciduous Shrubs
3 Feet to 15 Feet

Berberis thunbergii var. *atropurpurea* 'Crimson Pygmy,' Crimson Pygmy Barberry, 4–8, sun. Low growing, reddish leaf, most common.

Buddleia davidii, Butterfly bush, 5–9, sun. Summer flowers, cut flowers, attracts butterflies.

Callicarpa dichotoma, Purple Beautyberry, 5–8, sun or part shade. Attractive fruit in autumn, perennial in North.

Detail Purple Beautyberry.

Calycanthus floridus, Common Sweetshrub, 4–9, sun or shade. Fragrant foliage, open natural habit.

Clethra alnifolia, Summersweet Clethra, 4–9, sun or part shade. Fragrant white summer flowers, shrub border.

Forsythia x *intermedia*, Border Forsythia, 4–8, sun. Early flower, good slope planting.

Euonymus alatus, Winged Euonymus, 4–8, sun or shade. Fall color, grouping or hedge.

Fothergilla gardenii, Dwarf Fothergilla, 5–8, sun or part shade. Disease-free, shrub mass, interesting flowers.

Detail of Euonymus winged bark.

Hamamelis x *intermedia*, Hybrid Witchhazel, 5–8, sun or part shade. Winter flowers, yellows and reds.

Hydrangea quercifolia, Oakleaf Hydrangea, 5–9, sun or shade. Large leaf, fall color, white showy flowers.

Ilex verticillata, Common Winterberry Holly, 3–9, sun or part shade. Berries persist without leaves, mass plantings.

Detail of berries on Winterberry Holly.

Lindera benzoin, Spicebush, 4–9, sun or shade. Fragrant foliage, spring flower, fall color.

Lespedeza bicolor, Shrub bushclover, 4–8, sun. Rosy purple flowers summer, clover-looking leaves.

Pyracantha coccinea, Scarlet Firethorn, 6–9, sun. Outstanding berries, espalier plant.

Detail of Pyracantha berries.

Spiraea x *bumalda,* Bumald Spirea, 3–8, sun. Flowers in summer, has spring and fall foliage color, massing.

Viburnum carlesii, Koreanspice Viburnum, 5–7, sun or part shade. Beautiful fragrance and flower.

Viburnum dilatatum 'Oneida,' Oneida Linden Viburnum, 5–7, sun or part shade. Hedge, flower, fall color, bird-attracting.

Groundcovers

Ajuga reptans, Bugle Weed, 4–9, sun or shade. Deep green or rosy colored leaves, blue flowers.

Armeria maritima, Sea Thrift, 4–8, sun. Showy flower, bed edging, salt-tolerant.

Hypericum calycinum, Aaronsbeard St. John's-wort, 5–8, sun. Semi-evergreen, summer yellow flower.

Ceratostigma plumbaginoides, Plumbago, 5–8, sun or shade. Blue flower, fall color, good with bulbs.

Juniperus horizontalis 'Plumosa,' Andorra Juniper, 4–9, sun. Many forms in green and yellow, upright habit.

Epimedium species, Barrenwort, 4–8, part to full shade. Yellow, red, pink, or white flowers in spring, beautiful foliage.

Liriope muscari, Blue Lily-turf, 6–9, sun or shade. Broad-leaved, arching habit, low maintenance.

Lysimachia nummularia, Creeping Jenny, 3–9, sun or shade. Green or gold foliage, naturalized, from Europe.

Pulmonaria, Lungwort, 3–8, part to full shade. Interesting foliage, pink, blue, or white flowers early spring.

Nepeta species, Catmint, 3–8, sun or part shade. Blue flowers summer, silvery to gray fragrant foliage.

Rosa hybrids, Groundcover Rose, 4–7, sun. Groundcover, repeat bloomer, disease resistant.

Pachysandra terminalis, Japanese Pachysandra, 4–8, shade. Handsome under trees, fragrant flower.

Sarcococca hookeriana var. *humilis,* Sweetbox, 6–8, part to full shade. Fragrant flowers, dense groundcover.

Vinca minor, Common Periwinkle, 3–8, sun or shade. Blue flowers, lush shade carpet.

Clematis paniculata, Sweetautumn Clematis, 3–8, sun. Beautiful long-season flower.

Vines

Actinidia kolomikta, Kolomikta Actinidia, 4–8, sun or part shade. Large leaves, fast grower, produces kiwi fruit.

Dolichos Lablab, Hyacinth Bean, annual, sun. Fast-growing vine, purple or white flowers, purple pods.

Campsis radicans, Common Trumpetcreeper, 4–9, sun. Quick cover, orange trumpet flower.

Hydrangea anomala subsp. *Petiolaris,* Climbing Hydrangea, 4–7, shade. Winter flower, good climber.

Parthenocissus quinqefolia, Virginia Creeper, 3–9, shade. Quick cover, fall cover.

Passiflora x *allardii*, Passionflower, 7–9, sun or part shade. Vigorous woody plant, gorgeous complex flower.

Rosa species, Climbing Rose, 5–8, sun. Train for flowering overhead, many colors.

Schizophragma hydrangeoides, Japanese Hydrangea, vine, 5–8, part shade. Hybrid 'Moonlight' silver.

Perennials

Anemone x *hybrida*, Japanese Anemone, 5–7, part shade. Fall white flower, very popular, tall 'Honorine Jobert.'

Artemisia x 'Powis Castle,' Powis Castle Mugwort, 3–8, sun. Interesting silver foliage, prune spring, not fall.

Aster novae-angliae, Aster, 4–8, sun. Fall-blooming, many flowers, 4 feet tall.

Begonia grandis, Hardy Begonia, 6–9, part to full shade. Pink or white flowers, summer into fall, reseeds.

Chrysanthemum x *superbum*, Shasta Daisy, 3–9, sun. White flowers, fall-blooming, showy flower, cutting.

Cimicifuga racemosa, Snakeroot, 3–7, part to full shade. Tall, 3' to 4' nodding white flower late summer.

Coreopsis verticillata 'Moonbeam,' Threadleaf Coreopsis, 4–9, sun. Dainty yellow flowers summer, fine-textured ferny foliage.

Geranium species, Cranesbill Geranium, 3–8, sun or part shade. Many colors, rock gardens, fragrant foliage.

Echinacea purpurea 'Magnus,' Purple Coneflower, 3–8, sun. Rosy-purple daisy flowers midsummer to frost, butterflies.

Gypsophila paniculata, Baby's Breath, 3–9, sun. Tiny pink or white summer flowers, airy foliage, cutting.

Eupatorium species, Joe-Pye Weed, 4–9, sun or part shade. Tall, coarse texture, flowers late, butterflies, moist areas.

Helleborus foetidus, Bearsfoot Hellebore, 5–9, part to full shade. Blooms winter into early spring, lobed evergreen foliage.

Helleborus orientalis, Lenten Rose, 4–9, part to full shade. Blooms winter into early spring, leathery evergreen foliage.

Hibiscus moscheutos, Common Mallow, 5–9, sun. Brilliant red and white varieties, huge flowers, 4 feet to 5 feet.

Hemerocallis species, Daylily, 3–9, sun. Many colors and blooming times, attractive foliage.

Hosta species, Hosta, 3–8, part to full shade. Many sizes, leaf shapes, and colors, edging plant.

Heuchera americana, Coral Bells, 3–8, sun or part shade. Wide foliage selection, some evergreen, tiny flowers.

Kirengeshoma palmata, Yellow Waxbells, 5–8, part to full shade. Yellow flowers late summer, large maple-leaf foliage.

Lavandula angustifolia, Lavender, 5–9, sun. Entire plant fragrant, evergreen silvery-gray foliage, good for drying.

Phlox paniculata 'David,' Garden Phlox, 4–8, sun. White summer flower, fragrant, mildew resistant.

Liatris spicata, Gayfeather, 3–9, sun. Purple or white flower spikes summer, cutting, butterflies.

Pulsatilla vulgaris, Pasque Flower, 5–7, part shade. Ferny foliage, deep purple flower, early spring.

Perovskia atriplicifolia, Russian Sage, 5–9, sun. Blue flowers midsummer to frost, fine-textured foliage.

Rudbeckia fulgida 'Goldsturm,' Black-Eyed Susan, 3–9, sun. Yellow flower from midsummer to fall, borders.

Salvia pratensis, 'May Night' Sage, 4–8, sun. Good range of colors, habits, and blooming times, spiked flowers.

Solidago canadensis, Goldenrod, 3–9, sun. Golden yellow flower spikes in late summer to frost.

Scabiosa caucasica, Pincushion Flower, 3–7, sun. Light blue flowers, spring until frost.

Stachys byzantina, Lamb's-Ears, 3–8, sun. Silvery-gray woolly foliage, groundcover, yellow flower.

Sedum x 'Autumn Joy,' Showy Stonecrop, 3–9, sun. Grows 12 inches to 18 inches, blue-green foliage, red fall flower.

Courts for Sports

There are many ways to add fun, excitement, challenge, and relaxation to a landscape. One of the most popular methods is to install a surface that is conducive to playing outdoor games.

A Court for Every Sport

One of the main purposes of a garden is fun and recreation. When you're planning for these areas in your landscape, consider incorporating a variety of activities into the same space. You can include tennis, street hockey, volleyball, badminton, even soccer—something for every member of the family. And you can vary court sizes to fit your constraints.

Recommended standards for playing areas are usually set by a world federation that represents the sport, but you don't need to be tied to these dimensions. Modifications can be made for almost any restrictions that you have. For instance, you might be constrained by space and zoning. If a smaller swimming pool, basketball court, or tennis court were the only way you could have that activity at home, it would probably be fine.

Regulating Activities

As a starting point for making decisions about which activities will fit your property, it helps to know the universally accepted standards. Use these as maximum sizes, and reduce them as necessary to fit your space.

◆ **Badminton.** The recommended court size is 17 by 39 feet with an additional 18 inches to the sides and 30 inches at the back of each person's playing area. But the shuttlecock doesn't actually travel far. So it is a good activity for a small "postage stamp" property.

◆ **Basketball.** If possible, surround the court with a level lawn, planted fenced area, terraced retaining walls, or a mounded bed. Avoid long, downhill ball-chasing grades. A full-court game is played on a 37-by-84-foot area with a 3-foot out-of-bounds zone bordering the playing surface. Regulation half-court basketball is 37 by 42 feet. It isn't necessary to have a full-size basketball court. A backboard and hoop don't have any size limits. You can shoot basketball almost anywhere.

◆ **Croquet.** By federation standards, this requires a rather large course, 37 feet, 2 inches by 85 feet. However, a lawn that size could serve multiple uses, including a small football or soccer field, or a Frisbee playing area. And you can certainly set the croquet wickets so they'll fit almost any size space. Your ability to knock an opponent's ball out of view might be the only limiting factor.

◆ **Horseshoes.** The official measurement of a pitching court is about 6 feet wide and 50 feet long. Within this area, drive two, 1-inch steel or iron spikes into the ground, 40 feet apart. Each stake stands 15 inches high inside a pitching box that is 6 feet square. Fill each pitching box with soil, clay, or sand. Safety is a key consideration with this sport, so smaller horseshoe pits could have lighter shoes, such as those made out of rubber. You won't find yourself entering any championships, but it's still fun.

◆ **Shuffleboard.** The flat, slick, usually concrete surface is 52 feet long and 6 feet wide at its base line. This activity is associated with a park or resort, but is also the perfect complement to your driveway, basketball court, and hopscotch area. And it's an activity for all ages.

◆ **Swimming pool.** Typically, the minimum size pool for swimming laps is 16 by 34 feet. It could be narrower, but a shorter pool is frustrating for distance swimmers. The apron, or walkway, around the edge should be a minimum of 3 feet, plus a pad to support the pump and filter. Depth for swimming should be at least 4 feet. State-of-the-art water jogging and aerobics pools need a 5-foot to 6-foot depth, and 8 feet is necessary for diving. Locate your pool in a sunny spot away from shade trees if possible.

◆ **Tennis.** This game is played on a greater variety of surfaces than any other sport I know. They include clay, grass, asphalt, concrete, wood, fine gravel, and rubber. A singles court needs a 27-foot-by-78-foot area, and doubles are played on an area that's 36 feet by 78 feet. In addition to the court size, add 15 feet behind each player and 6 feet to each side. A tennis court could be made somewhat smaller, however, if necessary, to fit your property. Or consider a half court, with a backboard for practice.

◆ **Volleyball.** This is a favorite group sport and extremely popular at the beach. Volleyball is played in a relatively small area, 30 feet by 60 feet, with a 4-foot out-of-bounds around the edge. Any level surface will suffice: bare soil, grass, asphalt, concrete, sand, or wood chips. Smaller versions of volleyball courts are just as effective for entertainment and exercise.

For a Very Private Club

After designing the recreational feature of your choice, the challenge is to create a planting design to make the space fit your landscape. I favor woody shrubs and perennials in large beds with sweeping lines to break up the straight lines of a rectangular court or pool. Some people prefer a more classic approach and plant hedges to separate their sport activity areas from the rest of the landscape.

How about golf? You could at least have a putting green. There are companies that specialize in installing backyard putting greens, often with artificial turf, that are blended into the landscape beautifully.

In addition to areas for sports and outdoor games, you might want to install playground facilities, such as swings, slides, and climbing bars. You have full creative license to build a play feature, but heed the following safety considerations when designing them:

◆ The playing surface should be soft. Possibilities are lawn, shredded bark, peat moss, ground-up tires, and rubberized paving.

◆ The play gym should have a smooth finish.

◆ Follow age recommendations and other precautions, as advised by the manufacturer.

Index

G

H

M

purple coneflower, 37, 49
purple lablab, 212
pyramid-shape trees, 216

R

radical symmetry (landscape design), 55
railroad ties (landscape timbers), 160
repetition (landscape design), 58-59
Responsible Industry for Sound
    Environment. *See* RISE
retaining walls, 160-163
rhododendrons, 67
RISE (Responsible Industry for Sound
    Environment), 205
rocks, placement of, 185-187
Rogers, Elizabeth Barlow, 7
Rome, ancient gardens, 19
root zones, trees, 240
rosemary, 33, 136
Rosenfeld, Richard, 237
roses, 30, 33
Russian sage, 38, 231

S

sage, 38
santolinas, 32, 36
Sauer, Leslie, 43
saving water during waterings, 42
screened-in porches, 166
screening, 67
sculptures, placement of, 184-185

seasonal maintenance
    autumn, 249-253
    spring, 243-246
    summer, landscape maintenance, 246-248
    winter, 240-243
seating
    covered seating, 70
    placement of, 123
seating platforms, 70
Secret Garden, The, 27, 158
sedums, 36, 39
seeding lawns, 202
seeds, essential elements, 243
September, landscape maintenance, 249-253
sequence (landscape design), 59-61
shade trellises, 166
shelters, locations, planning, 167-169
shrubs, 222
    choosing, 222-223
    climbing shrubs, 210
    pruning, 243-244
    root zones, 240
    trees, compared, 222
sidewalks
    designing, 142-148
    dry-laid brick, 150
    gravel, 150
    landscaping around, 117-119
    mortared brick, 151
    mortared stone, 151
    mowed turf, 149
    mulch, 149
    stone, 150
    surfaces, 148-149
sites, assessing, 104

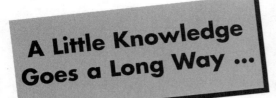
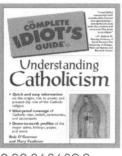

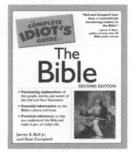

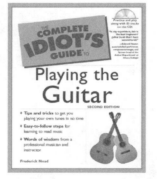